Native American Life-History Narratives

Native American Life-History Narratives

Colonial and Postcolonial Navajo Ethnography

Susan Berry Brill de Ramírez

University of New Mexico Press
ALBUQUERQUE

YEAR   PRINTING
12 11 10 09 08 07   1 2 3 4 5 6

Library of Congress Cataloging-in-Publication Data

Brill de Ramírez, Susan Berry, 1955–
  Native American life-history narratives : colonial and
postcolonial Navajo ethnography / Susan Berry Brill de Ramírez.
      p. cm.
  Includes bibliographical references and index.
  ISBN 978-0-8263-3897-6 (cloth : alk. paper)
    1. Navajo Indians—Biography—History and criticism.
  2. Storytelling—United States. 3. Oral traditions—United States.
  4. Ethnology—Biographical methods. 5. United States—History.
  I. Title.
  E99.N3B654 2007
  305.897'26—dc22
                                          2006035360

Book design and composition by Damien Shay
Body type is Trump Mediaeval 9.5/14
Display is Trump Mediaeval Bold

Contents

Introduction

Interrogations into the Ethnographic Colonization of Native American Stories

Since the arrival of Europeans on American shores, Native peoples have recounted stories about their encounters with the invading and colonizing outsiders.[1] Nevertheless, the vast majority of the published narratives about the colonization of Indian peoples and lands have been framed and controlled by European and, later, Euro-American chroniclers. The discursive power wielded by the colonizers granted them license to determine the orientation, content, interpretation, and diction of those articulations. As a rule, such depictions of the indigenous peoples of the Americas have portrayed them in objectifying terms that place their humanity and subjectivity under erasure—regardless of whether the presentations lean in idealized and romanticized directions, or are overtly derogatory in their ethnocentric and racist perceptions of non-European peoples. In contrast to the scholarly objectivity and objectification that have been definitionally inherent in most academic discourse, the accounts related by American Indian peoples about these encounters have often been related in orally conversive (conversative and relational) ways.[2] As this book delineates, the inevitable clash between textually discursive and orally conversive forms of communication has led to interpretive confusions on both sides—invariably yielding a questionable and, in many cases, a spurious record of scholarship on the indigenous peoples of the world. Insofar as the ethnographic enterprise was concerned, it was often the case that orally told stories were then translated (literally and symbolically) within the discursive constructs of the academy. As Pierre Bourdieu states in Language and Symbolic Power, "The question of performative utterances becomes clearer if one sees it as a particular case of the effects of symbolic domination, which occurs in all linguistic exchanges" (72). This has been all too often patently evidenced in the power relations involved in ethnographic fieldwork defined in terms of objectivity and objectification. However what Bourdieu does not address is that other class of communications that is not defined in terms of a discursive distance between persons that is bridged by symbolic language—namely, the conversive communications evidenced in traditional oral storytelling. Since conversivity is relationally centered, with language used as a means of expressing intersubjective relations, conversive communications serve as a means of bringing individuals together within a storytelling or conversive circle in which all involved persons, as points on the circle, are co-equal participants in the constructive coherence of the complete circle. Accordingly, to access and understand ethnographically constructed American Indian autobiographies requires that we first understand the processes involved in their orally conversive beginnings.

Much of the early construction of published American Indian autobiographies went through a linguistically and ideologically interpretive process that transformed conversive tellings into discursive texts that, more often than not, diverge substantially from their storied beginnings and instead present the ideologies, language, and discursive forms of the colonizing powers of the academy. As Irving Louis Horowitz states, "Whatever else autobiography is, it is an act of writing" (178). What this meant for generations of Native storyteller-informants was the colonialist reduction of contextually relational and symbolically complex stories into information and data constrained by the limiting boundaries of a life history narrative text. Filmmaker and critic Trinh T. Minh-ha trenchantly reminded us two decades ago that "Life is not a (Western) drama of four or five acts" (143). Discursive writing forms can represent stories as textual narratives (e.g., autobiographies), but these representations often result in little more than the trace of what their originating stories, in their actuality, never really were. Storytelling, when most successful, reflects the fullness and complexity of human life in ways that textual discourse can only hope to approach. The substantive differences between discursive and conversive communications strategies are especially evident in the various works of Euro-American ethnography about the various indigenous peoples of North America, and this divide requires categorically new methods to interrogate, interpret, and understand the underlying content of these texts.[3]

It is profoundly ironic that the range of scientific methodologies that required scholarly objectivity and distance in order to yield information that would be correct and valid all too often ended up preventing anthropologists and other ethnographers from listening to the stories told by their "informants," and thereby from actually getting to know the cultures and peoples those ethnographers sought to know. As Bourdieu explains in The Logic of Practice, "The objectivist relation to the object is a way of keeping one's distance, a refusal to take oneself as an object, to be caught up in the object" (19). Such objectification contrasts substantially with the more collaboratively relational models of either conversive or dialogic communications. Whereas dialogism privileges the logocentricity of the argument and the information that it positionally presents, within those conversively informed cultures that are strongly connected to their oral traditions one achieves knowledge about something (or someone) by virtue of being in relationship with it/her/him, not by a distancing or potentially oppositional process of external observation. As Vine Deloria Jr. (Standing Rock Sioux) strongly states, "I don't believe, in view of the awakening of the non-Western European peoples in this country, that an observational science can be a valid science if the person observing is not intimately tied in with the community that he's observing and shares some of the burdens and responsibilities for what's happening in that community" ("Some Criticisms"

97). Deloria even suggests that the problematic effects of such work can be seen in the work of those scholars who sincerely desire to represent Native America as accurately as possible. Deloria says that an anthropologist "can have the best of intentions of helping the Indians and the results of those actions may be bad for Indian people" ("Some Criticisms" 93, his emphasis). As this volume on Navajo ethnography demonstrates, one of the adverse results of such actions is scholarship that continues to misread orally told stories in terms of a colonizing science whose presuppositions redefine, redescribe, and reconstruct those stories into textual narratives that obscure the stories within the texts.

The colonizing encounters between Indian country and the academy have produced a wealth of written narratives that bespeak the divergent views of such encounters on the part of the participants. The period of the twentieth century has become an infamous site of contention for its production of much of the spurious scholarship on Native America. The rhetorical problematic within much of that work occurred as generations of American Indian storytellers told their respective ethnographers stories that the storytellers felt were relevant to share; the ethnographers, as a rule, then textualized those stories into the sorts of factual narratives that fit the respective agendas of the scholars. The interpretive and discursive error here lies in taking one sort of communicative event (a symbolic and metaphoric oral storytelling) and misreading it as an entirely different sort of communication (a literal and factual transference of informational data). The metaphoric medium of stories is conducive to the interactive sharing of mutual storied experiences and the reception, thereby, of meaning and insights that come from the fusion of story words and events with the real world's lived engagements between storytellers and their story-listeners. At the center of storytelling is the establishment of community, with all involved in the storytelling event coming together in their respective experiences as tellers and listeners. When there are those present who take discursively distancing stances (as did many ethnographers), there are two immediate results that impact the communications event: an incomplete storytelling circle, and a communications clash between discursive and conversive modes of speaking, listening, and understanding. Whereas in conversive relations, participants are co-equals, the presence of a colonizing academic-discourse structure upon the event creates the sort of hierarchized situation which Sherry Ortner has described as "contending discourses within a dialogic space" ("Resistance" 182)—and yet, as Ortner further affirms, the voices of those defined as subaltern resist their objectification in ways that are "more than opposition" and are "truly creative and transformative" (191). This differentiation between opposition and transformative creativity is the very discursive/conversive divide clarified herein.

Perhaps the most notable distinction between the oral stories and their textualized narratives (those stories transformed into the ethnographic record) is the presence or absence of objectification as seen in the portrayals of American Indian and non-Indian peoples, insofar as their agency, intentionality, and subjectivity are concerned. This precolonial communications mode has endured throughout the past five hundred years of European and Euro-American colonization throughout the western hemisphere, yet emerging, too, in textually conversive forms of a postcolonial articulation. Traditional oral storytelling circles demonstrate conversively inclusive frameworks that emphasize relationships and the connections between persons, peoples, cultures, experiences, times, places, and worlds. In contrast, it is the much more restrictive and op/positional discourse of textual narrativity that struggles to exclude, marginalize, erase, and thereby silence. Even dialogic inclusion is invariably at the expense of some other's exclusion as one speaker's voice and positionality prove to be the functional silencing and displacement of any other (even if only during the period of dialogue).

This volume demonstrates the extent to which such silenced decentering has been the case in many of those ethnographic encounters in Navajo country that have produced works presented as American Indian autobiographies. The process involved in the production of these texts is far more entangled than traditionally assumed by Western scholars. In fact, most of these narratives interweave the voices and discourses of all those involved in their production, including the ethnographers, translators, editors, and the originating storytelling informants themselves. And yet, as Angela Cavender Wilson (Wahpetunwan Dakota) avers, all too often scholars "dismiss our languages, our voices, and our stories in order to perpetuate their colonialist versions of history that facilitate the continuing subjugation of our people" (79). While the degree to which the scholars' voices are superimposed upon their informants' voices has been well documented, little attention has been given directly to the divergent colonial and postcolonial "language games" (in the Wittgensteinian sense of language use as a "form of life") involved in the encounter between the scholars and their storytellers or "informants." As this study of ethnographically produced Navajo autobiographies delineates, the extent to which chroniclers of the Navajo-white encounter objectify one side of that encounter or the other is a direct reflection of the perceptual, interpretive, and linguistic conflicts that arise when conversively told stories meet discursive science.

Over thirty years ago, Native American anthropologist Alfonso Ortiz (San Juan Pueblo) asserted that "anthropology is a science born of imperialistic and colonial powers and that, at best, all too many of its practitioners still approach their tribal and peasant subjects with a neo-colonialist attitude" ("An Indian Anthropologist's Perspective" 89). We see this in the textualization of oral tellings that forces events into the categorically divergent construct of the text, and as William M. Clements points out, such acts are always value-laden. He explains that "Transformations of Native American oral literary performances into European-language texts have tended to reflect the translators' preconceptions about 'the Indian' and about literature" (1). Here it is important to note that shifts from the oral to the written need not be definitionally understood as a colonialist problematic: two notable counterexamples are evidenced in the continued richness of the Jewish oral tradition that has intermingled with several thousand years of writing, and also the wealth of contemporary Native American literatures by writers such as Luci Tapahonso, Laura Tohe, Simon J. Ortiz, and Leslie Marmon Silko who interweave their respective tribal oral storytelling traditions within their creative and scholarly writing. These and other Native writers demonstrate powerful postcolonial voices that refuse the colonialist prescriptions for conformist speech that would put their respective tribal voices under erasure. Drawing upon any number of oral storytelling tools, these writers convey the conversive power of their tribal oral traditions through a range of strategies that they wield in service of their literary craft, such as line and paragraph breaks to express emphatic storytelling pauses and silences; voice shifts to the second person that address the reader directly; the protective coding of symbolism, minimalism, metaphor, and ambiguity; and the subjective personification of non-human persons (animal, planetary, historical, and mythical beings).[4] By means of such tools (oral and literary), the colonized have long been able to articulate their realities to postcolonial listeners and listener-readers committed to the co-equal subject status of those otherwise relegated to the subaltern.

Such textual affirmations of community and selves can be seen in the longstanding tradition of the Hebrew scriptures and Jewish literature, which are often expressly related orally as a means of enabling the listeners' participation in the story being told. For example, in the case of the Jewish Haggadah (the text that provides the foundation for the oral performance of the Passover seder), we see an example of a text that actually facilitates participants' entries into orally informed story-worlds. In the Passover story told during the seder, these words are heard: "When we were slaves to Pharaoh.... " These words and the conversive storytelling structures that pervade the story involve the listeners directly in the unfolding story, and the inclusiveness of conversive relations means that all present (Jews and any gentiles) are welcome and involved. Such relational equality is one of the central elements in traditional storytelling worldwide. As Jonathan Boyarin notes, "there is no reason to assume a priori that forms of authority grounded in an interaction between text and speech are any more repressive than those which are exclusively based in orality" (401). Even though the Passover story is often read from a text, that does not make it discursively distancing or oppositionally disempowering. The crucial element that determines the extent to which a written text is objectively distancing or intersubjectively relational is the degree of its discursive textuality and/or conversive orality.

This issue comes to the forefront in relation to the oral origins and textual construction of ethnographically produced Navajo autobiographies. The difficulty that arises in relation to such textualized tellings is when these orally informed texts are misconstrued in terms of textual conventions that presume degrees of facticity and factuality that do not apply in meaningfully helpful ways. The transference of oral stories into written narratives produces signifying complexities that arise both in their colonial or postcolonial constructions and in their subsequent interpretations.

By gaining a deeper and clearer view of the mediating transformations of stories into narrative texts, we will be able to learn how to approach those ethnographic texts in new ways. Rather than reading and interpreting orally informed ethnographies through discursively informational methods that can perpetuate colonialist preconceptions, a conversive listening-reading approach enables readers (as listener-readers) to listen through the texts and engage in meaningful ways with/in the underlying stories that are interwoven throughout the texts. In this way, listener-readers affirm the storyteller-informant as a speaking-subject while rejecting the colonialist privileging of the ethnographer's voice and the concomitant minimization of the indigenous voice, self, and culture. There is a familiarity inherent within conversive communications—what Nigel Rapport describes as the "naturally occurring" process of conversation—which thereby facilitates a deeper and more engaged access into stories (180). As an investigation and interrogation into ethnographically produced Navajo autobiographies, this volume offers both a broad and a close look at the ethnographic work developed upon the base of Navajo storytelling as a means of delineating the extent to which particular texts are more or less problematically colonialist or postcolonially reliable.

Chapter 1, "The Languages of Empire and Indigeneity in Ethnographically Constructed Native American Life-History Narratives," begins this study with an overview of twentieth-century ethnography in Indian country. Building on the last twenty years of anthropological interrogations, I provide a wide lens into the challenges and pitfalls that befell many ethnographers seeking information and facticity from conversive storytelling. Criticism of the past errors of earlier ethnographers is not new; what is new here is the introductory articulation of the conversive/discursive communications clash.

Chapter 2 introduces the volume's tribal specificity with a beginning overview of past academic depictions of Navajo lives, culture, and traditions. "Twentieth-Century Ethnographic Representations of Navajo Storytelling" provides an analysis of the nature, methods, facticity, and value of the legacy of several generations of ethnographic work in Navajo country. Most importantly in this chapter, I note the consequences of the communications differences that existed between non-Navajo scholars working within a scientific model of discursive facticity, and those Navajo storyteller-informants who were working within a cultural and tribal framework of conversive symbolism. After a brief historical overview of the early years of Navajo ethnography, the greater part of chapter 2 introduces a conversive method that enables readers (after the fashion of co-creative storytelling/story-listening) to read through editorially reorganized and constructed ethnographic texts as a means of accessing and listening to those texts' conversively rich stories. Here it is important to note that a conversive listener-reader can nowise resurrect or re-create the original storytelling event in which a storyteller-informant relates stories to an ethnographer and the others present (e.g., translator/interpreter, family members, other academics). However, as in the tradition of conversive storytelling, each time a story is retold and reheard, it is the very same story, and yet at the same time, there are meaningful differences. So, too, conversive listener-readers of textualized stories are able to enter into the storytelling circle of the Native storyteller-informants through an expansion and restoration of the conversive storytelling that had been interpretively frozen behind the barrier of the mediating text. By recognizing the permeable nature of that barrier, a conversive listening-reading approach enables recognition of and response to the various conversive storytelling cues that are, nevertheless, embedded throughout the story-texts. In this second chapter, the fusion of literary, folklore, anthropology, and Native-studies scholarship come together to offer a new way of approaching work that had previously been read textually, but now orally (or literarily)—even despite the mediation of the text that at times proves to be a barrier, and at other times an actual facilitation into a conversive approach. Several examples are presented in this second chapter to show the value of a story-listening approach to those texts whose origins are storied.

The next chapter continues the volume's increasing turns to greater specificity with its interrogations into the psychoanalytically oriented years of ethnography in Navajo country, thereby shedding light on much of the more seriously problematic interpretations of Navajo beliefs and behaviors. The evidence discussed in chapter 3, "Ethnography, Psychoanalysis, and Navajo Autobiography," raises critical concerns regarding much of the early foundations upon which later studies of the Navajo have been based. Additionally, this work on early Navajo ethnography serves as a beginning model for similar interrogations of the generations of psychoanalytically oriented ethnographic work conducted worldwide. The diverse psychological traditions of the first half of the twentieth century range from Jungian archetypal dream interpretation to Freudian psychoanalytic methods. It was the latter that served as the predominant model for the ethnographic work conducted by American-trained researchers. This chapter provides important contextualizing background for the succeeding two chapters that turn to well-known work by one anthropologist who was accordingly so trained and who is largely known for his ethnographic work with one Navajo. Those chapters demonstrate the clarifying corrective that obtains when ethnographic texts are opened up by means of conversive interpretive engagements—specifically, in this case, with the well-known, psychoanalytically informed Navajo "autobiography" *Son of Old Man Hat*.

Both chapters 4 and 5 focus very directly on issues of voice, subjectivity, and power as played out in the construction of the Navajo ethnography *Son of Old Man Hat*. The choice of this work is crucial in that the volume was viewed for many years as a model for other ethnographic life-history narratives (Kluckhohn, "Honest Insight" 6). Conversive access into *Son of Old Man Hat* illuminates stories whose content diverges substantially from the ostensive autobiographical presentation of the text. Both chapters articulate that a volume, once hailed as an exemplary ethnography, is in fact far from what it purports to be. Chapter 4, "Navajo Resistance to Ethnographic Colonization: *Son of Old Man Hat*," notes the wealth of cultural and tribal referents in the stories told by the old Navajo man "Lefty" (or Left Handed), while also raising serious questions regarding the autobiographical nature of the stories he told his anthropologist (e.g., Left Handed's initial avoidance of telling stories in the first-person voice; his inclination to relate stories with an unnamed primary third-person character; the emotionally challenging nature of his working relationship with the anthropologist Walter Dyk, which led to repeated work stoppages; and an eventual main character in the stories who is never named or identified as Navajo through any clan affiliation, is ignorant of even the most rudimentary knowledge expected in Navajo country, and is disrespectful of elders, especially women elders). This chapter shows the extent to which Left Handed's stories resist their textualized categorization as a Navajo autobiography and instead tell highly crafted stories about the academic colonization of Native peoples that reduces Indians to subaltern objects of the academy's gaze. These underlying stories are shown to be accessible via a conversively informed method of analysis.

Chapter 5, "Trickster Storytellers and the Elusive Identity of the Son of Old Man Hat," follows this thread even more closely, interrogating Left Handed's stories about a young man in Navajo country who never seems to find his footing there. Additional background information about various Navajo "informants" named Left Handed (or Lefty) indicate that the life-history "facts" in *Son of Old Man Hat* are in all likelihood not about Left Handed's own life, but are rather storied details about the main character or persona of the stories that he related to his young anthropologist. A conversive approach assists in bringing to the forefront Left Handed's stories as stories, thereby opening them up beyond the textual bounds of the purported life-history narrative. As chapters 4 and 5 delineate, while the stories within the text of *Son of Old Man Hat* are placed within the cultural and physical geography of Left Handed's lived Navajo world, the main character in the stories appears to be largely based on Left Handed's own anthropologist's attitudes and behavior in Indian country—including prejudging Indian peoples as ignorant, falling asleep in one ceremony and walking out prematurely from another, not recognizing fresh sheep tracks and mistaking them for deer tracks, being afraid of deer, etc. In *Son of Old Man Hat*, we see a Navajo storyteller offering a mirror to his anthropologist about the behaviors of outsiders who disrespect Navajos and other Indian people. Notwithstanding the levels of interpretive mediation between his originating stories and the eventual published "autobiography," Left Handed ensured his stories' accessibility through his skillful storytelling, which incorporates a range of conversive storytelling strategies such as coding, voice shifts, and episodic association. This purported life-history text, in fact, proves to be a collection of powerful and symbolic stories that require readers who resist the preconceived expectations of the text's presumed autobiographical facticity.

Turning from the range of problematic ethnographies produced under the aegis of the academy's colonizing objectification of the Navajo, the sixth chapter of the book introduces the wealth of ethnographic work conducted among the Navajo that stands out for its reliability, accuracy, and authenticity. The ethnographies delineated herein are distinguished for their postcolonial articulations that speak forth the realities of Navajo life and culture, notwithstanding the continuing Euro-American colonization of the Americas. For the most part, this is work that was initiated from within the tribal community, related through very open and forthright conversations and stories, produced through truly collaborative working relationships, and concluded with real-world benefits to the Navajo tribe and its members. Chapter 6, "Postcolonial Navajo Ethnography: Writing the People's Own Stories from within Tribal Culture," provides an overview of exemplary models of Navajo ethnography, including earlier work such as Franc Johnson Newcomb's stories and biography of Hosteen Klah (1940s), Irene Stewart's autobiography (work begun in the 1950s), and Tiana Bighorse's work with Noël Bennett on weaving and a biography of Bighorse's father (work begun in late 1960s), as well as the more recent work of Ruth Roessel on Navajo women (1970s), photographer John Pack on Navajo life in the Ganado, Arizona, area (early 1980s), photographer Kenji Kawano on the Navajo Code Talkers

(1980s), and the exceptional work that has come out of the Rough Rock Demonstration School and Navajo Community College Press (what is now Diné College). In observing the significant differences in the quality of such conversive ethnography, the role of women throughout many of these examples is acknowledged as a relevant, although not necessary, factor in the development of solidly relational ethnographic collaborations.

The book concludes with a final chapter that presents suggestions for future interrogations into and corrective readings of the West's colonialist scholarship about the Navajo and all other peoples whose cultures and lives have been similarly misrepresented. The epilogue, entitled "Future Directions for Interrogations into Orally Produced Ethnographies," includes a developed list of the various conversive strategies and storytelling elements that are evidenced in Navajo ethnographic texts. These conversive tools serve as important signposts to guide listener-readers through the texts and toward their originating storytelling bases.

Conversive investigations into the ethnographic record of the twentieth century offer powerful interpretive tools for opening up a wealth of stories, many of which are highly crafted symbolic works. One of the findings in my research is the fact that crucial to both the production and interpretation of the body of ethnographic work is an epistemological approach that incorporates meaning firmly within the bounds of a tribally conversive, relational experience and process of knowing. The oral storytelling traditions of Native America (and also those comparable oral traditions of the many other indigenous peoples around the world) offer a primer in conversive forms of communications that in turn will help guide readers of those other ethnographically produced texts whose origins are, as well, orally based. This relationally oriented method can guide future ethnographers in conversive forms of communications that will lead to the construction of truly collaborative and co-creative textual stories that will teach us far more about worlds, peoples, and cultures than can any text so constrained by the more superficial limits of the illusory representations of a logocentric facticity. Such an approach will further enable readers to unpack the layers of ethnographic mediation so that, as listener-readers, they will be able to plumb the depths of meaningfulness within the stories within the texts. As Deloria advises, "First corrective measures must be taken to eliminate scientific misconceptions about Indians, their culture, and their past. Second, there needs to be a way that Indian traditions can contribute to the understanding of scientific beliefs at enough specific points so that the Indian traditions will be taken seriously as valid bodies of knowledge" (Red Earth 60). Without indigenous interpretive guidance, the wealth of stories that lie beneath the texts of twentieth-century ethnography will continue to elude the grasp of scholars and other readers.

The controversy a few years back regarding the factual accuracy of *I, Rigoberta Menchú: An Indian Woman in Guatemala* demonstrates this very sort of confusion. In that book, Menchú relates stories about her life and times. She articulates the truths of her experience through story. Others would most certainly have related the same stories in different ways, even with some particular details changed, but this does not signify that any version of the stories would necessarily have been related untruthfully or without integrity. Menchú's stories speak the truths of her life and experience and those of her people. If we want to discern the truths of her stories and understand their meanings, we must approach and enter them as co-creative listener-readers, looking less for the more superficial and analytical facticity of details, and more for the deeper and larger meaningfulness that is at the heart of her stories. Stories are far more than bits and bytes of data, regardless of their textual presentation. Even when select facts in a story prove to be partially or wholly inaccurate insofar as historical data are concerned, it is crucial that we remember that this nowise invalidates the larger truths of a story. Orally informed stories need to be plumbed for their underlying meaningfulness, regardless of the extent of their texts' factuality. In the case of *I, Rigoberta Menchú*, this indigenous woman's autobiography was presented primarily as a historical work, yet its storytelling origins make it a work of autobiographical literature that needs to be read accordingly, regardless of its degree of historical accuracy.[5] In his analysis of early Mayan letters, William F. Hanks explicitly urges our reconsideration of "the methodology one uses in analyzing ambivalent documentary sources" (722). This is especially important in the arena of ethnography since the categorization that divides history from literature breaks down in the face of storytelling, which has been the historical and foundational center of both. Hanks further points out that "In the search for descriptive fact, scholars have overlooked the more basic questions of what kind of communicative acts...[such texts] embody, and to what ends" (722).

One of the greatest weaknesses of our academic disciplinarity lies in the extent to which we have prevented ourselves from understanding nonliterary texts whose origins are orally conversive. Whereas in the case of literature, scholars and readers understand that those written works need to be read in symbolic and figurative ways, if their depths are to be plumbed, so, too, must be read those ethnographic works with storytelling beginnings. If we misread a book like *Son of Old Man Hat* as nothing more than a factual life-history narrative of a Navajo man, or *I, Rigoberta Menchú* solely in terms of mere surface facticity, then it is we who are the losers, failing to have our own lives and understandings enriched through the meaningful lives, experiences, cultures, and stories of our fellow human persons; and yet it seems that even now, at the outset of the twenty-first century, the academy's recalcitrant refusals to recognize the limits of objective science continue to perpetuate the sorts of ethnocentric and interpretive errors made by generations of ethnographers working in Indian country. Looking back one hundred years to the time period that begins this volume's interrogation of early Navajo ethnography, Mary Louise Pratt trenchantly notes that "by 1900 [modernity] had become a European identity discourse" (444), even though, as Ann Laura Stoler adds, "What went into determining who was European and 'white' in the Indies in 1834 was not the same criteria as that used 100 years later" ("Political and Psychological Essentialisms" 105). Notwithstanding the past thirty years of feminist, cultural, ethnic, working-class, environmental, and indigenous studies, which have produced important critiques of the objectifying biases that are inevitable in the requisite distancing of objective science, the academy still clings to narrow academic methodologies that continue to impede our understandings of indigeneity, (and indeed perhaps

all of humankind—and at great cost as the world's increasing
unrest demonstrates daily).

How are we to read the past ethnography of Native America,
much less the vast majority of the world's orally informed texts
such as Herodotus and Thucydides, *Beowulf*, the *Iliad* and the
Odyssey, or Chaucer's *Canterbury Tales*, if we are not willing to
engage those works within the communications modes of their
storytelling origins? The question that we must ask is whether we
want to approach, engage, and understand such texts on their own
terms, from within their respective cultural frameworks, and
through their elicitive conversive communications—or are we so
committed to our own interpretive orientations and scholarly
methodologies that whatever is beyond our lenses is thereby
deemed irrelevant, unimportant, and unscholarly? As Max Weber
begins his classic work *The Protestant Ethic and the Spirit of
Capitalism*, initially published in German one hundred years ago,
"A product of modern European civilization, studying any problem
of universal history, is bound to ask himself to what combination
of circumstances the fact should be attributed that in Western civilization, and in Western civilization only, cultural phenomena
have appeared which (as we like to think) lie in a line of development having *universal* significance and value" (13). Such solipsis-
tic blindness in the face of global diversity has further perpetuated
appalling degrees of ignorance about the world, its peoples, and
their cultures. Linda Tuhiwai Smith (Maori) explains this, pointing
out that "The globalization of knowledge and Western culture con-
stantly reaffirms the West's view of itself as the centre of legitimate knowledge, the arbiter of what counts as knowledge and the
source of 'civilized' knowledge" (63). Insofar as Navajo ethnography
is concerned, the essentialist "othering" of the twentieth century
was so reductively self-reflective that the published ethnographic
record of that period often ends up saying more about Western
preconceptions of the Navajo than it does about actual Navajo
people's lives and culture.

Postcolonial and anticolonial thinkers such as Frantz Fanon,
Homi K. Bhabha, Simon J. Ortiz, Ngũgĩ wa Thiong'o, Tuhiwai
Smith, and Deloria speak forth the presences, subjectivities, lives,

and worlds of the indigenous peoples who have continued to survive despite the continuing global colonization of their lands, resources, lives, and cultures. Frantz Fanon articulated in his early and influential anticolonial work that efforts are required in the process of decolonization that involve "a genuine eradication of the superstructure built by these intellectuals from the bourgeois colonialist environment," explicitly pointing to the "narcissistic dialogue, expounded by the members of its universities" (37)—what Homi K. Bhabha has described as "an imperialist narrative and history, its discourse *nondialogic*, its enunciation *unitary*" (157). Fanon, Bhabha, and each of these thinkers open up discussion of the actual intellectual powers of the indigenous peoples of the earth, and the concomitant vacuity of much of the twentieth century's scholarship about those perceived as ignorant, powerless, and subaltern. Ortiz makes patently clear the fact that knowledge about indigenous people simply requires inquiry from the people themselves. As he reminds us about our articulations of peoples, places, and cultures, what is required, as in storytelling, is to speak, but also to listen: "A story is not only told but it is also listened to; it becomes whole in its expression and perception" ("Always the Stories" 57). Insofar as Navajo ethnography is concerned, the academy's inability to understand the conversive depths of oral storytelling has led to the erroneous presumptions that discursive power and knowledge were wielded by the scholars and not by the people themselves; but as Ngũgĩ wa Thiong'o states, "Imperialism is the power of dead capital" (*Moving the Centre* 110).

Living capital is evidenced in the real production of people's lives, as in the richness of their stories and other cultural creations. The profound irony in the past (and, alas, current) academy's information about the indigenous "others" of the world lies in the spuriousness of much of that knowledge (where figurative language has ended up being misconstrued in terms of facticity; where "information" is taught that actually originated as fictive jokes and stories; and where depth and complexity are altogether missed behind colonialist assumptions of the "other's" simplemindedness). Deloria's *Red Earth, White Lies: Native America and the Myth of Scientific Fact*, and *Evolution, Creationism, and*

Other Modern Myths: A Critical Inquiry present an indigenous turn that powerfully interrogates past and current scholarly assumptions about Native America; and Tuhiwai Smith explicitly articulates the problematic relationship between the academy and the indigenous peoples of the world. As Smith states, beginning her volume *Decolonizing Methodologies*, "From the vantage point of the colonized,...the term 'research' is inextricably linked to European imperialism and colonialism. The word itself, 'research,' is probably one of the dirtiest words in the indigenous world's vocabulary" (1). In this volume's overview of twentieth-century ethnography among the Navajo, the work that is factually reliable is that which is centrally informed by the Navajos involved in its production. This is not an essentializing turn to the Native, for as Pnina Motzafi-Haller points out, "the binary categories of 'native' and 'non-native' are themselves superfluous and misleading" and far more complex than assertions that all research must be conducted by in-group members (217). Southwest Native writer Simon J. Ortiz (Acoma) makes this poignantly clear in his poetry volume *from Sand Creek*, in which he affirms the conversive possibilities of coming to a deep understanding and knowledge about diverse peoples, times, and places. In the poetry collection, Ortiz gives a strongly voiced postcolonial assertion of the infamous nineteenth-century Sand Creek massacre of Cheyennes and Arapahoes, and of the enduring legacy of that and other such massacres. Ortiz is neither Cheyenne nor Arapaho, but in his conversive poetry and stories he demonstrates the power of such co-creative storytelling as a means of traversing otherwise impossible indigenous and diasporic distance. Thereby, his co-creative listener-readers can access a deeply informed understanding of the colonialist atrocity that occurred at Sand Creek well over a century ago. Comparable understandings can be achieved through ethnographic texts if readers bring to bear the range of interpretive strategies available by conversive methods.

Those who wielded institutional and societal power (namely, the academy, its educators and students, and the predominantly non-Native readership of the past generations of ethnographically produced Navajo autobiographies) have tripped up themselves with their colonialist, logocentric discourse and interpretive strategies. The foundational bases upon which their data, information, and "knowledge" lie often turn out to be parched and empty discursive mirages from the Southwest's deserts—traces and allusions mistakenly interpreted as facts and realities. French social theorist Pierre Bourdieu tells us that "the power of a discourse depends less on its intrinsic properties than on the mobilizing power it exercises" (*Language* 188). As my research has found, the intrinsic properties of an ethnographic "informant's" storytelling are largely centered in the storyteller's interwoven personal, familial, and tribal worlds; in the conversive elements that determine the intersubjective and relational accessibility, direction, and reception of her or his communications; and within the larger (post) colonial geopolitical rubric of the ethnographic storytelling context. As Edward Said has emphasized, "What matters more immediately is the peculiar epistemological framework through which the...[other] was seen, and out of wich Powers acted" (*Orientalism* 221).

Almost forty years ago, anthropologist Gerald D. Berreman offered us wise counsel that is decidedly relevant for us today: "In a world where anything we learn is likely to be put to immediate and effective use for ends beyond our control and antithetical to our values, we must choose our research undertakings with an eye to their implications" (394). In her novel *Ghost Singer*, Anna Lee Walters (Pawnee/Otoe-Missouria) relates a powerful story about the consequences of such scholarship insofar as the disciplines of history, anthropology, and archaeology are concerned. At one point in her novel, a tribal official from an Oklahoma tribe speaks with a younger Navajo student who is conducting research on his tribe in the holdings of a fictional natural-history museum and library in Washington DC (modeled on the Smithsonian Institution): "I was reading these unpublished manuscripts that were left here by writers decades agò. I guess they've been lying here all this time. It's a hell of a thing, the ideas they had 'bout 'red Indians.' It's enough to scare the crap out of you. What's even more spooky is that people acted on these ideas, made decisions based on them, decisions that still affect us guys. Willie, you and me's lucky even to be sitting around here at all" (80). The colonial consequents of voracious empire building agendas that descended upon the indigenous peoples of the world call for reparative textual efforts on the part of the academy.

Both Walters (in *Ghost Singer*) and Smith (in *Decolonizing Methodologies*) strongly speak to the need for corrective postcolonial histories that will present the truths of global indigeneity. Smith writes that we must "revisit, site by site, our history under Western eyes. This in turn requires a theory or approach which helps us to engage with, understand and then act upon history" (34). Conversive processes are a means toward that end, both in the production of ethnographies and in their analysis. Contributing to the ongoing critiques of the past scholarship about Native America, *Native American Life History Narratives: Colonial and Postcolonial Navajo Ethnography* offers a postcolonial corrective lens to the ethnographic record. Far from urging that the past work be wholly disregarded, what is argued herein is the need for new conversive tools to open up that record. As we develop the skills necessary to bring a storytelling ear and a literary eye to bear on a century of recorded, translated, transcribed, and reorganized stories, we can begin to approach and understand these texts in new, and often in categorically different, ways from the prior colonially logocentric, interpretive narratives. As Deloria tellingly asks in *Evolution, Creationism, and Other Modern Myths*, "So what is it that 'objective' science really knows?" (60).

Deloria and many other Native people (scholars, writers, storytellers) have urged us for decades, nay centuries, to listen to indigenous peoples' own stories about themselves and their worlds, including stories about the colonialist imposition of the academy upon Native America. Substantive scholarship means learning to listen and listening well, even when voices and stories are hidden within textualized documents and narrative texts. This effort to listen is an ethical imperative; it is a deep epistemological imperative as well. Our understandings of ourselves, each other, and our world depend upon this. As Robert Allen Warrior (Osage) asserts, "American Indian intellectual discourse can now ground itself in its own history.... When we take that tradition seriously, I will argue, we empower our work" (2). When those traditions are indeed taken seriously (including the vast global intellectual traditions of the diverse indigenous peoples of the world), it is the academy, the world, and its peoples that will be accordingly empowered and enriched with meaningful stories, accurate data, correctly understood information, tribally grounded interpretations, usefully applied knowledge, and collaboratively intersubjective scholarship that, ideally, arises from within its own tribal communities or, at the least, is wholly responsive to and centered within those communities. The larger argument of this book is that this is crucial for any scholarship about the Navajo, and more broadly, for scholarship on any peoples.

Rather than research that is bounded by the limits of a scientifically objective, ratiocinative methodology, this is a call for a future scholarship that is scientifically and logically rigorous, yet also relationally engaged and conversively intersubjective. Insofar as the past studies of the Navajo have shown, the more reliable indigenous research has turned out to be that which is integrally grounded in, informed by, and responsible to those persons, communities and worlds from which it originates. As chapter 6 shows us, even within the bounds of the continuing national colonization of Native peoples within the United States, postcolonial Navajo scholars and storytellers have articulated, and are continuing to articulate, the truths of their worlds, histories, and lives in powerfully conversive words and stories whose meaningfulness speaks through and within their textualized forms. Motzafi-Haller goes so far as to suggest the value of altogether "collapsing the categories of native and non-native, subject and object, researcher and subject of study... to go beyond the strict laws of the genre identified with traditional social-science practices" (219). As a conversive orientation clarifies, generations of Navajo storytellers have called into question such illusory dichotomies whose value and meaningfulness have long since lost whatever value they may have ever had. What is now needed are conversively engaged postcolonial readers capable of plumbing the storytelling depths of the very many Navajo and other indigenous ethnographies that were produced over the course of the past centuries' colonizations of the non-Western world by the "West." The broad relevance of this study of

Navajo ethnography is as a beginning guide for such revisionist interrogations into the past indigenous ethnography worldwide. Beyond its presentation of the pitfalls and errors of the prior colonialist ethnography among the Navajo, the volume depicts the expressive power and interpretive accuracy that pertains from the application of postcolonial conversive methods for the scholarly processes of research, writing, and reading.

The work in this volume owes its greatest thanks to Left Handed, whose intricately symbolic stories provided the original impetus for my investigations into ethnographically produced Native American autobiographies. Creative writer and professor Luci Tapahonso first introduced me to *Son of Old Man Hat* in a Native literatures course at the University of New Mexico in the 1980s. I remember one class in which she gave a very significant rhetorical apology for the volume. Noting the importance of the book for its lens into Navajo life a century ago, she then forewarned us about the language of the book, which would have been unusual for Navajos during Left Handed's time and which is more what one might expect in a gym locker room. In the 1990s, I followed Tapahonso's lead in incorporating the volume in my own Native literatures classes. The first time I did so, I was struck by the strong objections raised by one of my male students regarding the proliferation of sexualized language and content in the book. Understanding the intricate relationship between form and content, these two critiques of the book's language propelled me to consider the substance of *Son of Old Man Hat* in new ways. This work moved substantially forward when Native writer and critic Gloria Bird sent me a copy of the out-of-print Walter Dyk ethnography *A Navaho Autobiography*. The background information in this volume, and its own questionable autobiography alerted me to the perceptual, evaluative, and interpretive needs regarding ethnographically constructed Navajo life histories. It was clear to me that a conversive method combined with the tools of literary, folkloric, and linguistic analyses would provide a means of opening up those ethnographic texts as a means of accessing their indigenous storytelling origins. Additional research at the Newberry Library in Chicago provided valuable background documentation into Walter Dyk's life and work.

A sabbatical research year and a Research Excellence Summer Stipend awarded from Bradley University provided the initial time and funding to focus on the project, including time spent researching Navajo ethnographies at the Newberry Library; the Center for Southwest Research at the University of New Mexico Zimmerman Library; the Gallup, New Mexico, public library; and the library at Diné College in Tsaile, Arizona. It was in the Navajo Studies holdings at Diné College that I found *The Trouble at Rough Rock* with its Left Handed narrative, which led to further interrogations into the authenticity of the autobiographical claims regarding *Son of Old Man Hat*. Because of the important work that Diné College provides, not only for Navajo studies but also for indigenous studies globally, all proceeds from this volume will go to the library at the College. I also want to thank some of the very many people who have assisted this project in different ways: Jim and Roan Stone, Chester Kahn, Annie Kahn, Luci Tapahonso, Simon J. Ortiz, Laura Tohe, Della Frank, Gloria Bird, Serena Charlie, Ofelia Zepeda, Louise Profeit-Leblanc, Roseanne Willink, Mary Alice Tsosie, Arnold Krupat, Carl and Mary Gorman, Brenda Norrell, Alice Bathke, Harry Walters, Jeff and Helen Kiely, Sig and Yvonne Chapela Martinez, the Native American Bahá'í Institute at Pine Springs, Alvin and Joanne Bitsili, Peggy Franz, Alfred and Tina Kahn, Michelle Cusack, editorial assistant Lincoln Bramwell, copyeditor Barbara Fitch Cobb, University of New Mexico Press Director Luther Wilson who has championed Navajo studies at the press, my own English Department chair Dr. Peter Dusenbery who has come to understand and value the insights of Navajo Studies for broader literary study, my non-Native students both at Bradley University and electronically through BIHE in Iran who demonstrate the relevance of Navajo and Native studies for diverse students globally, and—most importantly—my patient and supportive husband Antonio Ramírez Sánchez Barron and our beloved son Jose Guadalupe Ramírez, both of whom have endured absences and the time-consuming process of academic research and writing. Chapter 4, "The Resistance of American Indian Autobiographies to Ethnographic Colonization: *Son of Old Man Hat*," previously appeared in an earlier and more condensed form in the journal *Mosaic* 32.2 (1999): 59–73.

Thanks also go to the various conferences and organizations where much of this work in progress was presented: Association for the Study of American Indian Literatures, Native American Literatures Symposium, Navajo Studies Conference, Native American Literatures Conference at the University of Oregon, American Culture/Popular Culture Association, Illinois Philological Association, American Folklore Society, and the Semiotic Society of America. Finally, I give thanks to God, for it was a passage in Bahá'í scripture ("Ponder this in thy heart") that led me to consider the process of conversive epistemologies that combine the tools of mind and heart for deepened knowledge, which in turn led to my studies of conversive communications, oral storytelling processes and their meaningful implications for ethnographic texts. Friend, scholar, and educator Bernard "Bud" A. Hirsch passed on as this manuscript was heading to press. This book is therefore co-dedicated to "Bud" and to Left Handed, honoring Professor Hirsch's commitment to the study of Native American Literatures and Left Handed's creative storytelling that teaches us that there is often far more going on in orally informed ethnographies than their narrative texts might otherwise indicate.

Chapter One

The Languages of Empire and Indigeneity in Ethnographically Constructed Native American Life-History Narratives

The personal life-history narrative is a literary construct that has no parallel articulation within American Indian oral cultures and traditions. In fact, the autobiography is a relatively recent literary construct in the history of the world, and insofar as the indigenous peoples of the world are concerned, the origins of autobiographical recording and writing were inextricably intertwined with the empire-building agendas of European and Euro-American expansionism. The exoticized views of Native America, whether framed within a Hobbesian negativity of the "savage" or a Rousseauian romanticization of the "primitive," nevertheless propelled a colonialist fascination with the presumably disappearing indigene. Perceiving the wholesale destruction of many indigenous cultures worldwide, ethnographers (both academic and lay) arose to write the cultural, historical, and life narratives of Native peoples and tribes. Such texts were part and parcel of the artifaction and museumification of indigenous peoples. While cultural belongings were appropriated for the static presentations of distant museums, people's stories were appropriated and reconstructed into the static texts of historical narratives. These ethnographic constructions provide poignant examples of the colonizing attitudes that reduced Native peoples to mere objects of study.

Ethnographically produced Native American autobiographies are particularly complex documents that require conversive analysis to unpack the mediative layers of editorial control. The very idea of a self-privileging narrative is traditionally alien to those cultures and peoples for whom orality, communal lifeways, ancestral lands, and the sacred are at the center of worlds and words. The oral primacy of the storytelling circle embodies the ideas of inclusiveness, relationality, and community that are realized and emphasized within the everyday intercourse of interpersonal relations; within such a framework, the centripetal base that holds listeners and speaker together is to be found in the unfolding story itself, and in the holistic and cohesive integrity of its interconnected participants (living and imagined). In contrast, the self-referentiality of the autobiography that authorizes primacy in one individual would be seen to represent an imbalance in which the individual places himself or herself at the center of attention, with all others decentered to varying points of periphery (as in many of the examples of coyote tricksters). As Arnold Krupat notes, "Autobiography as commonly understood in western European and Euro-American culture did not exist as a traditional type of literary expression among the aboriginal peoples of North America.... [And] to the extent that the life stories, personal histories, memoirs or recollections of Indians did finally come into textual form (traditional Indian literatures were not written but oral), it was as a result of contact with and pressure from Euro-Americans" ("Dialogic" 55). Not only did the early texts defined as Native American autobiographies come into contact largely through the colonizing ethnographic imposition of Euro-America, but the inherent heteroglossia of such texts seriously calls into question their constitutive autobiographical voices.

Beyond the extensive critiques of past ethnographic methodologies by feminist, indigenous, and postmodern scholars, as this chapter delineates, inevitable impediments in the ethnographic negotiations are to be found in the communications ruptures that presented themselves as discursively driven science clashed with conversively informed oral storytelling. Throughout the twentieth century, ethnographers were faced with problematic methodologies whose interpretive blinders could neither see nor understand the crucial role played by each person (including the ethnographers and translators) involved in the ethnographic encounter. It is only through serious misinterpretations of the underlying circumstances involved in the process that researchers could make presumptions toward scientific objectivity. Margaret Mead wrote in 1939, "The fieldworker is not in the field to talk but to listen, not there to express complicated ideas of his own that will muddle and distort the natives' accounts" (196). The psychoanalytically informed scientific method prevalent in the United States among many of the early ethnographers taught them the importance of being passive, distanced, and objective observers whose work was not to intrude on the worlds and words of their informants. Unfortunately, generations of anthropologists and ethnographers did not understand that their presence was an integral part of the conversive tellings of their storyteller-informants. In fact, the desired objective (and objectifying) distance between ethnographer and informant was so important that Franz Boas informed generations of fieldworkers of the "dangers of working with 'intelligent Indians' who 'may have formed a theory' about what [the fieldworkers] are doing" (quoted in Tedlock, "Analogical Tradition" 395). The imperialist attitude inherent in such a statement presumes a state of primitive ignorance on the part of the exoticized and marginalized indigenous "other," yet as Lee Maracle (Canadian Métis) avers most directly, "It's not that simple. We're complex people, just like any other human beings in the world, and people have to come to grips with us. Particularly when half of us don't want to talk to white people, and the other half likes to tell them stories that may or may not be true. We're not a simple people" (quoted in Kelly 83).

The great irony of twentieth-century ethnography is that over and over again, the simpleminded errors of perception, understanding, and interpretation were far greater on the part of the ethnographers, largely due to their disinclinations and inabilities to understand the articulate conversive communications of their storytelling "informants." Through an orally conversive approach to the ethno-graphically constructed texts purported to be Navajo autobiographies, readers will discern conversive listening skills and tools for accessing and opening up the respective stories within the reorganized texts. The impenetrable barrier that prevented generations of ethnographers from so doing lay in the conversive-discursive communications divide that led ethnographers to respond in superficially textual ways to the surface details (information, facts, and data) of Navajo (and other indigenous) stories while overlooking the deeper conversive significances that in many cases indicate divergent directions for storytelling analysis and understanding. Beginning with a brief review of the various revisionist responses to traditional ethnographic methods and methodology, this chapter introduces the form and substance of conversive communications and conversive relations, noting the crucial role of intersubjective relations and the relevant implications for ethnographic collaborations.

Brief Literature Review of Ethnographic Revisionism

As a brief overview of ethnographic revisionism demonstrates, the history of ethnographic fieldwork among the indigenous peoples of the world has left the more recent generations of ethnographers grappling with that history and making ongoing efforts to move ethnographic work in more collaborative, egalitarian, and empathic directions. Intersubjective ethnographers who have been able to step into the realm of conversive communications and interact with their "informants" as co-equals have begun to produce work that proves to be far more accurate and reliable insofar as its facticity is concerned. As Judith Stacey notes in a 1999 essay in the *Journal of Contemporary Ethnography*, "During the past two decades, many anthropologists have become hyperreflexive about epistemology and the politics of knowledge" (689). Where Stacey critiques anthropological content and understandings, discourse theorist James Clifford raises concerns regarding the evident heteroglossic imbalances of power, noting that "however monological, dialogical, or polyphonic their form, [ethnographies]

are hierarchical arrangements of discourses" ("Introduction" 17).
Bernard McGrane concurs with such a view, challenging the objectifying orientation of the field's origins: "By the nineteenth century
'anthropology' became, to a large degree, a discursive practice
whose systematic administrative function was to maintain belief in
the existence of exotic and alien worlds without fusing the alien
with our world" (3). And no less than Claude Lévi-Strauss in his
article "Anthropology: Its Achievements and Future" admits the
extent to which the development of the field of anthropology was
intertwined with the colonialist empire-building agendas of the
academy, the church, and the state:

> It [Anthropology] is the outcome of a historical process
> which has made the larger part of mankind subservient to
> the other, and during which millions of innocent human
> beings have had their resources plundered and their insti-
> tutions and beliefs destroyed, whilst they themselves were
> ruthlessly killed, thrown into bondage, and contaminated
> by diseases they were unable to resist. Anthropology is
> daughter to this era of violence...(126)

Commenting on the extent to which this historical process has
been perpetuated in the ethnographic practice of religious studies,
Armin Geertz states that "colonialism and imperialism nourish the
very attitudes and language that our discipline employs" (3). Lévi-
Strauss concludes his comments above by issuing his own call for
"a deep transformation" of anthropology (126).

Much of the history of ethnography among the indigenous peoples of the world has presumed a fascination with peoples and cultures viewed through the objectifying lenses of primitivism and
exoticization. Indigenous, feminist, and other revisionist scholars
have rightly interrogated the disturbing grounds upon which ethnographic studies have been based; as George E. Marcus notes, "When
the politicized nature of fieldwork has been highlighted in the past,
it has been developed by calling anthropology to account for its
colonial, and now postcolonial, complicities" (120). The problems
inherent in the various fields involved in ethnography's past (and to

a lesser degree, albeit continuing, in its present) have been well documented and critiqued over the course of the past twenty-five years; but as Patrick B. Mullen asserts, more is required than the mere identifications of past colonialist bias and blindness. In an essay in which he advocates the prospects of collaborative research methods, he points out that "From the ethnographer's side of collaborative research, it is easy to condemn the errors of the past from the 'enlightened' postmodern perspective" (211). While I would not be quite so quick as to question the value of postmodernity's diversity awareness and cultural sensitivities, I do agree that it is less helpful to focus on the errors of the past without understanding them within their respective historical contexts and as explicit lessons for current and future scholarship. It is especially important for us to learn from those errors by means of the increased knowledge that we can, in turn, bring to bear in understanding anew the past scholarly record that has been left to us. Yes, past and some current ethnographic methodologies have been seriously problematic, in some cases horrifically so, but this is not to say that the past record should be thrown out willy-nilly. In addition to the contemporary interrogations of past scholarship (as in the case of the close critical readings in this volume), also needed are meaningful revisionist readings that begin to decode that earlier research. Ngũgĩ wa Thiong'o states that this work is part and parcel of the struggle against dominant cultural colonizations of indigenous peoples' lives and voices (*Decolonising the Mind* 106). And yet, as the ethnographic record bears out, once a conversive lens is applied, that struggle is powerfully evident in the stories that lie beneath the mediating layers of editorial translation.

As this volume makes clear, even in the most hierarchically skewed fieldwork encounters, many indigenous storyteller-informants were nevertheless able to relate their own stories despite the discursively mediating lenses of ethnographic scrutiny. In an essay on Edward Sapir's linguistic work in Navajo country during the first half of the twentieth century, David W. Dinwoodie poses a crucial question: "Do these ostensibly ethnological materials present special interpretive problems and special interpretive possibilities?" (166). This is the fundamental question that this volume begins to resolve. The very nature of a discursively based ethnographic anthropology that transformed people's stories into texts created its own discursive barriers between readers and the originating stories. In an essay that explicitly addresses "the border between narrative and ethnography," Jaber F. Gubrium and James A. Holstein see this as perhaps the central issue in effective ethnographic work (561). They put forward the idea that "the challenge to ethnography lies in maintaining a balance with narrative analysis," namely, in recognizing "the need to curb ethnography's own representational excesses by letting indigenous voices have their own say" (569). The problematic barriers of ethnographic mediation have certainly prevented readers from accessing the storytelling voices of their indigenous storyteller-informants, but a conversive approach to those stories and texts demonstrates that ethnographic disempowerment has, in fact, been turned back upon academia all along. It is the academy that has misunderstood the told stories, misrepresented those stories as narrative data, and misread the texts as little more than historical information. Even so, the indigenous voices of the originating storyteller-informants have often permeated their textualized discourses in enduring and powerful ways, regardless of the overlaid levels of interpretive and editorial mediation. The problem has been that readers have not learned how to listen through the various ethnographies' respective textual covers to begin to hear the storytelling stories that lie within the texts, waiting to emerge to the attentive and interactive story-listening ears of conversive listener-readers.

Contrary to popular ethnographic critique, it has been far less the case that indigenous storytellers were disempowered and impeded from giving voice to the truths of their experiences. Native storyteller-informants often wielded the determining control over the sorts of stories they related to their respective ethnographers. The twentieth century's modernist silencing of subaltern indigeneity, and the more contemporary postmodern cultural critiques that respond to those past presumptions of indigenous silence have constructed mediating barriers of ethnographic practice that have, in fact, resulted in impairing the work of ethnographers, editors, critics, and readers who have been incapable of hearing

and understanding the vocalized stories due to the combined problem of textualized mediation, expectations of discursive narratives
rather than conversive stories, and an unfamiliarity with—and
thereby a deficiency in—conversive story-listening. In an essay on
consent in working with Native communities in Canada, Nathalie
Piquemal notes the extent to which confusions in modes of communication are central to the work of non-Native and/or outside
researchers in Native communities. Piquemal states, "One of the
most critical problems I foresee is that of differing communicative
norms and patterns of interaction. These communicative differences
can lead to misinterpretation of statements, including those of consent" (67)—hence Judith Okely's call for "an alternative theoretical
and methodological focus on persons as active subjects," not as
objects (230). When academic discourse meets conversive storytelling, stories become textualized into narratives, storytelling relationality becomes distanced and objectified as rhetorical devices,
and storytellers become informants, collaborators, and consultants
while story-listeners become audience, readers, and critics.

It is ironic that the very academic process attempting to shed
light on people's cultures and lives—namely, the textualization of
tellings into life narratives—has, in many cases, served to impede
both ethnographer-editors and other readers in their understandings
of and entries into the originally told stories. In this fashion, told
stories end up being misrepresented and misinterpreted as texts—
an especially problematic situation in the case of ethnographically
produced Native American autobiographies. As H. David Brumble
III comments about such American Indian autobiographies,
"Doubtless there are subtleties we miss as we make do with printed
translations of what were oral performances" (32). However,
Brumble notes that with ample background information about the
individuals involved and the nature of their collaboration, it is possible "to allow some pretty good guesses about where the Indian
leaves off and the Anglo begins" (12).

If I may amend Brumble's statement, what is needed is rather
for readers to be able to discern where the Anglo leaves off and the
Indian begins, so that we can focus less on the ethnographic text
and instead begin to listen to the stories told by the originating

indigenous storytellers. But to do so, it is crucial that readers of ethnographically produced Native American autobiographies understand the extent to which the individualist directions inherent in autobiography are definitionally problematized. In traditional Native storytelling, the primary focus is rarely self-referential, even when told in a first-person voice, but rather on the events and the relationships therein defined and expressed. Albert Yava (Tewa/Hopi) explains this point in *Big Falling Snow*, the ethnographically produced "autobiography" based on his stories and recollections:

> If I seem to say a lot about myself, it is really my times
> that I am thinking about. I am merely the person who hap-
> pened to be there at a particular time. It is hard to put
> down something with myself as a center of interest—that
> is, to say I did this or that. It makes me out as important,
> which isn't the way I see it. We Tewas and Hopis don't
> think of ourselves that way. (Courlander 4)

This perspective raises serious concerns for not only the ethnographic production of Native American autobiographies, but perhaps even more importantly for the interpretive reception of those texts. What are the implications for readers of these works where the reading is framed around the preconception of those works as definitionally autobiographical rather than as symbolically creative. Literary scholar David Murray points out that "The concept of an individual life as an unfolding story which can be isolated, recalled and retold, made into a product for contemplation, is not one necessarily shared by other cultures, and in particular not by oral cultures" (65).

What remains for readers is the responsibility to investigate the communications mode of the text in order to determine the most effective response. For conversive communications, a co-creatively conversive response is elicited, but all too often the mediation of the text obscures the symbolic and relational nature of the stories within the text. To read the texts for information is to miss altogether the symbolism of the stories. Livia Polanyi explains that oral storytelling manifests as much complexity as is more readily expected within the literary domain. She writes, "Everyday oral stories demonstrate the same complexities in manipulating point of view, identity or reference, and multiplicity of meaning which have hitherto been treated as special qualities of literary language" ("Literary Complexity" 155). Native-literatures scholar Alanna Kathleen Brown notes that "Written words are merely the extension of...a richly textured oral tradition,...not a reflection of a higher form of culture and sophistication" (173). In fact, *more* heteroglossic and paralinguistic complexity is possible within the oral storytelling process than through the stricter limits of textualized stories, and furthermore those literary works more immediately informed by their oral roots will demonstrate greater levels of complexity than those works which are more strictly textual. As Stephen A. Tyler reminds us, "Orality makes us think of many voices telling many tales in many tongues, in contrast to the inherent monologism of texts that only tell different versions of the one true tale" (136). For ethnographies that originate in conversively oral communications, any substantive interpretation of the published texts must negotiate among the degrees of literal facticity and symbolic creativity.

In her essay "The Significance of 'Literature' in Non-literate Cultures," Ruth Finnegan asserts that any interpretive approach must have at its center the cultural standards, aesthetics, and axiologic values from which any story (oral or written) is produced: "Thus to take as our yardstick the present circumstances of literature in Western Europe—or rather perhaps those of a generation or so ago—and assume that this is the standard by which we estimate all other literatures is to show a profound lack of historical and comparative perspective" (143). Arnold Krupat, author of several volumes on American Indian autobiography and ethnography, suggests that the "key to the Indian autobiography's discursive type" is to be found in its "bicultural composite composition"— here referring to the intertwined and culturally diverse worlds of the ethnographers and their Native informants (*For Those* 33). Brumble further emphasizes the importance of such narrative contextualization: "Responsible analysis [of these works], then, must largely wait upon descriptions of the assumptions and narrative conventions native to both the Indians and their editors" (18). Hertha D. Wong, author of *Sending My Heart Back Across the Years: Tradition and Innovation in Native American Autobiography*, develops this point, noting, "The roots of Indian autobiography, then, are not merely in the Western written tradition, but in the pre-contact Native American traditions of oral, artistic, and dramatic modes of self-expression" ("Pre-literate" 30). As she specifies regarding ethnographic autobiographies, "We can think of late-nineteenth- and early-twentieth-century Native American autobiography as a type of literary 'boundary culture' where two cultures influence each other simultaneously" (*Sending* 89).

Emphasizing the culturally complex origins of any ethnographic work, Gubrium and Holstein note the central importance of "the social patterning of the narratives that give diverse voice to shared experience, to the going concerns that shape and condition narrative constructions, and to the undernarrated and unnarrated mediations of the communication that is the grist of storytelling" (571). Inherent in such work are the underlying discursive structures that define such bicultural work—what Jean-Paul Dumont points to as the inherent dialectical nature of such ethnographic engagements: "What exists, however, is a concrete situation in which 'I,' the anthropologist, and 'they,' the studied people, came together in a series of interactions which deeply affected our mutual perception. By definition, the situation is dialectic, so that 'I' and 'they' transformed each other" (11–12). This transformation is the inevitable outcome of any relationship, but especially so in those relationships in which those involved come together consensually, equally, and conversively, as in the cases where the indigenous storytellers (ethnographic "informants") and their ethnographers are transformed through a conversive working relationship. June O'Connor refers to such change as "the dialogical, conversational nature of the inquiry [that] makes possible the expansion of my horizons, affections, valuations and therefore understanding" (9). This is so because in conversively informed communicative relationships, the storytelling circle broadens itself to include all listeners as co-participants—even those who step into the story-telling circle as listener-readers through the mediation of a text.

A number of scholars have discussed the complexities of pre-senting the relational event of storytelling via a textual medium. Literary scholar and writer Greg Sarris (Miwok-Pomo) extends the notion of a "cross-cultural" dialogue to include the presence of readers within a storytelling circle, and to explain how objective reading strategies have diverted readers away from the originating stories ("Verbal Art" 110). Building on the pioneering work of Ferdinand de Saussure that categorically differentiated speech and writing, David R. Olson explains the interrelational distancing inherent in logocentric writing: "In oral speech, the interpersonal function is primary.... In written text, the logical or ideational functions become primary, presumably because of the indirect rela-tion between writer and reader" (278). While this is generally true, writing is certainly not an insurmountable barrier to conversive communications, which generations of creative writers (and their readers) have known. Jonathan Boyarin, scholar of Jewish oral sto-rytelling traditions, asserts that we should not presume that the definitional limits of and the historical contexts behind any text signify greater degrees of repressive authority than might be evident in strictly oral communications (401). Indeed, within the Judaic religious tradition, the Passover Haggadah is a case in point, for the Haggadah is a written text designed explicitly to facilitate its con-versively oral, performative use during the Passover Seder (or din-ner). Specifically regarding Native American literary traditions, Sarris argues that scholars (and readers) need to move toward more explicitly dialogic approaches: "In my work I am attempting to open a dialogue with the text I am reading such that my history and critical activity inform and are informed by the text" ("Verbal Art" 111). Sarris's emphasis on the reader's role in the process is indeed crucial, but to achieve more fully the sort of conversation he sug-gests, we need to move beyond perceiving and approaching these autobiographies as texts, and begin reading them as the sorts of sto-ries that Sarris relates throughout his volume *Keeping Slug Woman Alive*. To approach the analyses of ethnographically produced American Indian autobiographies, it is necessary to begin with a

clear view of their orality. The next section of this chapter elucidates the conversive method that will enable readers to engage
more firmly within an orally conversive and collaboratively co-creative framework produced by the ethnographic storytelling process.
In this fashion, in accordance with Brumble's statement, it will be
possible to see where the Anglo text leaves off and the American
Indian storytelling begins.

Conversive Communications, Oral and Textual

Through a conversive method that is definitionally conversative
and relationally transforming, readers are able to read through narrative texts and back to the told stories, re-creating and listening to
them within the textualized narratives. In such a manner, the
scholar responds to and with the words of the text as would the
active listener of an oral storytelling event. The scholar as listener-
reader must understand that the words (text) of the story represent
only a small, albeit necessary, part of the story, and that the listener-reader has the responsibility to flesh out the story beyond its
textual skeleton. This involves the dual responsibility of gaining an
intimate understanding of the storytelling's context (including
related historical, biographical, mythical, cultural, tribal, familial,
and personal knowledge), and stepping into the co-creative role of a
listener-reader. A conversive listening-reading experience involves
the reader as listener coming into relationship with the storyteller
and story-characters and actually becoming part of the story. As I
discuss elsewhere, this "becoming" is at the heart of the transformative semiotics of storytelling: "Within a conversive model, the
emphasis is on the process and on the relationship between individuals or between the scholar and her subject of analysis.... Here
there is no oppositional nor objectified other, since the 'other' is
always in relation to oneself—and, through that relatedness, the
'other' is no longer 'other'" (Brill, "Conversive" 8–9; see also my
Contemporary American Indian Literatures for a more complete
discussion of this method). The conversive reader enters the indigenous world behind the writing (like a story-listener) and interacts

with the story-world from within. As anthropologist Rodney Frey points out about oral tradition among the Crow Indian people, storytelling is a process of "re-membering [that] involves a return to and a reuniting with the original" (134). "This is not a reader-response critical approach in which the reader completes the...story and thereby gains a position of privilege" (Brill, "Discovering" 64); unlike reader-response approaches in which readers construct texts in dialogue with fellow interpretive community members, in oral storytelling traditions the listeners co-create stories as fellow participants within the storytelling circle, thereby maintaining the contextual centrality of the indigenously originated and informed story. This internal participation is categorically different from external interpretive approaches to texts that shift primacy to the interpretations, regardless of the degree of subjectivity involved in those approaches.

In a conversively informed listening-reading process, it is most important for the listener-reader to engage closely and fully with the stories, vignettes, and words, listening to them within their evolving storytelling framework as best one can, struggling to hear the larger stories that emerge from within the printed or electronic text. To do this requires the understanding that at the heart of storytelling is relationality and love—the love that defines the relationship between the storyteller and the listeners. Storytelling is more about the development and strengthening of community and interpersonal bonds than about informational facticity. As Luci Tapahonso (Navajo) explains, "telling stories is very much a way in which affection is shown if a person is included within the circle. Then, in a way, it sort of implies that everyone within the circle thinks highly of each other, and so, it's a way to show affection and to be included within the listening to or the sharing of stories" (WCBU interview). To begin to listen to ethnographically recorded stories that have been textualized, readers must first come into a living (not merely a phenomenological) relationship with the others involved in the storytelling circle of those stories. This may appear at first to be a simplistic shift away from a distancing mediation of the text, but the conversive turn decidedly decenters the discursive control of the editor, as the story (not the storyteller) is re-centered and the storyteller-informant's voice becomes more audible and accessible. The recent revisionism of ethnography has moved much contemporary fieldwork in such conversively relational directions.

Over the last couple of decades, scholars have begun to recognize that the relationship between a fieldworker and his or her "informant" must be understood within the framework of a relationship among equals. Anthropologist Kenneth M. Morrison makes this very point regarding the relationships between anthropologists in the field and their informants, emphasizing the importance of "integrity" and true collaboration in that work (12). Leslie Rebecca Bloom writes that "mutual trust and reciprocity are critical" (118), while Helen Swick Perry warns against the "unconscious feeling of superiority" that can arise on the part of field researchers—thereby leading to the objectifying scientism that reduces indigenous persons to objects of study (323). In the earlier generations of anthropology, far too many scholars could not even see their own colonialist attitudes in their illusory presumptions of collaborative working relationships: as Margaret Mead confirms, "We do not treat human beings as subjects; we treat them as informants, which means colleagues and collaborators" ("American Indian" 69). Mead's discursive objectification of Native peoples as "informants" clearly contradicts her assertion that they are, indeed, "colleagues" (69). In his own field of archaeology, Gary White Deer critiqued this very attitude: "To archaeologists, the idea of consulting with potential specimens must seem annoying. For Native Americans, it's yet another version of this country's oldest and deadliest game: Cowboys and Indians" (38). And Native scholars Devon Abbott Mihesuah (Choctaw) and Angela Cavender Wilson (Dakota) tellingly ask, "Who will call attention to the reality that the 'famous' scholars of our histories and cultures do not use Indigenous perspectives in their analyses of histories and cultures?" (14). The extent to which scholarship about Native peoples is not indigenously informed is the extent to which that scholarship will continue to fall prey to the very colonialist biases and scholarly errors of the ethnography that has not been so grounded.

For decades, Native people and many folklore scholars have been arguing for a truly collaborative ethnography that demonstrates a responsibility to the communities out of which it arises. Storyteller and scholar of Jewish oral tradition, Peninnah Schram emphasizes what she refers to as the crucial "trust and bond between himself [the listener] and the storyteller" (43). The experiential "trust and bond" and "give-and-take between equals" are the reality of conversive relations in the world, whether they are among a storyteller and listener, a textualized story and its listener-reader, or two friends conversing over coffee or tea. Native writer and critic Gloria Bird (Spokane) explains in a discussion of American Indian literatures, "Everything depends upon something else. Our ability as readers to enter as participants of the story ultimately relies upon our ability to make those connections, to forego on an intuitive level the constricting notions we have of language and its use. We must also be willing to 'see the world differently'" (4). This is what novelist and storyteller Leslie Marmon Silko (Laguna Pueblo) refers to as "the boundless capacity of language which, through storytelling, brings us together, despite great distances between cultures, despite great distances in time" ("Language" 72). Insofar as this volume's analysis of Navajo ethnography is concerned, this means traversing time across a century and engaging with stories, persons, and places that one can only meet through the reality of story. Instead of coming together within a temporal, spatial, and interpersonal storytelling event, the conversive listener-reader must do so through the medium of the story to bring together the diverse persons, times, and places. Even though a physical storytelling event has individuals brought together physically in one place, even so, the storytelling circle is not a function of those persons' collective embodiment. What creates a storytelling circle is the extent to which the participants actually listen and imagine themselves into the story as they come together with their storyteller and fellow listeners as participants co-creatively engaged with and within the story. Such engagement occurs similarly through the medium of the written story as the listener-reader interacts with the characters in the story, the storyteller, fellow listeners, and/or listener-readers—thereby bridging the distances constructed by tendencies to objectify and distance those we want to know.

Past interpretive rubrics served to impede a conversive semiotics for fieldworkers and readers alike. Many of the early ethnographers and anthropologists struggled to interpret alien and/or ancient cultures and peoples in terms of a Western interpretive semiotics—the underlying assumption being that only such scientific interpretive systems could convey the realities of diverse peoples' lives, regardless of the fact that those peoples might, and often did, invest their behaviors, events, rituals, chants, and stories with meanings divergent from the significations externally imposed by outside scholars. At an interdisciplinary conference I attended a number of years ago, one researcher presented a paper focusing on a particular ritual that had been observed among one tribe. The scholar's observations were presented as being external to the ceremony, and yet within the conversive semiotics of the tribe, the scholar's very presence would have signified a degree of participation.

One specific example related in the talk is telling. Throughout the ritual, the researcher observed that at various times, a particular stick would be held. At the end of the ritual, the scholar asked the medicine man what the stick was—here seeking an abstracted interpretation of the stick as a sign. What did the stick represent or signify? This question makes sense within a Western interpretive semiotics, but not within a relationally conversive semiotics in which such abstractions do not hold meaning. As Dennis Tedlock notes about analyses of oral storytelling among the Zuni, "We will have to set foot on the threshold that separates the natural or physical science of language from the semiotics of language" (*Spoken Word* 199). Where signification is conveyed relationally, any particular object separated out as a sign would be understood as fundamentally meaningless. As David Moore explains, "Relationality across time and place entirely blurs the boundaries of subject and object, of humans and nature, of persons" ("Myth" 380). Since conversive relationships are between persons (subjects, not objects), meaning is developed intersubjectively. Jo-ann Archibald (Sto:lo) clarifies regarding indigenous storytelling, "In the oral tradition, the listener/learner is challenged to make meaning, gain understanding from the storyteller/speaker/teacher's words" (160). Folklorist John Miles Foley affirms the importance of the listener:

"Audiences, co-participants in implicitly dialogized speech-acts, will of course vary even for a highly focused traditional genre like the folk epic, and the role of the individual—the single performer or single members of the audience—must always be carefully considered" ("Word-Power" 284). Within this sort of a conversive framework, to divorce the stick from its place within the ceremony and the community of persons involved in the ceremony, and to thereby isolate it out as a sign, would be to lose the actual semiotic sense invested in it through its conversive relationality. In such a process of divorce, any semiotic meaning given to the object (stick) as sign would be, definitionally, the imposition of an alien Western semiotics incapable of comprehending significance that lies beyond its own definitional boundaries.

Simon J. Ortiz (Acoma) offers a powerful linguistic example that demonstrates such conversive relationality in which even the meanings of words are understood in terms of their interconnected use. When Ortiz once asked his father to break down a word into its parts, Ortiz relates that his father "looked at me with [an] exasperated—slightly pained—expression on his face, wondering what I mean. And he tells me, 'It doesn't break down into anything'" (*Song* 2). Ortiz explains his father's response much as we might imagine the medicine man explaining the ceremonial stick: that meaning is present when language [or, say, the stick] "is realized as experience as well, [that it] works in and *is* of that manner" (*Song* 3). Outside of its relationship within interpersonal communications and use, both words and sticks are empty, meaningless. It is through living and relational experience that signs are brought to life.

In the talk about the ceremonial stick, we were told that upon being asked what the stick used in the ceremony was, the medicine man looked at the stick and then at the researcher and replied, "It is a stick." What the medicine man communicated to the researcher was that in and of itself, the stick is nothing other than just that—a stick. Where meaning lies within its relational connections, so too must our understandings. As Marcus notes regarding the implications for ethnographic practice of such discursive confusions, "If there is anything left to discover by ethnography it is relationships, connections, and indeed cultures of connection, association, and circulation that are completely missed through the use and naming of the object of study in terms of categories 'natural' to subjects' pre-existing discourses about them" (16). While it would be possible to come up with a scholarly interpretation of the stick as a discursive sign, that would be other than the real meaningfulness of the stick within the ceremony. In fact, any interpretation that attempts to understand that which lies beyond its own interpretive boundaries invariably refracts back upon itself and ends up telling us more about its own interpretive system than about that which it attempts to describe. John Miles Foley explains, "An oral traditional performance...is...an experienced event that becomes a text only at the high price of intersemiotic translation" ("Word-Power" 289–90). As Rodney Simard points out, "Language is not necessarily a symbolic representation of reality; it can be an incarnation of reality in itself....What emerges is the distinction between language that affects and creates reality and language that represents and approximates reality" ("American" 247).

One literary critic who approached this sense of relational and contextual meaning is Louise Rosenblatt, in her assertions that even the reading of poetry is a communal event: "A poem, then, must be thought of as an event in time. It is not an object or an ideal entity. It is an occurrence, a coming-together, a compenetration, of a reader and a text" (126). Here, Rosenblatt focuses on the reader's relational connections to a text, touching on the deep and powerful effects of a story on a reader. However, what such a textual analysis cannot address are the broader intersubjective relationships and experiential learning that occur during a conversive storytelling event. This is evident in a story that folklorist Barre Toelken relates from his time among the Navajo. Toelken's example parallels that of the ritual stick in that it involved a non-Native scholar (Toelken) observing an indigenous cultural event. In contrast, Toelken includes an analysis of the situation from the Native elder himself—as well as further input and analysis by Toelken, who developed a substantive and enduring relationship with the elder and his family.

Toelken relates that the elder, Little Wagon, told a story about the origin of snow to his family and some members of a small family who, passing by, stopped for the night. The story centered around the importance of the sacred as manifested in the natural world, and the interrelationships that exist between this world and the spiritual world. At the end of the story, "there was a respectful silence" during which the listeners and storyteller were left to contemplate the deeper significance of the story (Toelken, "Poetic Retranslation" 73). Then, one of the traveling family's children turned to the storyteller, asserting that the story explained why there was snow in Montezuma Canyon, but that he wanted to know why it snows in Blanding as well. "'I don't know,' the old man replied immediately, 'You'll have to make up your story for that....' Little Wagon commented after the travelers' departure that it was too bad the boy did not understand stories" (73). Little Wagon's explanation of this event was that the child was incapable of grasping the underlying meanings of the story, and that was why the boy asked about surface details. Instead of considering the larger sense of the story, the boy sought the objective facts one expects within a Western informational semiotics. The difficulty was that the story was told within the bounds of a categorically divergent interpretive system, emphasizing understanding that comes through deeply felt empathic knowing that engages both mind and heart—what is often referred to as insight and inspiration. Regarding Little Wagon's story, Barre Toelken notes that "by seeing the story in terms of any categories ... our young visitor [had missed the point], a fact which Little Wagon at once attributed to the deadly influence of white schooling" (73).[1]

For Little Wagon and the medicine man, the more important concern is using and valuing language as a means toward the development and integration of relationships and community. Persons and things are understood by being in relationships with them, by understanding them as fellow subjects in relation to oneself. For example, in the Navajo language, there is no isolated word for mother, but there are words for "my mother" or "your mother." Here, language is understood as a crucial reinforcing element that knits together the fabric of a tribe, a community, and a family. As Wittgenstein reminded us over fifty years ago, "the *speaking* of language is part of an activity, or of a form of life" (*Philosophical Investigations* 23). Richard Bauman echoes this statement from the opposite vantage point, writing that "performance is a mode of language use, a way of speaking" (293). So, too, must our understandings of language be contextually informed by its respective system of meaning. The questioning Navajo boy and the anthropologist seeking the meaning of a stick used in a ceremony both had achieved a level of discursive understanding regarding the events surrounding them, and accordingly, they sought objectively factual significance within the framework of an alien (Western) interpretive system. As Wittgenstein writes about such miscommunications,

> We also say of some people that they are transparent to us.... one human being can be a complete enigma to another. We learn this when we come into a strange country with entirely strange traditions; and, what is more, even given a mastery of the country's language. We do not *understand* the people. (And not because of not knowing what they are saying to themselves.) We cannot find our feet with them. (*Philosophical Investigations* 223e, emphasis in original)

The difficulty here is in our attempting to understand different worlds by means of one conceptual and communications framework. To begin to understand how to approach storytelling (oral or textual) within a traditionally conversive worldview, we must investigate what it means to come into conversive relationships with others, especially those who are not in our physical presence due to distances across place or even across times, species, and worlds (such as spirit worlds).

Intersubjective (and Interspecies) Relations

A conversive orientation views those with whom one comes into relationship as co-participants who represent equal points on a conversative (or storytelling) circle. While the diversity of personal qualities and abilities is recognized, the important presence of each person involved is recognized and affirmed within any form of conversive communications. Such inclusiveness demonstrates the intersubjective and interpersonal relations among the participants, which can cut across species to include a broader ecosystemic biotic community. Barney Blackhorse Mitchell (Navajo) states that "the greatest sacred thing is knowing the order and structure of things" (quoted in Beck, Walters, et al. 95). By knowing the ways by which various elements of creation exist in relation to each other, human persons are permitted to take responsibility in the maintenance and restoration of balance and well-being for individuals and communities. The role that conversive communications plays in such perceptual inclusivity is crucial, for as Jack Goody and Ian Watt make clear, "The intrinsic nature of oral communication has a considerable effect upon both the content and the transmission of the cultural repertoire. In the first place it makes for a directness of relationship between symbol and referent" (Goody and Watt 306). Thus, knowledge of persons and things in the world comes from one's being in conversive relationship with them.

Such intersubjective communications between diverse persons (be they animate or inanimate—human, animal, plant, rock, star, etc.) occurs in relationally based interactions that are neither discursively nor dialogically oppositional, but conversively co-creative. For example, Peggy Beck and Anna Lee Walters (Pawnee/Otoe-Missouria) explain that when a medicine person wants to learn about a plant, s/he learns directly from the plant: "The plant has its own mind that you learn to know" (11). The process of learning emphasized by Mitchell, Walters, and Beck is not the observation of an object-thing by the subject-observer, but rather an interaction that involves more than Heisenberg's observer effect on the observed, but also the effect of the observed on the observer. Such intersubjective learning between human and person-thing involves two realities in the world possessing their own unique subjectivities and intentionalities concurrently and interrelationally. When we refer to a plant or human as a "thing" in the world, or both as "persons," we convey the dual senses of potentiality and actuality in the world. Descriptive psychologist James R. Holmes explains that the attribution of person-hood is an attribution of status and need not be restricted to human beings.[2] He writes, "Up to the present time, we have recognized as persons only those individuals who have the embodiment of homo sapiens, namely human beings. There is however, nothing about the concept of a person that requires persons to be human beings" (30). Native peoples (as well as many other peoples within conversively informed oral cultures) have historically referred to their ancestors as, say, the bear people or the bird people. In many Navajo stories, both from the oral tradition and in more recent written literatures, animals and humans interact conversively as equals. This does not mean that the Navajo or other indigenous peoples of the world did not differentiate human beings from other living creatures, but rather that they recognized and attributed a specific interactive status to a diverse range of nonhuman persons (such as animals and plants).

In one of her short stories, writer Anna Lee Walters explains this conversive relationship between animals and humans in a discussion between an old Indian man and a young woman. The old man tells her, "Old folks always say that the distance between two-leggeds and four-leggeds nowadays hasn't changed four-leggeds in any way. The distance has only changed us two-leggeds, made us worse off, more pitiful. They say that the four-leggeds still talk the way they always have. It's we who've forgotten how to listen. I guess we lost a lot when we quit talking Indian" (*Talking Indian* 32). This interpersonal intersubjectivity that cuts across species even has the potential to cross the boundaries of time and space. Not only can human persons come into relationship with animals or plants, but within a conversive framework of interpersonal inclusivity, human persons can also come into interactive and lived relationships with spirit persons (such as relatives who have passed on) and other human persons who are not physically present. This has great relevance for the reality of the storytelling circle that encompasses a storyteller, story-listeners, and story-characters all coming into relationship with each other within the realm of story. Within conversive relations, these interactions are lived experiences, not merely imagined. Human perceptions and interactions are complex in mysterious ways that a logically bounded and reasoned discourse can never fully explain. Such interpersonal communications and experiences that cross worlds and times and places can only be understood within the rubric of conversive relations in which knowing is relationally based.

Interspecies communications demonstrate the epistemological limits of a discursively based analysis that interprets communications at the surface levels of linguistic denotation, connotation, and argument. The very idea of communications across species calls into question such an approach, because only humans communicate and understand within linguistically based human language systems. When a human speaks to and with, say, a tree or a wild animal, whereas the human speaks with human language, the tree or animal communicates in the manner of its respective species. The attribution of personhood for nonhumans (including immaterial spiritual beings) demands an interpretive approach that can address communications and relationships that are not constrained by the articulation of human language and reason. The ratiocinative bounds of objective science preclude deep interpretation of such complexly symbolic, interspecific storytelling. The articulation of nonhumans is either trivialized and relegated to the realm of human imagination and interpretations of archetypal fixity, or further devalued to the infantile domain of children's stories and primitive fables. Discursive analysis hears the articulation of language that is discursively and ratiocinatively framed; a conversation among a human and a nonhuman would, thereby, be perceived as a monologue, with the nonhuman articulations interpreted as extensions of the human's imagination. The very presence of interpersonal communications among diverse forms of persons (human and nonhuman) holds great significance for the pitfalls that befell far too many ethnographers in Navajo country.

Colonizing perceptions and discursive forms of hegemonic communications raised the ethnographic structures that in turn predetermined the slant of the resulting oral and textual information. Diverse participants within stories (including animals and spirit beings) were perceived as mere objects. The romanticization, exoticization, and objectification of storyteller-informants placed their controlling creativity under erasure, denied their full subjectivity as co-equal persons in the world, and reduced their voices to little more than informational vessels. Ethnographers' lack of recognition of the subjectivity of nonhumans, also perceptually played out in the objectification of Native "informants," catastrophically prevented the ability to hear and engage indigenous conversiveness that included the ethnographers and the others present during the storytelling sessions as conversive participants in the storytelling. Subsequent chapters in this volume that address the *Son of Old Man Hat* and other psychoanalytically oriented ethnographic texts demonstrate the very problematic errors that the academy's interpretive blinders prevented it from either seeing or resolving. While I would recast the following statement in stronger terms, in his 1951 essay "Cultural Factors in the Structuralization of Perception," A. I. Hallowell rightly affirms, "It is of some importance to determine what aspects of culture are relevant to perception, how they become involved in the perceptual experience of individuals, the role they play in the total structuralization of the perceptual field and the consequences of this fact for the actual conduct of the individual" (170). Wittgenstein very astutely reminds us that *"Thought* can be of what is *not* the case," and that "our forms of expression prevent us in all sorts of ways from seeing that nothing out of the ordinary is involved, by sending us in pursuit of chimeras" (*Philosophical Investigations* 95, 94, his emphasis).

Ethnography as Collaboration

Over the course of the last few decades, many ethnographers have been redirecting their work away from what Susan Pierce Lamb describes as the "linear paradigm [that] manifests itself in separating self from the data base, in the preoccupation with being objective" (18). As Native American writer and critic Greg Sarris (Pomo) acknowledges, "Dialogue, self-reflexivity, polyphony, and bifocality characterize many of the newer ethnographic endeavors and textual recreations of oral literature" ("Verbal Art" 109)—what James Clifford defines "as a dialogical enterprise in which both researchers and natives are active creators or, to stretch a term, authors of cultural representations" (*The Predicament of Culture* 84). The oral storytelling mode at the origin of such work invariably points us in such conversive directions in order to access those stories, regardless of whether they are received orally or via a transcribed medium. Native writer Leslie Marmon Silko, who has studied and incorporated the oral storytelling traditions of her own Laguna tribe in her work, has explained the crucial role of listener co-creativity in any story's telling ("Language" 57). This has great bearing on the actual involvement of ethnographers in the development of story-teller-informants' tellings. Regarding the social processes of story-telling, Marjorie Harness Goodwin notes that the storytelling event or "drama" invariably comes out of "the *interaction* between teller and recipient" (811, emphasis in original). Linguist Livia Polanyi also emphasizes this crucial interactive element in storytelling, noting that "both teller and hearers have roles to play during the telling of a story" ("What Stories Tell" 98). Specifying this further, Lamb asserts that "the telling of a story (and perhaps the sequence of events within the story) is continually altered by the on-going interaction of the teller and the listener," which includes both ver-bal and nonverbal communication (17, 10); and Raymond F. Person Jr. even more strongly declares that "no element of interaction within conversation is to be ruled out a priori as arbitrary and/or meaningless" (3). Insofar as the ethnographic endeavor is con-cerned, this requires recognition of the inclusive wholeness of that storytelling circle. Stories and storytelling are not static; they are inherently transforming of themselves and of those persons partic-ipative in them. Stories continually grow and evolve with each additional new listener or contributive teller. The collaborative ethnographic process includes not only ethnographers and story-tellers ("informants") but all others involved at each stage in the telling, listening, or reading.

Readers who bring conversively informed interpretive story-lis-tening skills to bear on the ethnographic texts are needed to unpack the layers of meditative alteration, and to discern and decipher the underlying stories—what Peter Brooks refers to as "the oral in the written" (21). Many scholars have articulated the categorical differ-ences between writing and speech, from Saussure's delineation between "langue" and "parole" to contemporary analyses. As Jack Goody and Ian Watt explicitly state, "Writing establishes a different kind of relationship between the word and its referent, a relationship that is more general and more abstract" (321). While this is certainly the case, for those texts, however, whose origins are meaningfully conversive (which includes the majority of literature and, of course, textualized stories and other orally related communications), the structure of the written work can either facilitate or impede listener-readers' entries into the story-worlds of their conversive origins. Just as persons involved in oral communications actively co-create the worlds of their conversations, so too must readers engage interactively in relation to orally informed texts if the desire is to permeate the textual surface of the work and approach and enter the story-worlds within.

Dennis Tedlock has pointed out that "The anthropological dialogue creates a world, or an understanding of the *differences between* two worlds, that exists between persons who were indeterminately far apart, in all sorts of different ways, when they started out on their conversation" ("Analogical Tradition" 388, his emphasis). While much of the last quarter century's interrogations, critique, and revisionism of anthropology has focused on the methodological encounter between ethnographers and their indigenous "informants," it is crucial to address the interpretive relationship that readers have with the ethnographic texts. As James Clifford points out, "Experiential, interpretive, dialogical, and polyphonic processes are at work, discordantly, in any ethnography.... But this experiential world, an intersubjective ground for objective forms of knowledge, is precisely what is missing or problematic for an ethnographer entering an alien culture" ("Ethnographic Authority" 142, 128). This being true, what Clifford does not note is the extent to which conversive ethnographers and conversive listener-readers who step inside the unfolding storytelling circle literally do become part of that storytelling world, with interpretive accesses that are only available from within the conversive circle.

Central to this process is the co-creative nature of the story. The story is not a monologue whose storyteller wields total semiotic control, with listeners as passive audience members whose responsibilities are relegated to discerning the significance placed by the storyteller. Within a storytelling venue, there is no one story, for each listener brings her or his co-creative powers to the developing story. This also means that the story that a listener-reader participates in will definitionally diverge in significant ways from the story as intended and understood by the originating storyteller, and it will converge in meaningful ways. This is the nature of storytelling and literature. To look for the exact story as related by one storytelling "informant" would be to fall prey to the very errors of the intentional fallacy descried by the New Critics, for storytelling and literature manifest realities rich in conversive symbolism, and whose co-creative relationality requires engagements and interpretations that diverge radically from the more informational realm of discursive speech and writing. This is critical to our understandings of generations of ethnologically produced Native American autobiographies.

As fellow intersubjective participants, where all are co-equal points on the unfolding storytelling circle, indigenous peoples no longer are defined as "other" or "alien," but instead as fellow persons participative in the ethnographic story-world. In a discussion of such concerns in the study of African literatures, Mineke Schipper writes, "Scholars have become aware of the power factor that erects barriers between their own perspectives and an understanding of the Other as an object of research in (white, colonial, and/or male) culture and history" (40). By virtue of the traditionally objectifying barriers of scientific study, folklorist Susan Lamb laments that "we have removed ourselves from our research subjects, and in the process we have also removed our common humanity from what we study" (18). To engage with stories and understand them from within requires intersubjective relationships in which persons interact with fellow persons (whether embodied or storied). Far too often, as Lee Irwin notes, the Native storyteller has been reduced to little more than an informant: "What is missing here is the indigenous participant. . . . For Native Americans, what is at risk is the constant loss of self-representation through the overwhelming appropriation of indigenous discourse into narrow modes of scholarly analysis" (15). What also has been missing is the complete storytelling circle whose co-creative and co-equal participants include all listeners (ethnographers and listener-readers of the ethnographies) along with the storyteller.

One of the most challenging areas in the construction and reception of ethnographically produced autobiographies lies in the inevitable translation of orally conversive stories into textual life-history narratives. Many writers and scholars have noted the substantive communications differences between indigenous and non-indigenous peoples, as evidenced in the oral/textual divide. Silko has pointed out in the past that "Among the Pueblo people, a written speech or statement is highly suspect because the true feelings of the speaker remain hidden as he reads words that are detached from the occasion and the audience" ("Language" 34). In their analyses of interethnic communications in Alaska and northern Canada, Ron Scollon and Suzanne B. K. Scollon emphasize that the miscommunication they have observed is largely due to different "discourse systems," noting, for example, the longer and more frequent pauses in Athabaskan speech (12, 31). Linguistic anthropologist Keith H. Basso has offered some of the more thorough accounts of indigenous speech patterns in his work on the Apache, including an analysis of the importance of communicative silence, which he refers to as "giving up on words" (80–98). A conversive approach moves us away from categorization and primary foci on definition, difference, and signification (what Tullio Maranhão calls "mutually incommensurable modes of discourse" [265]) and toward a centering focus on relational engagement where even silence is a relational means of coming together through shared meaning. As Jane H. Hill and Ofelia Zepeda (Tohono O'odham) note, "'individuality' in its stereotyped form is rare in vernacular conversational narrative," further highlighting what they refer to as "the complex sociality of experience," which they identify as "critical to the social life of language" (222, 223). In contrast to interpretations of silence as definitionally disempowering, O'Connor writes that the linguistic pause in conversation is a connective link between persons and ideas "which always carries the potential of continuing in another time and place, always carries the potential of being resumed and sustained" beyond the "necessary pauses and breaks and silences," and that through the twists and turns of this conversive process, "there is always more to be learned and there are always more angles from which to see and understand and judge" (10), as shared insights lead to an enriched, more meaningful, and more accurate understanding of our worlds and each other (Lindfors 53–64).

The new directions in ethnography point in the direction of what Bob Scholte calls "a reflexive, critical, and emancipatory anthropology" ("Discontents" 781). For such work to be truly "emancipatory," it must arise from within its own communities. This does not deny the valuable contributions that non-Native scholars and writers can make, insofar as that work is collaborative from start to finish. As O'Connor comments about her own shifting work, "I myself see our work according to the model of a conversation.... As in a conversation, 'The Other' is seen as partner to and participant in the process" (9). But this demands a continued commitment to intersubjective and collaborative effort, not only on the part of ethnographers (Native and non-Native) but also on the part of editors and readers. In an essay entitled "Intelligibility and Meaningfulness in Multicultural Literature in English," Reed Way Dasenbrock discusses the co-creative involvement of writers and readers in understanding literary works: "Writers can therefore choose to make moments of their work more difficult to understand, less immediately intelligible, because they know that the reader will work for their meaning" (14). This needs to also be the case for readers of ethnographically textualized stories, for as Karl Kroeber explains, "Storytelling is a social transaction requiring, both in telling and receiving, an actively individualized participation" (*Retelling/Rereading* 192).

As this volume clarifies, such a co-creative and conversive effort is necessary to open up generations of ethnographically produced Native American autobiographies, which contain in varying forms highly creative and symbolic stories that, in some cases, may not even be autobiographical at all. Taking Dennis Tedlock's recommendation that "a translation of an oral narrative should be presented as a performable script," such a listening-reading response could thereby be greatly facilitated by writers, editors, autobiographers, and ethnographers in their crafting of such texts (*Spoken Word* 62).[3] Ngũgĩ wa Thiong'o explicitly encourages "the search for new directions in language, literature, theatre, poetry, fiction and

scholarly studies in Africa [as] part and parcel of the overall struggles of African people against imperialism" (*Decolonising* 106). The
remarkable power of a conversive approach to past ethnographic
work is in its recognition that ethnographic power relations never
really disempowered storytelling-informants. Rather, it has been
the academy that has been deceived and disempowered in the mis-
perceptions of conversively creative and symbolic stories as superficial repositories of cultural facts and historical data. If scholars
and other interpreters of indigenous-storytellers' stories misread
those stories due to discursive incapacities in engaging conversively
within the storytelling circle, it is the textual recipients who have
disempowered themselves by staying at the surface levels of the
texts and not delving deeply into the story-worlds below. What
scholars have scarcely realized is that the reductions of storytellers
into "informants" largely occurred at the discursive levels of interpretation. Scholars misinterpreted storytellers as informants and
stories as informational texts. By a conversive revisioning of those
texts, we will be able to begin to hear the texts' underlying stories—
not exactly as the storyteller or one of the other original listeners
would have understood the story, but nonetheless meaningfully,
accurately, and relevantly. Thereby, we will be able to open up told
and textualized stories, providing the needed conversive guideposts
to make them accessible to new generations of readers. The following chapters begin this process as specific textual examples are
engaged conversively and elucidatively.

Chapter Two

Twentieth-Century
Ethnographic Representations
of Navajo Storytelling

There may be no other Native American tribe in the United States that has been as studied and anthropologized as the Navajo. This is largely due to the period between the two World Wars when increasing numbers of ethnographers, representing a vast range of disciplinary interest, were sent to Navajo country to study, record, and (re)present information about the Navajo people, their language, their culture, their beliefs, and their everyday and ceremonial practices. During this period, and after World War II, Clyde Kluckhohn (the foremost academic scholar of the Navajo at the time) was at Harvard University, and he oversaw and actively encouraged the study of the Navajo by many of his colleagues and students. Additionally, the well-known linguist Edward Sapir was especially interested in having linguistic and ethnographic work directed toward a representative range of American Indian tribes and communities; he also actively encouraged work among the Navajo. One of the most active periods of ethnographic work in Navajo country was directed toward the Ramah Navajo community in New Mexico (to the southeast of Gallup and southwest of Grants). In just little over four years, from 1949 through 1953, literally scores of ethnographers and their students descended upon the Ramah Navajo community and their non-Navajo neighbors (including "the Zuni, Spanish-Americans, the Mormons, and the Texan Homesteaders" [Parsons and Vogt, 143]), to study their language, lifestyles, ceremonies, methods of healing, child-rearing, and even their sexual practices.

As introduced in the preceding chapter, regardless of the disciplinary training, scholarly interests, fieldwork practices, and resultant publications of the various ethnographers of the Navajo, arguably the most problematic difficulty that presented itself in the work of the vast majority of these scholars was the inevitable communications conflict that arose between the discursive informational data that they sought and the conversive storytelling symbolism extended by their informants. This chapter offers a beginning look at the conversive/discursive conflict evidenced in the fieldwork of four of the most well-known non-Native scholars of the Navajo: Leland C. Wyman (a Boston University medical-school professor who collected Navajo sand paintings and wrote about Navajo ceremonies); Father Berard Haile, O.F.M. (a cleric who studied the Navajo extensively throughout the course of his ministry among the Navajo); Clyde Kluckhohn (the most prolific and influential scholar whose work focused primarily on the Navajo); and Walter Dyk (known almost exclusively for his book *Son of Old Man Hat*). Following these examples of ethnographic practice in Navajo country, the chapter turns to the conversive strategy of protective coding to demonstrate the actual power that storytelling informants wielded thereby. The chapter concludes with a brief discussion of the subsequent effects of textualization upon those Navajo stories that were related in the course of the researchers' fieldwork.

A beginning example from the early twentieth century will clarify the conversive/discursive communications divide that led to questionable, and all too often spurious, conclusions. One of the scholars who spent a fair amount of time among the Navajo was Leland C. Wyman. He relates an early experience with Navajos where the conversive/discursive communications clash provided him with a wonderfully rich story, but with flatly erroneous information. He and his wife had taken a trip back in the 1920s to visit Mesa Verde, a site in southwestern Colorado with well-known ancient Anasazi ruins (McAllester 5). One evening when the Wymans were in their tent, they heard the voices of some Navajo men who were singing. The Wymans sought out the men, who were relaxing after their day's physical labor at Mesa Verde. The Wymans were enthralled by the men's singing in Navajo and asked them about their songs. At that time, the Wymans did not understand the extent to which such direct and exoticized inquiries of Navajos would be considered forward and untoward, if not insulting. Within a traditional Navajo framework (and among most peoples of the world), one usually does not approach groups of people one does not know, much less approach them as objectified and exotic curiosities that can be intruded upon with uninvited questions about themselves, their lives, or their behaviors. Within most cultures of the world, such intrusive inquiries would only be acceptable from persons with whom one is sufficiently familiar in order to talk in such personally inquisitive ways (e.g., close relatives, friends, or at least acquaintances).

In response to the Wymans' questions that night at Mesa Verde, one of the men looked at them and then proceeded to tell them a tall tale about how he and the other men were singing traditional Navajo "Bear Dance Songs" (McAllester 5). Due to the scientific training that demanded objectively detached observations and analyses, and the colonialist attitudes that, at the time, perceived Native people as exotic "others," the Wymans took the men's conversive stories at face value, overlooking the complexities of human interactions and the fact that Navajos (and many other peoples) might not respond to such questions in a purely discursive and informational manner. Mick McAllester writes that it was only later that the Wymans learned that what they had been told was not factually true, but rather "tantalizing misinformation" (5). This one story and memory taught the Wymans about the extent to which words and stories need to be taken within the framework and context in which they are uttered. McAllester has described the Wymans' later work in terms of the rigor with which they "carefully cross-checked data they were to record in the future from the Navajo ceremonial practitioners and intellectuals who collaborated in the preparation of scores of publications on Navajo ceremonial arts, symbolism and literature"(5).

The Wymans stand out among the earlier generations of outside scholars who have studied the Navajo in their commitment both to

the accuracy of their research and to a humble and continuing learning mode regarding that work—including the openness to reconsider
previous understandings and acknowledge past errors. Regarding
those many others who may not have been traditionally trained as
scholars (as in the cases of Father Haile or Franc Johnson Newcomb),
or those others who may not have been as committed to the sort of
rigorous accuracy that is demonstrated in much of the Wymans'
work, the published ethnographies of the Navajo (and the broader
global collection of indigenous ethnography) require careful scrutiny
and interrogation. To do so involves not only analysis of the written
record, but also inquiry into the paralinguistic communications that
surrounded the linguistic base of the told stories. Had the Wymans
picked up on the Navajo men's behavioral cues (laughter, smiles,
other mannerisms), they would have understood right away that the
one man's story about "bear dance songs" was more of a trickster
response to their inopportune inquiries. Ironically, in this case, it is
the Navajo men who were the more astute observers—responding in
knowing ways to the Wymans' objectifying questions and distancing
behaviors. Social theorist Pierre Bourdieu explains that the colonial
production and reproduction of symbolic power is evidenced not
only "through language and consciousness, but through suggestions
inscribed in the most apparently insignificant aspects of the things,
situations and practices of everyday life" (*Language* 51). In their pursuit of ratiocinative information, the Wymans overlooked the
broader aspects of their interactions with the men, thereby misinter-
preting what they were told. In contrast, it was the Navajo men who
were not the academically trained scholars who, in actuality,
observed more accurately and responded more appropriately to the
attempted academic imposition of discursive authority—even in its
interrogative manifestation.

    One other case that demonstrates the interpretive confusions
that arose for ethnographers working with the Navajo involves some
of the intriguing and variable work by Haile. In one representative
example of his work, he records what is presented as a traditional
coyote story in which the coyote desperately tries to procure a particular type of robe. In the story that was related to Haile (a member of
the Franciscan Order of Friars Minor), his informant describes the

desired robe with great specificity: "the black fabric, the white-on-black fabric, the black cotton robe, the white cotton robe, the skirt fabric, the many-fringed sash:...the Coyote robe" (*Navajo Coyote Tales* 65).[1] After listing the various parts of what he refers to as the "Coyote robe" (tellingly descriptive of a friar's or priest's own garments), Haile's storytelling "informant" then has the trickster character in his story exclaim, "'I wonder how one of them can become mine!'" (65). As we would expect in light of the co-creative nature of storytelling, any understanding of a story told in an oral event benefits from knowledge of the immediate context of the actual storytelling (including the listeners, the relationships between the listeners and storyteller, the initiating origin of the event, and its time and place). In relation to the Coyote robe story, we see the crucial role played by one listener's presence in the crafting of the story directed toward the storyteller's primary audience—the friar. It turns out that, quite understandably, Haile, too, wondered about the garments that were described with notable specificity. Haile queried his "informant" about the details of the robe. When he asked about the skirt fabric and sash with many fringes, the Navajo man responded by saying, "Oh, those are women's clothing" (125). This was a particular theme that repeated itself in other stories that various Navajos would relate to the friar. Haile later published a number of those stories about men who wear women's clothing, or who behave in other ways like women, in his book *Women Versus Men*, which purports to illustrate traditional gender relations among the Navajo.

Doubtless it will take generations of scholars—ideally, Navajo scholars and other scholars who live and work in Navajo country—to dig through the tremendous amount of ethnographic work on the Navajo and to guide us through such material. Back in 1955, Clyde Kluckhohn wrote that Haile "has studied the Navaho for more than fifty years and is universally regarded as the leading authority on this tribe," this notwithstanding the more consistently reliable work of trader and folklorist Franc Johnson Newcomb and, of course, knowledge possessed by the vast majority of the Navajos, who understood their own language, culture, and traditions with the intimacy, familiarity, depth, and engagement that Haile could only approach (386). Here it is helpful to have Charlotte J. Frisbie's reminder about Haile's valuable contributions to the Navajo tribe in deliberations and determinations of land rights ("Tales" 189). Haile was a friend to the Navajo in many ways over the course of his many years on the reservation, despite what was nevertheless his colonizing commitment to the imperial mission-building that framed his ethnographic work, including "pre-Vatican II theology and early twentieth-century anthropology" (Frisbie, "Tales" 188). Haile's volume *Women Versus Men* is still used as a source for its portrayal of traditional Navajo gender distinctions and relations. Only by bringing a conversive ear to that work will we be able to recognize the intricately symbolic storytelling indicators evident in the stories that were told to Haile and many other ethnographers of the Navajo whose academically colonialist attitudes skewed their interpretive access into those stories. As Bob Scholte states regarding the increasingly apparent problematized and convoluted history of ethnography:

> [E]thnographic authority (existential credibility, empirical comprehensiveness, descriptive adequacy, etc.) and ethnological legitimacy (scientific insight, theoretical acumen, disciplinary value, etc.) are, in fact, *constituted*, that is, they are not merely descriptive (imitative) of reality or analytic (logical) manipulations of the real, but they are also and perhaps more fundamentally literary, poetic, inventive, imaginative, and constitutive *deeds* of a metaanthropological (political, historical, aesthetic, etc.) kind. ("Literary Turn" 36, emphasis in original)

Vincent Crapanzano, who wrote *The Fifth World of Forster Bennet: Portrait of a Navajo* (recently reprinted in 2003), echoes this recognition of the literariness of the life history, noting, "It is, as it were, doubly edited, during the encounter itself and during the literary re-encounter" ("Life History" 4). But even here, for both Scholte and Crapanzano, the focus is on the "literary" and editorial nature of ethnography, rather than on the literary or creative quality of the stories related to ethnographers. A literary and storytelling approach to the ethnographic record is necessary to assist readers in beginning to decipher both the constructed ethnographic texts and their respective originating stories by freeing them from the imperial bounds of discursive control wielded by their ethnographers and editors.

The ethnographic interrogations and engagements in this and the subsequent chapters are designed to contribute to the larger intertwined and discrete analyses of Navajo history, psychoanalytic anthropology, ethnography, modern and postmodern critical interpretations of texts, conversive relationships with stories, and conversive reading strategies for ethnographic texts. The earlier generations of academic study of the Navajo offer a strongly representative example of the colonial ethnographic encounter as it was more often than not practiced during much of the twentieth century. The various ethnographers of the Navajo, like the Wymans, brought to their respective work the scholarly and scientific methods and expectations of their disciplines and times, and the published Navajo ethnographies reflect that range of backgrounds and training. As Ruth Finnegan points out, "We naturally have a bias in favour of the associations and forms that we know—especially if this is combined with ignorance of those of other peoples" (114). Navajo historian Jennifer Nez Denetdale points out that this has been especially true of those "autobiographies [that] have been used to validate and endorse anthropologists' interpretations of Native life as well as to further their own hidden agendas" (17). The vast majority of early ethnography on the Navajo was conducted within a colonialist rubric that largely served to further the ends of ethnographic ivory towers productive of work that was bounded by the interpretive and evaluative theories and methods of their times. By bringing a conversive ear to the ethnographic record, corrective readings of past ethnographies become methodologically possible, analyses of the miscommunications that can occur in the production and construction of those ethnographies become rhetorically clear, and a conversive model for a relational and intersubjective science is introduced. Corrective readings provide a way to work with the past record (even when ethnographers' actual field notes are unavailable); rhetorical analyses help to articulate a rationale for the importance of conversively informed ethnography; and the conversive models point the way forward for a scholarship that is definitionally relational, methodologically intersubjective, and tribally and ethically responsive.

Regardless of the past demands of disciplinary scholarship, the communications conflict that invariably arises when discursive approaches interact with conversive ways is especially problematic for the work done in Navajo country, in light of the degree to which appropriate language use was culturally held in great esteem by traditional Navajo elders. As Gary Witherspoon explains in *Language and Art in the Navajo Universe*, "It is through language that the world of the Navajo was created, and it is through language that the Navajos control, classify, and beautify their world" (7). Therefore, fundamental differences in the mode of communications would have great bearing on both the respective speech acts themselves and their resulting ethnography. One Navajo storyteller-informant Barnie Bitsili tried to explain this problem to no other than Edward Sapir when Bitsili was employed by the Laboratory of Anthropology Field School in Linguistics, based on the Navajo Reservation in 1929. In one story that Bitsili related to Sapir, Bitsili has one character say, "If our languages are alike, let it be that we shall go about together. If they are not alike, it will (prove) that we are not one" (Sapir 57). Commenting on this statement, Bitsili as storyteller then speaks directly to his listener (Sapir) with a conversive storytelling voice-shift to second person, saying, "You see, these languages of ours are not alike. You there talk in one way, I also talk in a different fashion" (57–59). James Dinwoodie notes that "For some reason, Sapir does not register the possibility that Bitsili is speaking to him, in particular, about differences between the two of them" (186). Sapir, like many anthropologists of his time, worked in a largely discursive mode, in search of objective data and information. Being presented with conversively informed stories by various Navajo storyteller-informants, Sapir and his fellow anthropologists were unable to understand the deeper, storied symbolism and meaningfulness of the stories they heard. Instead, since the outside academics were looking for facts and information at the surface levels of the narrative "texts" given to them, the stories they received were perceived as merely the means toward the "greater" ends of data and information, and not the means toward actual understanding and deep meaningfulness. As Dinwoodie further points out about Sapir's work in Navajo country (like the example of the made-up bear-dance songs related to the Wymans), "Evidence from

Sapir's *Navaho Texts* shows that informants did not always restrict their activities to 'informing'" (188).

It is especially illuminating to see the extent of this communications conflict as it is reflected in the work of the preeminent academic scholars of the Navajo, those who for several generations have been widely regarded as the experts on Navajo language, culture, traditions, and lives. Non-Navajo and non-Native scholars such as Edward Sapir, Clyde Kluckhohn, Dorothea C. and Alexander H. Leighton, Leland C. Wyman, Gladys A. Reichard, William Morgan, Karl W. Luckert, W. W. Hill, Ruth M. Underhill, Walter Dyk, and Fr. Berard Haile largely established the foundation of scholarship on the Navajo. Representative examples from their work demonstrate again and again the communications confusions that prevented the accuracy and reliability that these scholars presumed. Therefore any reading of their work must take into account these conflicts. Understanding that published ethnographies may diverge greatly from their originating storytelling events is not new, yet few ethnographers (regardless of their disciplinary training) have been overtly trained with an awareness of either oral storytelling traditions or conversive communications. Considered the leading scholar of the Navajo in his day, any review of past ethnographic work among the Navajo must address representative examples of the conversive pitfalls that tripped up Clyde Kluckhohn.

The Problematic Interpretive Hegemonics Evidenced in Clyde Kluckhohn's Navajo Scholarship

Clyde Kluckhohn, who had spent time in the Southwest as a boy, later focused much of his anthropological studies on the Navajo. The extent to which Native America has been viewed through the objectifying lenses of the exotic is poignantly clear in the work of a man like Kluckhohn, who, unlike so many other anthropologists, had lived encounters with some Navajos prior to his academic studies. Even so, Kluckhohn's presumptive expertise about the Navajo led to a number of remarkably obtuse interpretations about the people's lives and culture. One example from Kluckhohn's work is telling. In 1945, he published "A Navaho Personal Document with a Brief Paretian Analysis." This article focuses on a story told by one of

Kluckhohn's Navajo informants in response to Kluckhohn's request for "the story of his life" (262). Kluckhohn presents this story as "the life story of an old Navajo Indian precisely as I got it in 1936 from the interpreter who was translating his words" (262). It is significant that even though Kluckhohn presents the man's storytelling as a sufficiently reliable autobiographical narrative text upon which Kluckhohn bases his "Paretian analysis," he later qualifies the credibility of the man's story in a small footnote: "More correctly it may be described as what an old Navaho Indian told me when I asked him to tell me the story of his life" (262). Kluckhohn then continues the footnote by directing his readers' attention to two volumes that he does recommend as "true autobiographies," namely Walter Dyk's *Son of Old Man Hat* and the Leightons' *The Navaho Door* (262).[2] (Chapters 4 and 5 directly focus on Walter Dyk's *Son of Old Man Hat*, interrogating the authenticity of an autobiography that Kluckhohn praised so highly.) In Kluckhohn's positive valuations of both the Leightons' and Dyk's work, he contrasts a story about his informant (a man he refers to as "Mr. Moustache") with these other two works, which he saw as exemplary Navajo autobiographies.

At the time of Kluckhohn's work with "Mr. Moustache," he was a young anthropologist, and this was his first effort in ethnographic autobiography. Kluckhohn's access to prospective "informants" was made possible due to his familiarity with the region, having spent many summers in the area where he returned to do his fieldwork. This being so, it is notably curious that Kluckhohn's ethnographic research, writing, and analyses demonstrate the scholarly hegemonics of control that discount the attempted directives on the part of Navajo storyteller-informants to assert and affirm their own worldviews and agendas. Kluckhohn relates that the old Navajo man "Mr. Moustache" was the first Navajo he had come to know (265). Kluckhohn explains that in his work with Mr. Moustache, he approached the old man in the manner in which he had been taught as an ethnologist: "My approach to him with the request that he tell me about his life was not only the first time that I had talked to him as an ethnologist but also on the first day I ever did formal ethnological work among the Navaho" (265). Even though Kluckhohn uses his occasional connections with the old man in order to procure a suitable Navajo informant, in his efforts for scientific objectivity, Kluckhohn attempts to recast that relationship into the expected professional forms (e.g., scholarly discourse, scientific methodology, detached observation, etc.). Immediately after explaining his desire for the old man's life story, Kluckhohn tells Mr. Moustache that he will be paid—"So every day that you work, telling me about your life, I will pay you two dollars" (265)—thereby redefining their time together as an academic trade encounter. The old Navajo man, untrained in the objective and objectifying scientific method of the 1930s anthropologist, instead responds to Kluckhohn in the interpersonal and intersubjective manner of conversive relations and conversive storytelling.

Kluckhohn attempted to artificially distance himself from the old man to achieve the requisite objectivity of scientific research. Kluckhohn's discursive stance contrasts with the old Navajo man's conversive manner of co-creative storytelling. In the course of the old man's storytelling, his listeners would have included not only the young anthropologist and his interpreter, but also any other family, clan, or tribal members who came and went, listening for various periods of time. The storytelling that ensued was co-creatively informed by those present during the storytelling, and also by the old man's recognition of his possibly broader audience through Kluckhohn's work. The older man further explains to Kluckhohn that his stories are not purely his own, and that his tribal responsibilities necessitate that he ensure the propriety of his storytelling with Kluckhohn. He tells the young anthropologist, "I want to help you. But I've got to be sure that it would be all right for the people for me to talk with you like this" (265). It is ironic that in this one statement, it is the objective ethnologist whose individual subjectivity is evidenced more directly than that of the old Navajo man, who sees his words as less his own and more responsive to and within his tribal community. Notwithstanding Kluckhohn's objectively distanced academic discourse and positionality, it is his Navajo storyteller-informant who makes it very clear that, in his work with the anthropologist, determinate primacy is to be wielded not by Kluckhohn, not by the academy, nor even by the present storyteller-informant, but by the larger Navajo communities of family, clan, and tribe.

Even though the men's fieldwork communications reflect the anthropologist's academically discursive orientation and the old Navajo man's inclusively conversive approach, it is Kluckhohn who places his trust in his informant, assuming that "Mr. Moustache" will relate his own personal life story openly, honestly, and factually to the anthropologist. Both men speak forthrightly with each other; yet because of their divergent intentions and ways of communicating, they misunderstand the other's concerns, intentions, and words. The old man senses this problem when he questions Kluckhohn as to whether he can really be trusted with his stories. The old man shares his immediate and broader concerns openly with Kluckhohn, particularly noting areas of recourse in which a white academic might be able to help the Navajo people: "Lately since we've got this new Indian commissioner the government has sent some white people out here to ask us questions. Then they started to take our sheep and goats away. The people don't like that" (265–66). In these three sentences, the old man communicates to us the past and enduring United States governmental colonization of the Navajo people, here specifically referring to the government's livestock-reduction policies. The livestock-reduction efforts that attempted (largely ineffectually) to minimize the problems of overgrazing on Indian lands in the Southwest not only had the real-world effects of herd reduction and the continued governmental intrusions in the lives of Navajo people, but these policies also served to perpetuate the external domination and control of the Navajo. Whereas the government approached the livestock-reduction programs from an agricultural and economic standpoint, to the Navajo, these programs were painful and living reminders of past historical brutalizations such as the Long Walk, the internment of the Navajo at Ft. Sumner, and the prior destruction of the Navajos' crops and herds to starve them into submission and surrender during the horrific years of the 1860s.

As discussed in the previous chapter, for those persons whose lives and worlds have been largely defined within orally informed cultures, social communications are often conversively informed such that the developing or established relationships among those involved in the speech act (whether physically present or not) are placed at the center of the interaction. The words serve as the sign of the individuals' relationships and their affection for each other, whereas within a more discursively oriented communications model, language is primarily a means of conveying information and demonstrating the varying power relations between participants. In textually based cultures, which are increasingly predominant throughout the world, we still will see shifts toward conversive communications, but generally these occur within those interpersonal relationships where communication is empathic and comes "from the heart." Regardless of Kluckhohn's ostensively distanced scientific approach, his storyteller-informant "Mr. Moustache" nevertheless spoke very openly of his peoples' struggles and needs to the young anthropologist, who apparently neither understood nor appreciated his responsibilities to the tribe whose stories propelled his career forward. Kluckhohn, as an objective scientist, did not intervene in governmental affairs, nor did he attempt to present the concerns of the Navajo to authority figures who might have been able to alleviate the conditions to which the Navajos were subjected during the first half of the twentieth century.[3]

One other example from Kluckhohn's work with the Navajo points out the sorts of difficulties evidenced in his work with "Mr. Moustache." During the following summer of 1937, two other Navajo "informants" related to Kluckhohn what they said were parts of a traditional Navajo Eagle Way ceremony. Aside from the fact that for most Navajos, it is considered inappropriate to share sacred ceremonies outside of their actual sacred practice, Kluckhohn admitted that what his informants shared with him diverged almost in its entirety from the reliable description of the Eagle Way by folklorist Franc Johnson Newcomb. Unlike Kluckhohn's limited and distanced connections to the Navajo, Newcomb spent twenty-five years of her life living on the Navajo Reservation, where she and her husband ran a trading post. Having learned the Navajo language, and being very involved in the events of her Navajo community, Newcomb's ethnographic work stands out for her rigor and consistent reliability. In her essay "Origin Legend of the Navajo Eagle Chant," she asserts that the Eagle Way was a chant/prayer/song specifically used for hunting eagles. In contrast, Kluckhohn's two informants told him that the "Eagle Way" had nothing to do with eagles, but was a traditional ceremony for curing illness. Discussing the disparities of his informants' stories, Kluckhohn asks, "But because the two episodes recorded by me contain so much not even alluded to in Newcomb's recording, are we justified in inferring that my informants are utterly ignorant on this topic or even charlatans?" ("Notes on Navajo Eagle Way" 11).

Kluckhohn then proceeds to offer dubious and convoluted support to confirm his representation of the chant as part of a healing ceremony that is wholly unrelated to eagles. To do so, he references a popular (and possibly spurious) description of an unnamed Navajo healing ceremony discussed by George H. Pepper in an intriguing article entitled "An Unusual Navajo Medicine Ceremony." In the essay, which appeared in a 1905 issue of *The Southern Workman*, Pepper does not identify the "unusual" ceremony as having anything to do with eagles, eagle hunting, or any sort of "Eagle Way" ceremony. Nevertheless, the similarities between the odd ceremony related to Kluckhohn and the "unusual" ceremony described by Pepper in his popular (and unscholarly) presentation are used by Kluckhohn to support his own assertion about the facticity of this ceremony and its use for healing purposes: "A brief description (almost certainly of this ceremonial) in rather popular vein has been given by Pepper" (Wyman and Kluckhohn 29). It is most telling that Kluckhohn qualifies his reference twice in the very same sentence that he uses as support for his claim: first with a parenthetic qualification ("almost certainly"), and second in noting that Pepper's article is not scholarly ("in rather popular vein").

As I've found in researching much of the extensive academic study of the Navajo during the 1930s and 1940s, I must admit to having been surprised at how much of the scholarship on the Navajo at that time was based upon prior unscholarly, unscientific, and popular presentations of Navajo culture and traditions. In most cases, the earlier sources came from either outsiders who spent very brief periods of time in Navajo country, or work by individuals (frequently without scholarly training) who lived on or near the Navajo Reservation but who did not develop the sort of conversive relationships necessary for achieving solid work in Navajo country. The reliability of the early ethnographies appears to be very variable, determined in large part by the type and degree of relationship established between the ethnographers and their Navajo "informants." It is absolutely crucial that future scholars interrogate the reliability of such published information. In some cases, presentations of what are presumably traditional cultural practices of the Navajo prove to be based on earlier sources that in turn offer no original sources of their own, but merely cite even earlier sources that turn out to be highly questionable early twentieth-century or late nineteenth-century popular presentations about the Navajo (e.g., the early discussions that present homosexuality as a traditionally accepted practice among the Navajo).[4] While today there are Navajos who identify themselves as homosexual, in reviewing the exhaustive scholarship on the Navajo conducted during the early part of the twentieth century, I have found no solid substantiation of this practice in the published record of traditional Navajo culture, nor any substantiation of such behavior as traditionally accepted among the Navajo, notwithstanding the stories told to Father Berard Haile about men (as in the case of priests' robes) who wear women's clothing. The next chapter discusses the psychoanalytic tradition of anthropological scholarship that heavily investigated issues such as sexuality, and which led to much of the published scholarship focused on such topics.

Regarding Wyman's and Kluckhohn's classifications of the Eagle Way Chant as a healing ceremony, they both note that their various informants explained which ailments the chant was used for. It is significant that their different informants mentioned wildly divergent ailments (e.g., head diseases, swollen legs, lack of appetite and vomiting, boils and sores, sore throat, and itching) (29). In Kluckhohn's defense of his and Wyman's 1938 paper asserting the use of the Eagle Way Chant for curing and not for eagle hunting, he discounts Newcomb's explanation as anachronistic and outdated, even though Newcomb's paper was published two years after theirs. Addressing Newcomb's discussion of the ceremony, Kluckhohn states the following: "Newcomb implies that the Eagle Way Chant was used only as an aid to success in hunting eagles. This may once have been true, but there is no doubt that at present it is carried out for curing" ("Notes on Navajo Eagle Way" 11). Newcomb's work on the Eagle Way Chant was published in the *Journal of American Folklore* in 1940; Kluckhohn's subsequent critique and variant presentation was published in *New Mexican Anthropologist* one year later, in 1941. Kluckhohn's citations demonstrate a greater acceptance of more questionable work by male writers (even nonacademics) than the consistently thorough work of a woman and folklorist who developed substantive and enduring relationships with the Navajo among whom she and her family lived for many years.

Walter Dyk and the Disjunctive Consequences of Objectifying Methodologies

The best-known ethnographically produced life-history narrative of a Navajo is *Son of Old Man Hat*. The book's ethnographer and editor, Walter Dyk, who worked with a number of different Navajos over the course of his several visits to Navajo country, produced three published ethnographic volumes that are presented as Navajo autobiographies (*A Navaho Autobiography*, *Son of Old Man Hat*, and *Left Handed*—published posthumously by Dyk's wife). Dyk arrived in the Navajo Nation having relatively little knowledge of the Navajo and negligible Navajo language facility. In the established scholarly models of academic colonial superiority and informant subalterity, Dyk approached the Navajos with whom he worked via a discursively op/positional distance and a perceptually objectifying objectivity. Unfamiliar with more orally informed cultures, Dyk was unprepared for the conversive communications model that presented him with deeply meaningful stories about a range of issues important to the Navajo. As in the preceding examples that demonstrate the consequences of the conversive-discursive communications divide, Dyk sought information from the very people who were, in turn, pushed away due to his perceived, articulated, and behavioral objectifications that reduced his Navajo storyteller-informants to the subaltern artifaction of what Dyk and the academy perceived as an exotic and disappearing culture (salvage anthropology). In his interactions with one Navajo woman "informant," this communications clash results in the devaluation of the woman's stories to little more than a mere monetary payment. Her verbal and behavioral response is telling.

In this one example, after the Navajo woman told him some stories, instead of responding to her in a conversive manner that would demonstrate that he has not only heard but also considered what she has said, Dyk responds as if the woman's words are merely part of a sterile trade encounter in which the woman (objectified in Dyk's text as "an informant") exchanges her stories for a financial payment of $1.50. Such a monetary view of the interaction devalues and attenuates relationally told stories into mere objects of trade. Fortunately, Dyk recounts his interaction with this woman storyteller sufficiently to give conversive listener-readers enough background and text upon which to flesh out the larger unfolding story of their interaction:

> I had given an informant a dollar and a half, and she laughingly said, "Thank you, I'll get me a cup of coffee with this." My interpreter added, "That's what they say, when you give them any money...." ("Notes and Illustrations" 110).

When I first read Dyk's description of this encounter, I paused on the word "laughingly." The word struck me as odd within its context. It did not seem to make sense in this context, especially when followed by her subsequent comment. The term "laughingly" has the connotation of a light and happy response. In contrast, Dyk's statement "I had given an informant a dollar and a half" demonstrates his distanced objectification of the woman. Furthermore, his reference to her merely as "an informant" disappears her as a living person, instead portraying her as little more than a receptacle of Navajo cultural information. Here, it is the information and the interpreting ethnographer that are privileged, and the role of the informant is marginalized, if not absented altogether. Additionally, Dyk's choice of the indefinite article "an" disappears the unspecified woman even further from her interpersonal role in providing Dyk with Navajo stories.

As Kevin Dwyer writes, "In the pursuit of the 'concrete' or 'abstract' Object, the anthropologist denies either the subjectivity of the Self, or of the Other, or of both, and refuses to attend to the conditions which shape the pursuit itself; and in those efforts which focus on the research process, the authors strive to cleanse that process of its historical dimensions and their own particular presence and/or refuse to relate the unique, specific experience to the impersonal, generalizing impulse which they oppose" ("Ethnology" 210–11). When I initially read Dyk's statement "I had given an informant a dollar and a half," I laughed at the painful irony of a storytelling event reduced to little more than a business exchange where stories are told but not heard, and metaphor and symbol are disappeared in favor of information, facticity, and payment. A reception of stories whose appreciation is evidenced solely in terms of a small monetary payment demonstrates an insensitivity that devalues a woman's stories to little more than the objectified and sanitized encounter of an exchange—her stories reduced to the level of a cheap trade, her person disappeared beyond her receipt of $1.50. Then I read that the Navajo woman, too, had laughed at Dyk's monetary response to her stories.

The woman's verbal response, "Thank you, I'll get me a cup of coffee with this," made all the sense in the world to me. Perhaps this is due to my years of working as a waitress. I thought long and hard about what it might mean for a woman to receive a quantity of money that would be worth the cost of fifteen or more cups of coffee, and yet reply with her coffee-purchasing comment. While a cheap cup of coffee can cost a dollar or more today, back in the 1930s and 1940s, when Dyk visited the Navajo Reservation area, a cup of coffee would not have cost much more than a dime at most. The comparable situation today would involve an informant being offered, say, $25 for an hour or so's worth of storytelling, then looking at the money and the absence of any other valuative appreciation of her stories or self and uttering, "Thanks. I'll get me a cup of coffee with this." The woman's response clearly indicates her perception of the extent to which Dyk devalued her—perhaps not even listening to her stories, but mainly interacting with the male interpreter; perhaps ignoring her until the moment of payment. Regardless of Dyk's verbal and behavioral interactions with the woman, in her recorded response to him we see her evident indignation about that payment. As Kenneth M. Morrison points out, the ethnographic "literature does show that, even when couched in benevolent terms, paternalism and ethnocentrism are close cousins, genetically linked to individualism, capitalism, literacy and authoritarian politics" (12). In this vignette, we see the real-world effects of the intrusion of a capitalist, colonialist, and ethnocentric paternalism in Dyk's work with this woman.

Dyk's choice of the descriptive word "laughingly" demonstrates his perception that the woman's laughter reflected her joyous pleasure with his payment—when the woman's laugh, in all likelihood, was her response to the objectification of her stories and herself. By conversively slowing down the text by means of close reading and listening strategies, the potentially deeper story of the woman's encounter with Dyk emerges. Regarding the importance of hearing such slight yet crucial changes in wording, as in the difference between "laughingly" and "laughed," Deborah Tannen points out that words provide clues into "the relationship between communicator and audience" ("Oral and Literate" 2). At the time, Dyk was a bit perplexed by the woman's laughter and comment. Upon asking his interpreter what she meant, his Navajo interpreter merely replied, "Oh, that's what they say" (110). Dyk's later choice of the word "laughingly" to describe the woman's laughter communicates much to us about the extent to which he misunderstood the woman's response to his payment, and also about his working attitude, cultural awareness, and perceptual cognizance. Such linguistic descriptors can serve to facilitate, or in this case impede, the readers' accurate assessments of the encounter. Dell Hymes tells us that "Mostly what is required is to 'listen' to the text in all its details" (*In vain* 7). Through such a conversive method, Walter Dyk's woman informant is finally enabled to tell her textualized story to listeners who are willing to go beyond the surface discourse of Dyk's text. As Joel Sherzer writes, "The ethnography of speaking must be able to analyze the most subtle of communicative behavior of the type that occurs every day, what Goffman has aptly call the laconicity of talk, the fact that most often in social life it is the unsaid that lies behind the said that must be analyzed" (52).

In this and the preceding brief examples from the work of ethnographers among the Navajo, we see the questionable, if not completely spurious, conclusions that have been made about the Navajo "other" as told stories are forced into preconceived interpretive frameworks. Regarding the consequences of narrative reconstructions, Hayden White explains that "narrative strains to produce the effect of having filled in all the gaps, to put an image of continuity, coherency, and meaning in place" (15). This illusion of narrative wholeness and coherence requires more beyond the simple deconstruction of textual structures, for such literary critique cannot open up the deeper realms of conversive storytelling meaning. Ironic in the objective methodologies of ethnography is the fact that more often than not, the more the outsider ethnographers wrote about the Navajo, the more the actual lives and culture of the Navajo receded from public view. Regarding Western representations of non-Western cultures, Sally McLendon notes that "In these societies there are different conventions from ours which condition expectations about the types of information which are: (a) assumed and not specified; (b) considered irrelevant to the narrative told; (c) obligatorily included in a well-formed narrative of a given indigenous genre; (d) optionally included for stylistic effect" (155). A lack of awareness of such differences leads to the problematic presentation of those texts as autobiographical narratives that were scarcely, if at all, self-referential in their original tellings. Chapters 4 and 5 of this volume explicitly address this issue in relation to the reliability and authenticity of Dyk's well-known volume *Son of Old Man Hat*.

Conversive Coding and the Actual
Controlling Subjectivity of "Informants"

The work of linguists, folklorists, discourse theorists, and anthropologists has shed much light on interpersonal orality, especially regarding how meaning is made and understood. Much of this recent scholarship is enormously helpful in our reassessments and reevaluations of past ethnographic fieldwork. For example, John J. Gumperz explains that any speech event "is governed by norms of behavior specifying such things as who can take part, what the role relationships are, what role people are acting, what kind of content is admissible, in what order information is to be introduced, and what speech etiquette applies" (193). Accordingly, our readings of textualized oral tellings must take into account the range of aspects relevant to those originating speech events. This is particularly important when the persons involved in the event bring to it radically divergent expectations, discourses, and semiotics. Communications specialists Richard Ellis and Ann McClintock point out that when groups are artificially constructed, with diverse members having divergent aims (as in the case of ethnographic fieldwork), "there may be external pressures on the members of the group which make it difficult for members to behave as they would wish. They may have to carry out their roles according to the rules, or they may have to work alongside other group members whom they dislike or would not naturally wish to associate with" (103). This describes the very artificial and awkward groupings evidenced by the conjunctions of more traditional monolingual Navajos, bilingual translators/interpreters whose experiences straddled Navajo and Anglo worlds, and the alien Euro-American ethnographers.

Even more serious than the often discordant diversity of the fieldwork encounter are the exigent power relations that such groups display, and the fact that the wielding of subjective determinacy has a discursive and actual complexity far beyond the more evident presumptions of imperial power. As Bourdieu affirms, "the relations of communication *par excellence*—linguistic exchanges—are also relations of symbolic power in which the power relation between speakers of their respective groups are actualized" (*Language* 37). James C. Scott clarifies this specifically regarding those communicative encounters that display divergences in worldly positions of power: "The dominant never control the stage absolutely, but their wishes normally prevail. In the short run, it is in the interests of the subordinate to produce a more or less credible performance, speaking the lines and making the gestures he knows are expected of him" (4). Therefore, Scott asserts that if we seek to understand the communications of the powerless (e.g., "rumors, gossip, folktales, songs, gestures, jokes, and theater"), we need to recognize that "they insinuate a critique of power while hiding behind in anonymity or behind innocuous understandings of their conduct" (xiii). Accordingly, the exigencies of power wielded by outside academic ethnographers necessitated that Native informants resort to protective means to assert their own subjectivity in the face of an imposed and presumed discursive alterity, for as Bourdieu notes, "the use of language, the manner as much of the substance of discourse, depends on the social position of the speaker" (*Language* 109).

Whereas the power of ethnographers permits them to openly express their desires, intentions, goals, and methodologies in the process of the working relationship—where informants' interests, desires, and aims diverge from those of the researchers—in the vast majority of cases, those wishes were either denied or not even allowed articulation. Nevertheless, the storyteller-informants and the Navajo translator/interpreters would find other ways to assert their subjectivity from their subaltern position, often doing so in speech that was protectively encoded. Joan N. Radner and Susan S. Lanser explain some of the ways by which women have coded their communication with diverse levels of signification: "Coding allows women to communicate feminist messages to other women; to refuse, subvert, or transform conventional expectations; and to criticize male dominance in the face of male power" (423). In other words, in one communication there could be a range of semiotic levels, with each level accessible to certain readers and/or listeners. The responsibility of the scholar, as Gumperz notes, "requires, first of all, judgments of expectedness and then a search for an interpretation that makes sense in terms of what we know and what we have perceived" (204). As Radner and Lanser further point out, individuals often resort to such coded language in those mixed groups where certain members of the audience would be perceived as dangerous or untrustworthy. Therefore, the communication is coded so that only in-group members will understand the message, and those who are not trusted will not understand the coded message that is communicated around them (414)—what Scott refers to as "a politics of disguise and anonymity that takes place in public view but is designed to have a double meaning" (19). As Radner and Lanser quote from Emily Dickinson, "Tell all the truth but tell it slant" (quoted in Radner and Lanser 419).

Even in conversive settings where there may not be a personally protective need to disguise and deceive, coded communication is often utilized for diverse audiences (listeners or readers) with a range of capacities for understanding different concepts and situations. Coding enables such complexly crafted stories to offer multiple interpretive accesses for listener understanding. For example, one story might communicate underlying ethical teachings within a much lighter humorous frame as a means of making a serious story more appealing to listeners. Coding also serves as a protection for younger listeners not yet ready to understand certain aspects of a story that might be more appropriate for adults. As Leslie Marmon Silko explains, "The stories often contain disturbing or provocative material, but are nonetheless told in the presence of children and women" ("Landscape" 93). In my own family, whose Jewish, Middle Eastern, and mixed-blood Appalachian storytelling traditions came together in many familial storytelling events, it was not unusual for stories to be related with similar age-appropriate protections. Even now, I can remember back to stories that were told when I was a child, but whose encoded meanings were inaccessible to me at the time. As Peggy Beck and Anna Lee Walters (Pawnee/Otoe) explain,

> The "coding" has another advantage, the stories appeal to more people. For instance, many of the teaching stories are very funny sometimes. This humor might be "light," on one level of telling the story, for children; a little heavier on another level, perhaps with sexual references that older children would understand. And for adults, the storyteller might add tricks of language and references to a wider range of knowledge and perhaps other sources of humor. (60)

Beck and Walters further note that "the story is like a code which, the more it is listened to over the years, the more it reveals" (59). Hence the value of conversive-reading approaches to virtually any text or telling, for each conversive reading replicates the interactive storytelling experience in which listener and teller co-create the story, which in turn changes from telling to telling and from listening-reading to listening-reading.

The importance of coding becomes particularly necessary in those tellings that involve the oppositional power relations among colonialist participants, clearly evident within ethnological fieldwork practice. As Talal Asad points out, "The structure of power certainly affected the theoretical choice and treatment of what social anthropology objectified—more in some matters than in others"

(17). The responses of the objectified subaltern more often than not led to what Scott describes as "sanitized official transcript[s]" that could be misread regardless of the "techniques by which, against heavy odds, subordinate groups infiltrate the public record with dissent and self-assertion" (87, 138). Even though, as Radner and Lanser correctly note, the ambiguity created by coding runs the risk of "reinforcing the very ideology it is designed to critique" (423)—as in the case of Left Handed's coded stories that still are read and interpreted as his own life-history experiences, as this volume makes clear—a conversive method of literary and storytelling engagement provides readers and listeners a powerful means of interpretive decoding to avoid the errors that misread coded stories as autobiographical narratives.

When scholars such as Clyde Kluckhohn or Walter Dyk misinterpreted the linguistic, paralinguistic, and behavioral cues of various Navajo storytellers, the subsequent ethnographic texts invariably substantiated and reiterated the researchers' colonizing biases and assumptions, regardless of the extent to which their master narratives diverged significantly from the stories that they had been told. As Dennis Tedlock warns about ethnographic communications, "Conversations will stand or fall on their own merits as the meeting ground of two worlds, not on the basis of whether the investigator got what he claims he had been looking for (and at whatever cost). The danger lies to either *side* of the dialogue, and it is just as near in the armchair as it is in the field" ("Analogical Tradition" 395, emphasis in original). The op/positional nature of discursive or dialogic communications creates the disjunctive "sides" that are altogether absent within the inclusive relationality of the conversively informed storytelling circle. Even where storyteller-informants communicated in conversive manners in their respective fieldwork engagements, the ethnographers' stances of ethnological scientific objectivity constructed the discursive distancing that positioned the ethnographers outside the storytelling circles. This is a choice that readers of ethnographic texts also are faced with. Both listeners in the field and readers in the armchair can choose either to engage intersubjectively, or to textualize stories and storytellings into narrative texts. Unfortunately, the requisite distancing inherent in much of the twentieth century's science led to the production of ethnographies whose discursive voices impede readers' entries into the stories within the texts. As Dwyer asserts, "Anthropology is today a major vehicle for this [objectifying] discourse. It too creates otherness and objectifies it" ("Case Study" 143). One of the consequences of such anthropological objectifications is that most readers of ethnographic texts approach their readings with the expectations of reliable facticity, informational accuracy, and narrative coherence—thereby overlooking the symbolic codes, episodic meaningfulness, and colonizing resistance evident in the conversive stories.

It is naive to assume that those texts ostensibly marketed as Native American autobiographies are solely what they appear to be, for Native storytellers exercised far greater control in the direction and content of their ethnographically elicited stories than the academy has recognized to date. As Dwyer further explains, "The informant became, for the anthropologist, an instrument to aid in the pursuit of an abstract object.... Here, the objectification of the informant disguises itself as his disappearance" ("Case Study" 144). Yet this is a disappearance of interpretive perception and the deafening of the academic ear, not the actual silencing of the indigenous voice. The discursive power relations that are at the heart of most ethnographic encounters reflect the divergent agendas, aims, intentions, and understandings between the individuals involved (most notably the differences between the indigenous informants and their outside scientist-observers), and over and over again, "informants" speak forth their assertions of subjectivity and articulation. As one Moroccan villager forthrightly explained to Dwyer during his fieldwork in Morocco, "As for me, I know that I'm not concerned with a single one of your questions. I know that these questions serve your purposes, not mine" ("Case Study" 144). One Native informant, Agnes Savilla (Mohave), who worked with a number of anthropologists in the American Southwest, noted how informants would actively attempt to subvert the ethnographic process. One Mohave "informant" who spoke English pretended that he did not and insisted on having Savilla as his translator. Savilla relates that throughout his sessions with one anthropologist, the male informant would crack jokes and make fun of the female anthropologist, leaving Savilla in the awkward position of having to explain away his comments (quoted in Officer and McKinley, 104).

Savilla expressly points to the profound irony that in many cases, greater articulative disempowerment has been on the side of the academy, whose ethnographers, students, and other readers have misconstrued conversive stories as narrative texts, storytelling devices as historical facts, and symbolic complexity as straightforward recounting. Vincent Crapanzano, an anthropologist who, as a graduate student, spent a summer on the Navajo Reservation, discovered the communications divide that impeded his initial desire for a scientifically objective ethnography. In the published volume based on those experiences, *The Fifth World of Forster Bennett: Portrait of a Navajo*, Crapanzano made the challenging decision to craft the ethnography in a first-person voice, owning that his observations could not be differentiated from his presence as an (often intrusive) outside researcher in Navajo country. In the foreword to the recently reprinted edition of the book, Crapanzano notes that the explicit subjectivity of his book was criticized by fellow anthropologists when it first appeared in 1972, but that he now affirms his choice with one emendation: "I still stand by the importance of the 'I' in social scientific research and description, but today I would focus on the dialogical relationship, in fact and in fantasy, that constitutes the 'I' as it is constituted by the 'you,' and on the discursive constraints that govern that relationship" (ix). Crapanzano's volume is an important transitional example that moves ethnography away from the decidedly colonialist discursive divide of his time, even as he declares that the scholarship of "anthropologists, as stipulated outsiders, can never gain full entry into the lives of the people they study" (xi). This is true insofar as anthropologists and other scholars study peoples, cultures, and worlds from a discursively relational distance.

Interpretive Impediments in the Textualization of Navajo Ethnographies

Not only have the empire-building agendas of academics and other ethnographers led to the misrepresentations of people's stories, but the textualized products of such work perpetuate colonialist views of the indigenous "other" while constructing interpretive and editorial layers that obscure the underlying stories, possibly even disappearing them altogether. Readers who approach these texts are thereby misguided away from the storytelling base upon which the texts have been erected. As Ethel B. Gardner points out in relation to the misreading of stories told by First Nations people in Canada, those stories that have meaning for indigenous peoples have been "collected and analyzed by a multitude of anthropologists and other academics" simply as "curios" (105). The process of their textualization is the process of objectification, of transforming telling events into the exoticized and artifacted "curios" that have fascinated Europeans, Euro-Americans, and Euro-Canadians over the course of the past five hundred years of American colonization. Since, as John Miles Foley states explicitly, "any and all aspects of traditional oral narrative are concrete parts that stand for untextualized and untextualizable wholes," readers must bring orally informed conversive tools for story ingress ("Explaining" 52). The necessity for this is paramount, especially in light of two central consequences that accrue through textualization of orality: "First, [writing] is static; it freezes words in space and time. It does not allow the living story to change and grow, as does the oral tradition. Second, though it potentially widens a story's audience, writing removes the story from its immediate context, from the place and people who nourished it in the telling, and thus robs it of much of its meaning" (Hirsch 1). The construction of the narrative text from the oral telling often produces texts scarcely recognizable in the telling, and vice versa, but insofar as orally informed texts are concerned, it is the storytelling and the stories that are most important. The text can tell us about the text and about the result of textualization, but it is the storytelling that opens up those worlds of meaning that are inaccessible at the more surface level of the text.

Reaching ethnographically yielded stories requires the recognition of the substantive differences between orality and textuality, and how those differences inform the origination of the published texts; yet few readers of ethnographies have brought to bear conversive methods as a means of delving below the surface presentation of information (be that factual, questionable, or spurious). As Richard

Bauman notes, attention to the storytelling event is rare, with the majority of scholarly attention being given to the text: "Only occasionally... is attention given to the immediate circumstances of folkloric performance; when the dominant conception of folklore is as collective representation, the expression of society as a whole, the circumstances of performance, while perhaps colorful, are not seen to be of much analytical importance" ("Linguistics" 17). Throughout the twentieth century, one of the more immediate problems involved in the transcription and editorial analysis of oral stories has been ethnographers' relative lack of familiarity with both the respective indigenous languages and the tribal storytelling traditions of their storyteller-informants. In 1981 Hymes noted, "There are no chairs of Native American languages and literatures. Literary scholars have mostly assigned the subject to folklore and anthropology, and American anthropologists and folklorists are not much for knowing or working with languages" (*In vain* 7). While the study of Native American languages is much more widely recognized today (even with the increasing threats to the survival of many tribal languages), few scholars of Native American literatures study Native languages or tribal oral traditions, and far fewer anthropologists study examples of Native literatures where the intricacies of conversive language use are brought to the page. Written versions of oral tellings thereby slip through the cracks of literary study, still relegated to the interest of folklorists, anthropologists, and the occasional linguist, yet without the literary interpretive skills needed to decode the figurative language of, and the symbolic allusions within, the stories.

The dilemma for literary scholars who are trained in strategies of textual interpretation is that literary criticism works well in decoding the various texts produced by ethnographic scholarship, but literary theories and methodologies alone are insufficient for oral and performative interpretation. For example, Susan Hegeman notes that the work by mixed-blood Native American writers is "generally speaking, easily assimilable into established [literary] criteria of evaluation" (265). She explains that these writers provide works that are more accessible to audiences within textually based cultures, but she continues, "Many traditional works by native Americans are far less accessible" (265). While literary and critical training is clearly useful for literary scholars who study texts within the burgeoning canon of Native American literatures, recently specialists in Native literatures have begun to articulate the importance of tribally informed methods for opening up those literatures (Brill de Ramírez *Contemporary;* Womack; Warrior). This is even more necessary regarding the analysis and interpretation of complex ethnographic works informed by the conflation of Western scientific discourse and tribal oral traditions. It is crucial that scholars take into account both of these traditions (Western science and tribal storytelling) as a means of avoiding what Finnegan refers to as a "natural...bias" that orients a scholar's perspective in terms of "the associations and forms" of his or her own world view and experience (114).

Three current scholars who have grounded their scholarship firmly within its Navajo origins are Kathy M'Closkey, James C. Faris, and Jennifer Nez Denetdale (Navajo), each of whom has produced important studies that delineate some of the more egregious scholarship about and appropriations of Navajo culture, while pointing the way forward toward responsible and accurate Navajo study. Denetdale provides additional guidance, directing her readers to the wealth of reliable information that is available about the Navajo, including the more recent work of Navajo scholars, and of non-Navajo scholars who work from within tribal culture. Cultural and gender familiarity, scholarly rigor, and tribal realism come together in shaping Denetdale's overview analysis of the scholarship on Navajo women. M'Closkey's *Swept Under the Rug: A Hidden History of Navajo Weaving* reviews the history of Navajo weaving, illuminating the commercial undercurrents that have perpetuated the impoverishment and anonymity of weavers while enriching traders, exoticizing Navajo culture, and popularizing a people's art form to the point of insignificance in the face of the increasing encroachment of fake "knockoff" rugs (Navajo-style rugs cheaply made by non-Navajos in other parts of the world). While mainly focusing on the economic appropriation of Navajo weaving, M'Closkey additionally notes that anthropologists have overlooked the deeper aspects (e.g., sacred, creative, and artistic) of Navajo weaving by relegating it to the categories of cultural tradition and "material culture" (1, 205–33). Faris's volume *Navajo and Photography: A*

Critical History of the Representation of an American People provides a thorough overview of the archival photographic representations of the Navajo from the years of the Long Walk up to contemporary images. As Faris notes toward the end of his volume, "Navajo subjecthood is always defined by outsiders" (279). While this has often been the case insofar as colonialist, non-Navajo perceptions are concerned, Faris spends less time noting the actual subjective control that Navajos have wielded in the course of outsiders' objectifying efforts. While Faris also appears to be unaware of the superlative photography of John Pack done on the reservation in the early 1980s, he does mention Kenji Kawano, who has also produced wonderful photography of the Navajo Code Talkers (Faris 279–80). Both of these photographers and their work are discussed in chapter 6.

A noticeably different tone from that of either M'Closkey or Faris is set in Denetdale's "Representing Changing Woman: A Review Essay on Navajo Women," in which she provides a thorough overview of the scholarship on Navajo women. In contrast to the critical revisionism of the M'Closkey and Faris volumes, Denetdale takes a broader view, interrogating "the ability of cultural outsiders to produce and translate adequately the epistemic values of other cultures" (7), while reviewing and introducing emergent tribally based presentations by recent Navajo scholars, educators, and writers. Denetdale points out the possible new directions and shapes that tribally informed scholarship might take, as scholars (Navajo and tribally connected non-Navajos) facilitate rather than impede the respective articulations of Navajo culture, history, governance, and worldviews. Additionally, the Cultural Resource Compliance section in the Navajo Nation government's Historic Preservation Department now oversees scholarship about the Navajo, providing licenses for research on the reservation and among the Navajo. This insures the reliability and accuracy of current work conducted under the department's aegis. Insofar as the past hundred-plus years of problematic ethnography are concerned regarding the Navajo, as the next chapters further delineate, a conversive method of reader engagement facilitates crucial degrees of cultural discernment. Our interpretations of the past ethnographic work produced about the Navajo need to be centrally informed by knowledge that comes from within their respective tribal cultures and traditions, and as M'Closkey, Faris, and Denetdale make very clear, there is much work to do to correct the past misrepresentations of the Navajo. Additionally, our interpretive methodologies used for understanding those ethnographic texts require literary skills that are capable of opening up the interwoven layers of symbolic oral storytelling complexity. In such a fashion, our critical approaches to such oral tellings (either in their performative acts or in their transcribed texts) will be developed along the conversive lines that straddle both oral and literary worlds, as stories are reclaimed from the residues of textual fixity and restored to their storytelling center by listener-readers who step forward to complete the storytelling circle broken by the ends of narrative textuality. Through such interactive and interrelational reweaving, we access and become part of the range of storytelling meaning that lies within and behind artificially constructed life-history narratives. This is very much the sort of process that Angela Cavender Wilson (Wahpetunwan Dakota) calls for in remembering and reclaiming indigenous ways of knowing: "The recovery of traditional knowledge is deeply intertwined with the process of decolonization because for many of us it is only through a consciously critical assessment of how the historical process of colonization has systematically devalued our Indigenous ways that we can begin to reverse the damage wrought from those assaults" (72). This volume offers conversive tools for this work.

The subsequent chapters demonstrate such a methodology by offering applied conversive listening-readings of Walter Dyk's *Son of Old Man Hat* and several other ethnographically constructed Navajo texts. Chapter 3 turns directly to the range of ethnographic Navajo studies that were significantly informed by the psychoanalytic model prevalent in the 1930s, 1940s, and 1950s (including analysis of the implications of this approach for Dyk's scholarship and that of other scholars who studied the Navajo at that time). Chapters 4 and 5 focus explicitly on the *Son of Old Man Hat*, not only because it is a representative mid-twentieth-century ethnography, but also because it has been one of the best-known Native American "autobiographies." Since this book was held up for many years as a model for other ethnographic autobiographies, it serves as an especially useful model for a demonstration of the ways by which a conversive reading can elucidate a text in new ways, and with—in this case—surprisingly corrective results. The larger argument of the next three chapters is that while a discursively informed approach can teach us much about discursively constructed texts, insofar as *Son of Old Man Hat* is concerned, conversive methods are necessary to inform us more deeply about Left Handed's stories, including deeper insights regarding Left Handed, Walter Dyk, the son of Old Man Hat, their interactions, their respective worlds, and the ethnographic enterprise.[5]

Chapter Three

Ethnography, Psychoanalysis, and Navajo Autobiography

The Objectification of People's Stories and Lives into Textual Narratives

Much of the early ethnography in Navajo country was performed by psychoanalytically trained scholars working in a range of disciplines. This chapter interrogates the psychoanalytic anthropological tradition of ethnography specifically as it was played out in Navajo country. The work of these early generations of psychoanalytically trained scholars informed much of the ethnographic work during the first half of the twentieth century; this academic tradition is especially important in that this work encompassed a significant amount of the enduring anthropological and other ethnographic work on the Navajo. To delineate both the limits and value of such work, this chapter will take a close look at the work of several psychoanalytically trained scholars who studied the Navajo people. While the actual stories behind those early generations of ethnographic recording remain to be told in their entirety, this chapter's conversive discussions begin to open up the discourse on some of this scholarship, most notably the work of Walter Dyk and Clyde Kluckhohn.

In light of the problematic origins inherent in early twentieth-century anthropology, it is important that psychoanalytic anthropology, too, be understood within its own respective legacy of academic colonization. In an essay that interrogates the potential dangers of shifting elites even within multiculturalist studies, Terence Turner warns that "The result, in anthropological terms, can only be rebellion rather than revolution: specifically, the replication of the hegemonic pattern of cultural elitism through the creation of new hegemonic elites comprised of academic specialists" (417). This very concern of Turner's is, ironically, a danger inherent in the fabric of the ivory tower and other exigencies of power. Insofar as the psychoanalytic tradition of anthropology is concerned, even though the ethnographers' "informants" often proved to be highly skilled storytellers whose stories turned the ethnographic agenda on its head, storyteller control is still not widely recognized within the halls of academe, largely due to the patronizing presumptions of indigenous disempowerment within much of early ethnography. In a discussion of the colonialist representations of the indigenous "other," Paul Rabinow notes the "dialectic of domination, exploitation, and resistance" that defined the social fact of the ethnographic encounter (259). As this chapter addresses, substantive resistance to the ethnographic appropriation of Navajo culture existed throughout the twentieth century in the form of highly crafted and coded stories that often subtly subverted the psychoanalytic agenda—even into present times, as tall tales and spurious information continue to be misread and misinterpreted as fact. The work of Walter Dyk and a few other representative ethnographers from the last century will serve to exemplify some of the more egregious errors that occurred.

Walter Dyk's Training and
Early Ethnographic Work

Born in Germany, Walter Dyk and his family emigrated to the United States when he was a boy. After two years of military service during World War I, he attended the University of California at Berkeley, graduating in 1928. He studied with Edward Sapir at the

University of Chicago, where he earned his M.A. He then contin-
ued his studies at Yale when Sapir moved there, receiving his Ph.D.
in 1933. Thereafter, Dyk did his fieldwork on the Navajo
Reservation in 1934 with a fellowship from the National Research
Council, and he also received fellowships at the Harvard
Psychological Clinic. He finally ended up as a professor at
Brooklyn College from 1942 to 1961, when he retired due to devel-
oping Parkinson's disease. The volume *Left Handed: A Navajo
Autobiography* was published posthumously through his wife's
editorial assistance. Other than his two previously published
ethnographic works, *Son of Old Man Hat* (1938) and *A Navaho
Autobiography* (1947, edited from stories related by a man named
Old Mexican), it appears that Dyk published relatively little else in
his lifetime, including a short three-page article, "Stress Accent in
Wishram Chinook," coauthored with Dell Hymes in 1951;[1] and the
longer essay "Notes and Illustrations of Navaho Sex Behavior,"
published in 1951 in the volume *Psychoanalysis and Culture*,
edited by G. Wilbur and W. Muensterberger.[2]

Dyk's early work on Wishram grammar (the subject of his doctoral dissertation at Yale) provides an important key to an under-
standing of his work with Native informants. In his obituary in
American Anthropologist, Fred Eggan and Michael Silverstein
relate that "Dyk lived in 1930 and 1931 with the Kahclamet (or
Charley) family at the village of Nixluidix across the Columbia
River from The Dalles, Oregon....Dyk fired up [his informant
Philip] Kahclamet's interest in linguistic research, and the latter
spent the 1932–33 academic year at New Haven with Dyk and
Sapir" (87). Actually, it turns out that during Kahclamet's brief
tenure at Yale, he was not welcomed as an equal coworker or as a
fellow student of language, but rather as an objectified in-house linguistic informant for Sapir and his students. Prior to arriving at
Yale, Kahclamet assumed that he would be working collaboratively
with Dyk on his tribe's language. At Yale, he soon realized the cat-
egoric divide between his conversively intersubjective approach and
the discursively objective science that was marginalizing and
silencing him as little more than the scholars' informant. Dell
Hymes, who later worked with Dyk's Wishram data, fills out the

story of Dyk's work with Kahclamet in his volume *"In vain I tried to tell you": Essays in Native American Ethnopoetics*. As Hymes relates, "When in 1930 Sapir sent a student of his own, Walter Dyk, to work with the language [Wishram], Dyk went to Spearfish and there obtained the aid of a brilliant young man, Philip Kahclamet. Kahclamet learned to write the language himself, helped Dyk obtain information from older people, corresponded with Dyk, and returned with him for a semester to a seminar by Sapir at Yale" (19).

In this short description of Dyk's work on Wishram, we see the central role of Philip Kahclamet, who was instrumental in providing older informants and also in helping Dyk to understand the meanings and structure of "Wishram."[3] Here I put "Wishram" in quotes, since it appears that the presumably distinct language that Dyk defined as Wishram is not, in fact, a separate language. Rather, "Wishram" is the Wasco language as spoken by the people who lived in the village of Wishram, which was across the river from the Wasco village where scholars had previously studied the Wasco language. For whatever reasons, it appears that Philip Kahclamet did not correct Dyk and Sapir about their error in believing that the peoples on opposite sides of the river spoke different languages— even though any apparent differences were so slight as to make the different "languages" indistinguishable (Hymes 19). Nevertheless, Dyk developed a grammar of the language he referred to as Wishram, and after going to Yale, Philip Kahclamet referred to the language as Wishram, according to the linguistic and demographic borders accepted by the scholars. Dell Hymes comments as follows on this fact: "I cannot help thinking, however, that the literature of anthropology, linguistics, and folklore is deceiving in writing as if there were distinct peoples, Wishrams and Wascos, one on the Washington, the other on the Oregon side. People on either side today trace kin and property often enough to the other, and the surviving speakers of the language use only Wasco, whether at Yakima or at Warm Springs, as its name" (*In vain* 18).

There are two additional side notes about Dyk's work with the Wishram people that shed light on the problematic relationships that developed between the anthropologist and a number of his Native informants. The first involves Kahclamet's experiences at

Yale. Dell Hymes notes that "Mr. Kahclamet had gone to Yale as an informant in Sapir's class for a semester, but he broke with Dyk and returned, having destroyed, it is reported, his copies of what he had written for Dyk" ("Breakthrough into Performance" 88). Kahclamet's response to Dyk's ethnographic and linguistic work was such that over twenty years later, when Dell Hymes worked with Kahclamet in 1956, Kahclamet "was forthcoming in matters of lexicon and grammar, but resistant to requests to dictate connected text or to tell narratives in either Wishram or English" (89). Perhaps while at Yale, Kahclamet had learned of the Yale scholars' psychoanalytic interpretations of the stories he had written down, or perhaps he was offended about his objectified role as an informant. Regardless of the ostensive cause of his break with Dyk, the effect was Kahclamet's refusal to continue working with Dyk, his destruction of their work, and his later refusal to share tribal stories with other anthropologists.

One other offhand comment about Dyk's work adds to the increasingly disturbing picture of his scholarship on, and work with, American Indian peoples. In his obituary in *American Anthropologist*, Eggan and Silverstein note that Dyk "made such an impression [with the Kahclamet family] that the half brothers of his late informant, Philip Kahclamet, still recall the unfolding linguistic research" (87). Eggan and Silverstein do not describe the nature of that impression, but they further note that Dyk falsely presented himself as an Indian to some of the Indian people he encountered. They write, "Dyk had apparently learned enough Wishram to pass himself off as an Indian at the Pendleton, Oregon 'Round Up,' convincing the management of this even though he wore a full beard at the time!" (87). This statement gave me great pause for thought when I first encountered it. Approaching that comment with the cocreative response of a conversive listener, I considered the situation of an academic German-American with a full beard who spoke some "Wishram" but who was far from fluent, and who believed that he had successfully passed himself off as an Indian and was proud of that misrepresentation. I have tried to make sense of this telling ethnographic referent. I have worked to reweave the strands of this vignette back into a full story, imagining Walter Dyk arriving at the

"Round Up" and speaking some of the "Wishram" that he had learned. I further imagined one or more of the Indian people observing this white man trying to speak Indian, and some trickster person making fun of the white man by asking him, "Are you Indian?"—not out of confusion about Dyk's ethnicity, but simply asking a leading question about this strange white man trying to speak an Indian language. I then considered the response of the white outsider anthropologist misconstruing the humorous (but perhaps not necessarily mean-spirited) intentions behind such a question. As I continued to weave the story's strands together, I imagined the alien scholar discursively misreading the text of the question and eagerly responding (and thereby lying) that he was, yes, Indian.

In light of Dyk's clearly European appearance, his negligible ability to speak the tribal language, and the fact that the local Native people would have been familiar with their fellow tribal members, I really doubt that any of the Indian people ever believed that Walter Dyk was Indian, but in light of Eggan and Silverstein's statement, it seems clear that Dyk believed that he was so perceived. Regardless of the actual historical events that transpired when Walter Dyk misrepresented himself as an Indian (either premeditatively, or at the very least in not correcting others' misinterpretations), according to Eggan and Silverstein, Dyk did "pass himself off as an Indian"—a fact that indicates his willingness to lie to Native people (87). It is this lie that serves as a sign of the foundational ruptures that this and subsequent chapters show to have permeated much of Dyk's ethnographic work.

Dyk's 1951 Psychoanalytic Essay on the Navajo: "Notes and Illustrations"

There is one other fact surrounding Walter Dyk's work with his Indian informants that stands as possibly the preeminent sign of his anthropological stance toward the Native other. This is his article "Notes and Illustrations of Navaho Sex Behavior," published in 1951 in the volume *Psychoanalysis and Culture*, edited by George B. Wilbur, M.D., and Werner Muensterberger, Ph.D. There are several aspects of this article that underscore its very problematic existence. But first, I want to begin with a brief disclaimer. The subject matter is clearly of a sensitive nature, and to me is very disturbing. I discuss the topics because they can help us understand the range of cases of anthropological work that have grossly misrepresented the Navajo and other indigenous peoples—cases that I would argue were and still are far more frequent than many scholars are prepared to admit. By way of an introduction to Dyk's essay, a few comments on his language use are called for.

Throughout his published work on the Navajo, situations are depicted and terms are used that are notably salacious. This is especially evident in the book *Son of Old Man Hat*, in which profane language is used extensively, and especially that which would appeal to prurient sexual interests. Wilson Follett discusses this in his *New York Times Book Review* piece on *Son of Old Man Hat*: "Left Handed, when he recounts, for instance, his early adventures in sex, does so with a blunt physiological particularity, reproduced for us by a liberal use of the ancient four-letter colloquialisms.... The terms in question are conventionally unprintable in English.... Are we, then to presume that Left Handed resorted to a vocabulary conventionally inadmissible in Navaho and invested with the same sniggering associations? ... A man, Navaho or Nordic, does not go into unreserved detail about a sexual experience without disclosing in the very words he uses what he thinks of the experience and of himself in connection with it" (33). This holds not only for the individual initially using such language (whether that was Left Handed in his Navajo-language storytelling or in the translated/interpreted versions related to Dyk by his Navajo-to-English interpreter), but also for those who would retell such stories with the same choice of language (in this case, the interpreters, ethnographers, and editors). I find it mystifying that individuals who were presumably experts on the Navajo (e.g., Dyk and Kluckhohn, who described the book as the "Navajo as he really is" ["Honest Insight" 3]) did not know that such prurient language choices were not possible in the Navajo language. Oliver LaFarge, the non-Native author of the "Navajo" novel *Laughing Boy*, also comments on the surprising word choice in *Son of Old Man Hat* in his review of the book in the *Saturday*

Review: "More startling, and equally unnecessary, is the lavish use of the strongest of our four-letter words. Navajos are frank about sex; it is not shocking to them, wherefore they do not need by-words or pet names for its aspects" (6). Due to Dyk's relative ignorance about the Navajo, he was incapable of realizing that the choice of words used by his translators may have grossly twisted the original Navajo-language stories related by his informants. In Dyk's work on the Navajo (including *Son of Old Man Hat* and Dyk's "Notes and Illustrations" article), the psychoanalytically trained anthropologist consistently presents the Navajo as singularly obsessed with sexual activity—especially the abnormal.

"Notes and Illustrations of Navaho Sex Behavior" presents eleven passages from the range of stories told to Dyk by his various Navajo informants. Seven appear to be from Left Handed; three are from women informants. Dyk went to the Navajo Reservation specifically to record life stories, and the information in his article is culled from those purportedly autobiographical tellings that are actually collections of stories that individual Navajos chose to tell Dyk. It appears that the majority of stories which Dyk published as autobiographical narratives may not have really been about his informants themselves. Dyk insisted that the stories his informants told had to be about their own lives, so in a number of cases, his "informants" obliged by proceeding to tell him the stories they wanted to tell him in the first place, only doing so in a first-person voice. Regarding Left Handed, the Navajo man with whom Dyk worked the longest, Dyk admits that it took a great deal of effort on his part to get Left Handed to tell stories that were presumably about himself—namely, stories that Left Handed related in the first-person voice. Of course within literary and folklore studies, it is well understood that a first-person voice on the part of a persona of a story or poem is not necessarily the voice of the writer or storyteller, but for scholars trained in social-scientific fields, such discriminations were far less clear. Dyk does not appear to have questioned whether any of the stories related to him in a first-person voice were indeed autobiographical or not.

As indicated by the 1951 essay's title, the stories and vignettes that Dyk presents in the article have sexual activities as the predominant focus. They are all exhibited outside of their storytelling

contexts, with little background information about the circumstances under which the respective tales were told. What we can
reconstruct about the tellings is that each of the stories comprised
a Navajo teller with a psychoanalytically informed anthropologist
listener. As Bruce Mannheim and Dennis Tedlock explain, "A narrative told to an ethnographer is a joint construction of the ethnographer and the storyteller" (13). In the co-creative and interrelational
act of storytelling, the stories told exist by virtue of the particular
context that was created due to Walter Dyk's presence as listener.
With his psychoanalytical interest in sexual matters, it is not surprising that his informants would tell him the sorts of stories that
they believed Dyk sought. Seven of these stories involve what Dyk
defines as the traditional Navajo practice of "prowling"—namely,
the supposedly normal and common practice of individuals (usually
males) fondling the genitals of individuals who are asleep.

According to Dyk's research, "prowling" is an "established custom" (112) among the Navajo, which, he writes, reflects the people's
response to their sexual frustrations that result from the cultural
taboos against nudity. As Dyk explains, "Exposure, or sight, of any
part of the body, except in a limited number of rigidly defined situations, incites shame, embarrassment and ridicule. Exposure of the
human genitals always does so. Even among members of the same
sex, or between mates, exposure is rare. Consequently the very natural desire to touch, and to see is systematically frustrated" (112).
Therefore, according to Dyk's Freudian analysis, the degree of physical modesty among the Navajo leads many to transgress those
restrictions to the extent that "Such efforts, if successful, . . . in turn
become established forms of behavior" (112). Apparently, this "custom" involves the practice of individuals getting up in the middle of
the night when everyone else is asleep and going to where other people are asleep, in their own hogans or the hogans of others, and then
looking under the clothes of sleeping individuals of the opposite sex
and then molesting them while they are asleep. Personally, I find it
mystifying that any scholar could actually believe such a practice to
occur as a "custom" among the Navajo—or among any people, for
that matter. When I have shared some of this early ethnographic
material on the Navajo with diverse Navajos, the response to the

material in Dyk's article ranges from laughter and ridicule to various forms of stoic disbelief to outright anger. One woman, who affirmed that such behavior was neither customary nor accepted, exclaimed, "Who do these anthropologists get for their informants anyway? The local pervert?!" One reviewer of this manuscript did note that parents might use such a story to warn young people about such possible aberrant practices, perhaps as Mexican children are warned about *La Llorona* (the ghostly woman who tries to abduct children)—in both cases, stories to teach children to stay close to home and safety.

I have found no evidence whatsoever that substantiates "prowling" as customary among the Navajo. While anthropologists who were trained in the psychoanalytic school would be especially interested in early childhood behavior and in sexual matters, among the Navajo, questions about sexuality and sexual practice would be addressing topics that would have traditionally been considered inappropriate for such casual conversation with a non–family member. Perhaps within a family there might be some discussions of topics of such a sensitive nature—perhaps parents teaching their children about human sexuality, or perhaps private conversations between a wife and her husband. But the open discussion between Walter Dyk and his Navajo informants of such sensitive topics as sexual promiscuity and deviant sexual behaviors struck me as puzzling, and as discussions that demand interrogation and explanation—especially since the early sexual research on the Navajo and other indigenous peoples is still taught in colleges and universities and has been accepted as factual presentations of Navajo belief and practice.

As a literature professor who has worked extensively on orality in American Indian literatures, it became apparent to me that Walter Dyk and many other ethnographers erred by misreading conversively complex stories as discursively factual narratives. As noted in the previous chapters, when stories are taken in the most simplistic and superficial manner as straightforward textual sources of factual information, the stories then end up being little more than the raw data for anthropological analysis. Therefore, even if an anthropologist were to ask a direct question about Navajo sexual practices, this nowise ensures that the storytelling responses are, in fact, relating such sorts of practices at all, even if the stories *appear* to be about such matters. As Agnes Savilla (Mohave) comments about her work with the anthropologist Ruth Underhill and other anthropologists,

> Sometimes, though, you do feel like a little bug under a microscope when they come in and ask you questions. Some can be very foolish questions, but you have to remember that they don't know us. How else are they going to know unless they ask and we tell them truthfully?
> I have done some interpreting for anthropologists. I did some for Ruth Underhill and I had an informant who spoke English very well—but she [Underhill] didn't know that—and he insisted that I interpret for him, so I did. I mean I tried. I sat there and she would ask a question and he would look at her and start making remarks about her—he just made fun of her—and she would turn around to me and ask, "What is he saying?" I couldn't tell her, so I said, "Nothing." I never would tell her because I didn't want her to feel badly. (In Officer and McKinley 104)

As Savilla makes very clear, the relationships between anthropologists, their informants, and translators/interpreters are complex and involve a range of agendas and concerns that impact the process at every point. As in the case of Agnes Savilla's work with Ruth Underhill, Walter Dyk and other ethnographers in Navajo country were told lots of stories in response to their scholarly inquiries—stories that may have been quite divergent from what the fieldworkers were seeking. The power relations inherent in the objectifying process of objective science elicit what James C. Scott refers to as "a hegemonic public conduct and a backstage discourse consisting of what cannot be spoken in the face of power" (xii). As Linda Alcoff explains in her critique of the discursive practice of speaking for others, "What is said turns out to change according to who is speaking and who is listening" (12).

While postmodern critiques of the globalizing master narratives of modernity have helped us to better understand the relationships involved in the creation of meaning and significance, far too much of the work of the early anthropologists is still tacitly accepted as accurate and factual. Not only must this work be looked at anew, but as Alcoff further explains, "Meaning must be understood as plural and shifting, since a single text can engender diverse meanings given diverse contexts" (12). Additionally, the very co-creative nature of stories invites conversively informed strategies of listening, understanding, and responding. Since a storyteller and his or her listeners co-create a story suited for the particular time, place, and group of participants, the stories told to ethnographers in Navajo country were stories specifically aimed at their particular audience—namely, the ethnographers and their translators. The meaning within such stories must be understood within the respective storytelling event. The relational quality of storytelling is such that to approach the meaningfulness of a story, we must understand the larger constitutive context of the storyteller's "subjective stance"—what literary theorist E. D Hirsch explains as necessary in "the imaginative reconstruction of the speaking subject" (478). Therefore, it is important to investigate the relationship between the ethnographer and his or her informant, and the relationships between them and the translator. In most cases, such relationships do not reflect the degree of intimacy one would normally expect to find in which sensitive and private topics would be broached among the Navajo. What this means for our approaches to the Navajo ethnographic record is that any meaningful understanding of that record necessitates our reconstruction of, and engagement with, the originally told stories, and with their respective storytelling events that lie behind the ethnographically produced texts.

Rather than reading the words and sentences and understanding them on a ratiocinative level (be that via a scientific means or through the literary textual approaches of the New Criticism or the more contemporary poststructural criticisms), a conversive approach means reading through the text and listening in a co-creative manner to the stories with the deliberation, responsiveness, and skill that a listener brings to a storytelling event—picking up on the storyteller's cues, such as voice shifts, episodic and associational interweaving, repetition, and pauses and silent periods for listener reflection and co-creative fleshing-out of the skeletal words into an evolving, meaningful story. In this way, the modernist literary training in close reading is conjoined and transformed through the listening strategies of the oral tradition into a conversive approach to the written material. In relation to Dyk's essay about the practice of Navajo "prowling," through a conversively informed method we can see the storytelling cues that alert listener-readers to not take certain stories as serious sources of information about Navajo sexual behavior. Clearly, the stories tell us much about some informants' willingness to pull the legs of their ethnographers, and in all likelihood, the stories tell us far more about the colonial encounter between the academy and the Navajo than they do about the informants' personal lives and sexual practices.

For example, one of Dyk's storyteller-informants relates a long and involved story that includes the practice of "prowling," but to do so, he begins with a storytelling frame designed to help guide his listeners' (and listener-readers') interpretive responses to his prowling stories. The Navajo man says that one evening he was asked, "Grandfather, tell us a story of some kind, about your life, or anything" (115). Even without literary or folklore interpretive skills, the direct parallels with the ethnographer/informant storytelling situation are obvious. Continuing the storytelling frame as follows, "I said, 'All right, I'll tell a story. Yes, yes, I will, I will tell you a story.' So I started with my story. This was just a made-up story. They were so happy. They were enjoying my story" (115). With such a storytelling frame, the Navajo grandfather explicitly alerts his listeners to the fact that the story he is about to tell is "a made-up story." Such an explicit introductory directive functions as a protective frame to ensure that his "made-up" story would nowise be misconstrued as a factual depiction of accepted Navajo behavior. Even though the older man adds this proviso about the story's fictional nature, in the article, Dyk presents the old man's story as one of his factual sources for the "established custom" of late-night "prowling" among the Navajo. Dyk's colonial biases blind his perception such that he readily accepts the story as confirmation of "prowling" as traditional among the Navajo, a people whom he objectifies as fundamentally different from Euro-Americans and therefore likely to engage in otherwise aberrant behaviors that Dyk presumes to be normative for Navajos. In a footnote, Dyk does note the older Navajo man's odd comment about telling "a made-up story." In Dyk's response, he offers a rather unconvincing and, I would hazard, disingenuous explanation of the grandfather's assertion that his story is fictional: "Unfortunately I failed to make this clear, but my belief is that he meant he was telling a story about himself, that he had not told before, and so was making up as he went along" (115). Thus, Dyk offers a convoluted interpretation to permit a most dubious acceptance of the story's facticity. In one other example of Dyk's "prowling" narratives, he notes that one woman storyteller-informant could not keep a straight face throughout her storytelling; her demeanor would switch back and forth from a more serious expression to evident smiles and outright laughter. In the vignette from this older woman, Dyk explains away her behavior by interpreting that her laughter meant that she "enjoyed herself immensely in the telling" (117). He does not interpret this woman's smiles and laughter beyond the remarkable assumption that they reflect her pleasure in her own past sexual ventures of "prowling." Dyk's ignorance of Navajo language and culture, his objectification of Navajos, and his lack of training in literary or folklore analysis made him incapable of discriminating between historical fact and storytelling creativity. Dyk wholly overlooks the distinct possibility that the Navajo woman storyteller-informant was telling a tall tale that the young anthropologist took as literally true. In his search for psychoanalytically anthropological facts, Dyk either overlooked or misunderstood the range of interpretive storytelling cues (verbal and behavioral) strategically placed throughout the stories related by his storyteller-informants.

Linguist Deborah Tannen reminds us of the importance of words as cues to "the relationship between communicator and audience" ("Oral and Literate" 2). While the language used by ethnographers is now recognized as emblematic of the researchers' colonial or postcolonial attitudes, positions, and relationships, less acknowledged have been the deliberative language and storytelling symbolism as they reflect upon the fieldwork encounter. Hymes concurs with Tannen's emphasis on linguistic attentiveness, noting the significance of a storyteller's words even when those words have been textualized: "What is required is to 'listen' to the text in all its details" (*In vain* 7). Going even further, Joel Sherzer states that the paralinguistic elements in oral communications are of paramount importance for interpretive accuracy: "The ethnography of speaking must be able to analyze the most subtle of communicative behavior of the type that occurs every day, what Goffman has aptly called the laconicity of talk, the fact that most often in social life it is the unsaid that lies behind the said that must be analyzed" (52). Far too many ethnographers have misunderstood their "informants'" communications as little more than informational data—which in turn has led to their blindnesses regarding the complex and symbolic levels of communication that lie behind the more superficial levels of the skeletal text. One example that demonstrates the intersubjective relationality that is possible even via the mediation of a text can be seen in Alanna K. Brown's essay "Pulling Silko's Threads through Time: An Exploration of Storytelling." In this essay, Brown co-creatively interweaves her experiences with Mourning Dove's novel *Cogewea*, Mourning Dove's family, and an elderly great-aunt within a scholarly presentation of Leslie Marmon Silko's stories. As Brown explains, "I was being asked to hear and think about language, dialogue and integrity in a new way. How one said something, what one said, were certainly important, but the omnipotence of the writer was gone. A human voice was speaking to another human voice" (174). Here we see the sort of postcolonial intersubjective relations that Dyk's academic colonialism kept him from achieving.

In Dyk's essay, it appears that his female informant's story about her own and her aunt's "prowling" is in response to an inquiry about whether she ever engaged in the act of "prowling." She begins her story by saying, "It happened once..." (116). The indeterminate pronoun "it" indicates that she is referring to an antecedent referent. She then relates that her aunt used to do this activity, so she thought that she would try it, too. Her story, along with the others, is very sexually explicit. Dyk paid his informants for their stories, which provided the primary (if not sole) motivation for their storytelling; nevertheless, it makes no sense to me that an older Navajo woman of the 1930s would have 1) sexually molested sleeping men she did not know; 2) admitted such behavior in public to the ethnographer, translator, and other people present during the storytelling; and 3) enjoyed such a public confession. This story, told by a storyteller-informant who could not keep a straight face during the telling, appears to be another of the made-up stories "informants" told Dyk. These are the sorts of representative stories upon which Dyk based his thesis that "Prowling, in Navaho society, is a custom, recognized as such, if not approved. It is an attempt on the part of the male to satisfy his frustrated and inhibited desire to see and touch the female genitalia" (119).[4]

Dyk represents "prowling" as a traditional Navajo practice, even though he correctly notes that for the Navajo, "Exposure of the human body is rare" (108). Apparently confusing modesty with puritanical inhibition and shame, Dyk asserts that for the Navajo, "Exposure of the human genitalia is shameful and embarrassing" (108)—this notwithstanding the fact that, as Dyk notes, infants and young children were often naked, and that women openly and comfortably breastfed their children in public. Dyk further concludes that physical modesty among the Navajo leads to 1) a "compulsive" focus on sexual bantering in Navajo discourse, 2) a systematic frustration conjoined with the obsessive desire to touch others' genitals, 3) the recognized custom of "prowling," and 4) Dyk's assertion that "aggressive seduction, by both men and women, is common" (111). Throughout Dyk's presentation of Navajo sexual mores, he imposes his own psychoanalytic interpretive framework upon a culture and people for whom that framework scarcely applies. Such interpretive blinders led the anthropologist to make even more disturbing assertions about the Navajo, for example that "Rape, in fact, is hardly a recognizable offense" (111). Dyk even goes so far as to claim that "there is little stigma attached" not only to rape, but even to gang rapes among the Navajo (111). Regardless of the time period during which Dyk was conducting his research, I find it mind-boggling that any scholar could assert that women of any cultural background would not see rape as a horrific violation. In fact, one of the most painful aspects from the European and Euro-American colonization of the Navajo and other Native peoples was the sexual abuse of women. In his short story "The Blood Stone," Navajo writer Irvin Morris gives voice to this horrific side of the colonial domination of the Navajo during the period of the Long Walk and the Navajos' internment at Ft. Sumner. This one story affirms a powerfully and categorically divergent view from that which Dyk erroneously held and presented about the Navajo.

Even more problematic than Walter Dyk's assertions that rape and "prowling" are accepted practices among the Navajo is the fact that Clyde Kluckhohn, supposedly one of the foremost anthropological authorities on the Navajo, also accepts these as traditional Navajo behaviors. In fact, Kluckhohn concludes his essay in the collection *Sex Habits of Men: A Symposium on the Kinsey Report* not only by referring to the suspect practice of "prowling," but even describing it in a very graphic (and, I would add, prurient) manner. While I will not repeat the more salacious and disturbing parts of Kluckhohn's discussion, I will share one tame passage that indicates the slant and tone of his discussion. Kluckhohn begins his narrative by noting that at night, "a man will steal across to the side where the unmarried or temporarily single women are sleeping" (104). He then continues with his graphic description of the man's "prowling" behavior. In Kluckhohn's description of the man who "will *steal* across" (my emphasis), his language choice hardly bespeaks the detached objectivity of a scientist, but rather the dramatic language of someone clearly fascinated with this behavior. In fact, Kluckhohn's description of the behavior is more graphic than Dyk's descriptions. Concurring with Dyk's acceptance of this practice, Kluckhohn concludes his essay by telling us, "The whole process is a recognized pattern and has a special Navaho name" (104). Here, I want to repeat that not one of my Navajo friends and informants affirmed that any such practice is or has been accepted and common among the Navajo, and they were mystified that anyone would believe such behavior to be normative among the Navajo—or among any people, for that matter. In any case, Kluckhohn and Dyk believed this to be true. The importance Kluckhohn gave to this topic is underscored in the conclusion to his essay, in which he graphically relates one such molestation—this in an essay that also includes discussions of bestiality (with one "informant" asserting that bestiality was commonly practiced, even with porcupines!).[5]

Interpretive Blinders and the Need for Corrective Intersubjective Research

What past scholars such as Walter Dyk and Clyde Kluckhohn did not understand is that when stories are given within a conversive mode, any interpretation (psychoanalytic or otherwise) that is discursively rooted in textual facticity is bound to misrepresent the stories in terms that are not their own. Since the text of a story is merely the surface level of storytelling, textual signification can be gleaned from the text alone, but there are deeper levels of meaningfulness that are invested in stories that cannot be accessed solely through textual analysis. As Leslie Marmon Silko (Laguna Pueblo) explains, "We don't think of words as being isolated from the speaker, which, of course, is one element of the oral tradition" ("Language" 55). To understand a story conversively requires listeners or listener-readers coming into interactive relationship within the story, analogous to the creation of meaning in conversations (Gumperz 195). While Heisenberg taught us about the effect of an observer upon that which is observed, scholars now understand the extent to which this holds equally true within the ethnographic encounter. Kevin Dwyer points out that "the inevitable tie between what is studied—the 'Object'—and who studies it—the 'Subject': neither can remain unaffected by changes in the other" ("Dialogic of Ethnology" 205). Noting that this was an especial problem in anthropology in the early part of the twentieth century, Mick McAllister writes, "However, much of the anthropological collecting was tainted by a kind of naiveté about the effect of the collector on what was collected" (3). Insofar as the psychoanalytic influence on anthropology and the other social sciences was concerned, the questions and topics raised by the researchers predetermined not only the informational reliability of their storyteller-informants but also the factual and/or imaginative nature of their stories.

Especially within the framework of conversively informed oral storytelling traditions, it is crucial that listeners of stories and readers of the written versions of those stories both step into the inter-subjectively conversive roles expected of actual participants in an oral or literary storytelling event. Otherwise, we run the risk of attempting to understand words by means of an interpretive framework that is outside the bounds of the system of meaning from which those words originated. As the philosopher Ludwig Wittgenstein writes,

> We also say of some people that they are transparent to us.
> It is, however, important as regards this observation that
> one human being can be a complete enigma to another.
> We learn this when we come into a strange country with
> entirely strange traditions; and, what is more, even given a
> mastery of the country's language. We do not *understand*
> the people. (And not because of not knowing what they
> are saying to themselves.) We cannot find our feet with
> them. (*Philosophical Investigations* II, 223e, his emphasis)

First Nations writer Lee Maracle made it very clear in her statement about Native people's responses to their encounters with white people that there are far more complex "language games" going on in these interactions than would be evident in a superficially textual analysis of the language of those encounters. As Maracle affirms, Native people are human persons in the world "like any other human beings in the world," and they need to be recognized as such (in Kelly 83). The colonialist blinders of the ivory tower that presumed objective and objectifying lenses prevented generations of scholars from achieving their desired knowledge of the diverse peoples of the world. As in the case of Dyk's assertion about Navajo "prowling," which has been cited as substantiated documentation of the practice by other scholars such as Kluckhohn, even today there is scholarship that is based upon the questionable, if not altogether spurious, scholarship of prior researchers. One example of such confusions originated in the work of Gladys Reichard, was later discussed by Walter Dyk, and most recently has been cited by Mary Shepardson. In her early work *Social Life of the Navajo Indians*, Reichard relates a supposedly customary Navajo behavior that one of her informants communicated to her. She was told that among the Navajo, "obscene teasing...[that] includes twitting about sex matters" is permissible between male and female relatives as long as they are "cross-cousins [who] are not potential mates" (72). Walter Dyk accepts Reichard's information as factual, referring to the "special sanction in the cross-cousin joking relationship" (110), and Mary Shepardson pursues this thread in her recent work. She writes, "Obscene teasing is permitted between both maternal and paternal cross-cousins who are not potential mates (Reichard 1928: 72). It is called 'joking in the clans' and involves clan relations of exogamy" (169). Shepardson tellingly adds that "Whenever we got on this subject our informants were convulsed with laughter" (169). I can confirm Shepardson's experience, for my inquiries on this topic have generated a fair amount of laughter. While it is true that there are relational limits that determine the appropriateness of sexual teasing between men and women, I have not found confirmation of the specificity that Reichard was told. The larger issue that is crucial for scholars conducting any degree of interpersonal research is a deep awareness of the complexities of human communications, so that linguistic and paralinguistic cues that signify in meaningful ways are neither overlooked nor discounted.

One final vignette demonstrates the problematic confusions that resulted from such miscommunication, resulting in what Dyk took as evidence of "compulsive...sexual banter between men and women" (110). Dyk relates that "Once when visiting a hogan where they were holding a little ceremony for a baby, they asked the interpreter how long I had been around. He said, 'A month.' Whereupon they turned to me and said, 'Well, I guess you have a baby by now.' Everyone laughed. 'That's what they say,' said my interpreter" (110). Dyk then interprets this passage as support for his thesis that the Navajo have a compulsive obsession surrounding sexual matters—ignoring the extent to which his own psychoanalytically oriented interpretive prompts elicited such topics. In this one passage, what is communicated is the Navajos' perception of either Walter

Dyk's apparent obsession with sex, his own sexual activity, or that of other Anglo outsiders in Navajo country. It is the young researcher who is accused of producing a baby-on-the-way during his first month among the Navajo. The statement "Well, I guess you have a baby by now" points to Dyk's own behavior and/or interest in sexual matters, and also to Dyk as the sign representing the behavior of white outsider males who, for five hundred years, have come to Indian country and forced themselves on Indian women. Significantly (and, I might add, very disturbingly), it is on the very next page of Dyk's article that he discusses the existence of gang rapes of drunken women on the reservation—behavior that he states has "little stigma attached" to it (111). He then describes the men who gang-rape a woman in these words: "the men who enjoy her" (111). For Native women who have endured the horrific histories of individual and gang rape at the hands of European and Euro-American men, any story told by American Indian people about similar behaviors to a foreign Euro-American male must be taken within the context of that history. It is appalling, even during the time of Dyk's work, to have a presumably objective scholar describe the men who gang-rape a woman as "the men who enjoy her"—a clause that tells us far more about Dyk and his work than about the Navajo. Additionally, the laughter about Dyk already having a baby on the way on the reservation offers a clear example of how his objectifying interpretation prevents him from understanding that in this case, the joke is not only on him, but that it is about him as well. Throughout the twentieth century, presumptions of scientific objectivity prevented generations of scholars from understanding that their presence in a storytelling event meant that they were as much a part of the conversive telling as the storyteller and the other characters in the story.

In his discussion on the value of narrativity, Hayden White tells us that efforts to craft what appear to be cohesively clear and meaningful narratives are often futile attempts to avoid "fantasies of emptiness, need, and frustrated desire that inhabit our nightmares about the destructive power of time" (15). In the essay "Navaho Sex Behavior," it is the imposed ethnographic narrative that gives us the illusion of coherent meaning across a range of divergent stories and vignettes that need to be understood within their own conver-sively meaningful frameworks. Twentieth-century mono-logic (or at best dia-logic) anthropological work has sought to fulfill its desires to explain the Native "other"; but in the process of objecti-fying living human subjects, the ethnographic enterprise ended up frustrating its own ends. As Richard Handler explains, "The invisi-bility of the ethnographer, together with the depersonalization of his or her interlocutors and their replacement by a reified culture, fundamentally distorts the narration of cross-cultural interactions and leads as well to an inadequate theory of culture" (173–74). Specifically referring to the objectifying effects of scientific studies of American Indian peoples, Roger Buffalohead (Ponca) says, "Many of the objections that Indian college students and Indian people today have to the social sciences—not limiting it to anthropologists but involving all the social sciences—is that the cumulative effect of social science research on Indians has been the rape of Indian dig-nity" (in Officer and McKinley 99). As this chapter depicts, the ethnographic generations largely influenced by the psychoanalytic method most definitely fit within Buffalohead's critique. Such scholarship befits neither the dignity of the lives and traditions of the Navajo people, nor the dignity of what is valuable in academia.

While all of this is a serious criticism of Dyk's work, and the work of many other ethnographers and other scholars of American Indian culture and history, it is not intended to be an attack on Walter Dyk, or on scholars whose work is informed by a particular theoretical approach. The colonialist positions of researchers pre-vented collegial and collaborative fieldwork engagements. This being so, there still remains the larger interpretive problems that accrue due to the scholars' lack of training in the interpretive methods of literary criticism and the oral tradition. This is a prob-lem that endures even today. Dyk's work is clearly representative of his time, even though there were those whose work at that time is exemplary (some of which is discussed in chapter 6). Dyk con-ducted his fieldwork in accordance with the training he had received, and he interpreted his interactions and the stories he was given in light of the psychoanalytic framework accepted at that time. As a scholar, he approached his "informants" objectively as objects of study. Dwyer points out the questionable benefits that accrue for the scholar who maintains an objective and academic distance from those whom he seeks to understand, noting the extent to which the scholar is thereby implicit in the construction of his object of study: "The denial of a dialectical relationship between Subject and Object hides the influence, and thus the responsibility of the Subject in 'creating' its Object" ("Ethnology" 206). As Dwyer emphasizes, human persons are not objects, but living, breathing, intentional agents in the world. As a conversive approach clarifies, when human persons are not recognized as such and, in turn, are objectified through the ethnographic agenda, complex and symbolic storytelling is misunderstood as textualized narratives portraying presumably factual and literal life histories; thereby, the people and cultures behind those stories end up being misrepresented and misinterpreted through the lens of such externally imposed interpretive agendas.

Because Walter Dyk misunderstood the relational communications between himself and his informants, his analyses of his "data" and their subsequent publications are, in turn, misconstrued and misconstructed. Such ignorance of the challenges of intercultural communications and relationality prevented him and other scholars from recognizing the colonialist boundaries that generally circumscribed the ethnographic encounter. Insofar as Dyk is concerned, it appears that he may have had the opportunity to produce some reliable scholarship, since he was welcomed by some (but definitely not all) of his informants. In one example from his published article, we learn that he was invited to one family's baby ceremony, and in his short recounting of that interaction, it is also clear that in everyone's joking around with him about his behavior that, from the viewpoint of the Navajo people there, he was being welcomed, at least to a degree—even if the joke of having a baby on the way was at his expense. Either due to his training or personal inclinations, Walter Dyk was not able to permit himself to become a part of the worlds he hoped to understand, notwithstanding his sometime lies about being an Indian. Dyk's lived experiences in Navajo country unfortunately ended up transformed and deformed by virtue of the interpretive frameworks of an objective and objectifying colonialist psychoanalysis, anthropology, and ethnography.

The Limits of Objective Science in Accessing Intersubjective Orality

The preceding examples introduce the importance for readers to step into new roles as active participants in the re-creation of the storyteller-informants' stories and the respective contexts that lie within and beyond the actual written texts based upon those told stories. There is a terrific wealth of stories that exist within the bounds of the ethnographic record, but these stories still remain to be conversively approached as stories and understood within their storytelling frameworks. As Rodney Frey comments, storytelling is a process of "re-membering [that] involves a return to and a reuniting with the original" (134). When knowledge of the other is reformed into the co-creative act between storytellers and listeners, then the alien other will no longer be defined as "other," and instead will be recognized as a fellow person in the world. This is why many Native scholars have explicitly called for the indigenization of scholarship about tribal persons and communities. Angela Cavender Wilson (Wahpetunwan Dakota) writes that "A reaffirmation of Indigenous epistemological and ontological foundations, then, in contemporary times offers a central form of resistance to the colonial forces that have consistently and methodically denigrated and silenced them" (71). Devon Abbott Mihesuah (Choctaw Nation of Oklahoma) and Cavender Wilson (2), and also Daniel Heath Justice (Cherokee) have raised explicit calls to "indigenize the academy" (101), which has for centuries privileged colonialist non-Native knowledge over that of Native experts. The conversive turn in communications offers us a methodological shift away from such empire-building hierarchies of discursive power. While Dwyer has argued for the importance of keeping "open the possibility of hearing the challenges to the Self that the Other may voice" ("Ethnology" 216), a substantive turn to the conversive requires intersubjective relationships between the self and the other such that the other is no longer perceived as other. This is what Kenneth M.

Morrison describes as "the integrity of interpersonal discourse as constituted in a real give-and-take between equals" (12), and what Peninnah Schram emphasizes as the crucial "trust and bond" in storytelling settings that determine the conversive holism that brings all involved together within the community of the storytelling circle (43). This heartfelt and empathic wholeness is virtually impossible within the distancing structures of a detached and objective science.

Walter Dyk was certainly not alone in his psychoanalytic, ethnographic approach to the Native "other." His article "Notes and Illustrations of Navaho Sex Behavior" appeared in the Wilbur and Muensterberger–edited volume *Psychoanalysis and Culture*, in which diverse cultures and peoples are interpreted in terms of psychoanalytic frameworks; a number of preeminent scholars of the time also appear in the volume. Some representative articles include George Devereux's "The Primal Scene and Juvenile Heterosexuality in Mohave Society" (90–107), Marie Bonaparte's "Some Psychoanalytic and Anthropological Insights Applied to Sociology" (145–49), and Karl A. Menninger's "Totemic Aspects of Contemporary Attitudes toward Animals" (42–74). Bonaparte and Menninger are well known for their psychoanalytic work. Devereux was also widely known, having previously published a number of other articles on the Mohave people (e.g., "Institutionalized Homosexuality of the Mohave Indians," *Human Biology* 9 [1937]: 498–527; "Mohave Zoophilia," *Samiksa* 2 [1948]: 227–45; and "Mohave Indian Autoerotic Behavior," *Psychoanalysis Review* 37 [1950]: 201–20). As problematic as many of the articles in the Wilbur and Muensterberger volume are, one of the most troubling is the one other essay on the Navajo.

In "Some Notes on Navaho Dreams" (120–31), Clyde Kluckhohn and William Morgan relate a number of dreams (actual or, in all likelihood, made-up dreams) told to them by five members of one Navajo family. These tellings include the Navajos' interpretations of their own dreams—interpretations that Kluckhohn and Morgan minimize as psychoanalytic "associations").[6] The sections delineated as "interpretations" are reserved for the scientifically objective psychoanalytic interpretations of the writers. Their interpretations not only present their own psychoanalytic readings but also include statements indicating the naive inaccuracies of their storyteller-informants' interpretations ("associations"). What is particularly disturbing about this article is that Clyde Kluckhohn and William Morgan have long been considered to have been two of the foremost scholars of Navajo life, culture, belief, and traditions—and yet this article, along with the previously discussed work of Kluckhohn and Dyk, demonstrates the errors that arise when a colonizing scholarly discourse, objectivity, and objectification clash against conversive storytelling, relationality, and intersubjectivity.

As it turns out, more often than not, the ignorance and error was on the side of the scholar. In an essay on relations among archaeologists and Native peoples, Alan S. Downer writes, "The Indians I spoke to made it clear that they *did* understand exactly what the archaeologists were saying. They kept asking their questions because they could not believe that what they were hearing was so stupid" (31). Over and over again, scholars misinterpreted what they were told largely by virtue of the fact that their colonialist prejudices made them incapable of understanding those they viewed as subaltern. In his important interrogation of Franz Boas's psychoanalytic work among the Tsimshian people, Ralph Maud reminds us that what generations of storyteller-informants offered their listeners are first and foremost stories.

> These are *stories*, not Rorschach tests where the hidden neuroses of a people are going to reveal themselves to professors....We should not gut the stories for supposed empirical evidence for tribal traits; instead we should bring to the stories all the wisdom about human nature, both universal and tribal, that we have at our disposal. The meaning resides first and foremost in the context of the narrative event. (119)

Oral stories (like written literature) are far more complex than the range of critical theories (modern or postmodern) can address. As Agnes Grant explains, "Critics often apply criteria from the dominant culture while overlooking the unique qualities of Native literature. We need a new theory of criticism, or at least new perceptions of existing critical theory as applied to Native American writers" (5). More recently, Taiaiake Alfred (Kanien'Kehaka) calls for Native scholars "to generate and sustain a social and political discourse that is respectful of the wisdom embedded within our traditions; we must find answers from within those traditions, and present them in ways that preserve the integrity of our language and communicative styles" (143). One needed method that Grant and Alfred seek can be found in the tools of conversive listening-reading strategies, which are the ancient tools of storytelling-listeners, only now transformed for literary and scholarly listening-reading.

It is the orality that is and always has been at the center of literature that distinguishes literature from the more strictly textual forms of writing. William Bright points out, "It must be recognized, then, that the difference between speech and writing is not necessarily basic to a definition of literature" (171); and in discussion about new media technologies, Robin Tolmach Lakoff notes, "The contemporary introduction of oral devices into written communication suggests the merging of the oral and literate traditions" (260). As we have seen in the ethnographic examples discussed in this chapter, the fusion of the oral and the written is evident throughout the ethnographic record. While the developments in contemporary new technologies may bring the oral and the written together in new ways, such a convergence is nowise dependent upon those technologies, for the entire history of literature, including those works defined as Native American autobiographies, is the history of that convergence and its all-too-frequent conflict. As Grant further notes, "It is not inevitable, however, that a literary tradition will automatically destroy the oral tradition. The two can exist side by side, as is demonstrated by Native cultures that have made a point of keeping their oral traditions alive" (6).

Not only do the traditions coexist within Native cultures as two separate threads, but they are also evidenced within the interwoven fabrics of Native American literatures and of the oral stories textualized in the form of anthropological ethnographies. Most scholars generally recognize the metaphoric nature of Native American written literatures, but this is not the case for oral stories, which even today garner scant attention by literary scholars. Scholars (literary critics, historians, anthropologists, and others) need to recognize and articulate the very sophisticated structures and significations within indigenous stories (both those that are oral and those that have been written). As James Ruppert tells us, "Once the distinctions that separate oral literature from written literature are banished, new fields of discourse increase the possibilities of mediation, of new insight, and of experiencing new world views" (*Mediation* 37). This is especially crucial in light of the very different "language games" participant in conversively informed storytellings (oral or written) and discursively constructed texts (which can also be in written, oral, and performative forms). Susan Bordo explains that fundamentally, all cultural formations are "complexly constructed out of diverse elements—intellectual, psychological, institutional, and sociological. Arising not from monolithic design but from an interplay of factors and forces, it is best understood not as a discrete, definable position which can be adopted or rejected, but as an emerging coherence which is being fed by a variety of currents, sometimes overlapping, sometimes quite distinct" (135). This is the very conjunction (albeit, at times, disjunctive) that is at the heart of those Native literatures that "continue the expansion of stories to enable Native peoples to encompass assimilation pressures within their oral tradition" (Brown 177). Over fifty years ago, Wittgenstein categorically rejected the usefulness of externally "preconceived idea[s] to which reality *must* correspond" (*Philosophical Investigations* I, 131, his emphasis).[7] As the examples discussed in this chapter demonstrate, the imposition of the externally preconceived assumptions of psychoanalytic ethnography upon the words and worlds of Navajo people resulted in scholarship that, while representing the interpretive biases of the researchers, represents Navajo lives and culture most problematically.

The past generations of ethnographers have recorded innumerable stories that remain for listener-readers to resurrect as stories. Perhaps Walter Dyk's work in Navajoland can serve as a warning sign for future generations of scholars. Conversively told stories hold meanings that need to be accessed through the relational connections made by their respective listeners. While externally imposed theories may offer discursive insights that appear valuable within the theories' interpretive frameworks, the significance of those insights must be called into question when they have been directed at conversively informed cultures and peoples for whom the theories do not apply. Whether the interpretive lens is that of psychoanalytic ethnography or other colonialist methodologies, such orientations will always tell us more about the academy and its theoretical orientations than they will about the stories, cultures, and peoples we seek to understand. The next two chapters turn to Dyk's well-known Navajo "life history" *Son of Old Man Hat*. Conversive negotiations are shown to open up that text, demonstrating that a presumptive volume of Native American autobiography may, in fact, communicate very little information about its storyteller-informant himself—instead relating very interesting stories that tell us much about the colonial encounter between the academy and Navajo country.

Chapter Four

Navajo Resistance to Ethnographic Colonization

Son of Old Man Hat

Any close investigations into the stories within and behind the ethnographic text *Son of Old Man Hat* require attention to the multiple mediative layerings of translators, ethnographers, and editors that have reduced the voices of Native storyteller-informants to little beyond their textual traces. Recent generations of anthropologists have been very open regarding problematic layers of academic mediation that, ironically, work against the very ethnographic agendas that erected them in the first place. As Bernard McGrane explains, "Anthropology, in short, does not simply describe its subject matter; it systematically constructs and produces it" (4). Malcolm Crick goes further in noting the distance between the stories of particular storyteller-informants and any "ethnographic monograph," which he states "is precisely *a piece of writing*" (35, emphasis in original). Whereas poststructural theory has taught us the extent to which discursive meaning is "plural and shifting" (Alcoff 12) and thereby resistant to monologic interpretive grand master narratives, such shifts are especially evident in those anthropologically constructed narratives that have been at the expense of peoples and cultures whose realities have been misrepresented or even altogether disappeared. In his essay "The Dialogic of Field Work," Kevin Dwyer provides examples from his own fieldwork to show the objectifying processes that turn informants into discursive "otherness," quoting Levi-Strauss that "the ultimate goal of the human sciences is not to constitute man but to dissolve him" (144). This is why increasing numbers of scholars now recommend corrective processes that resist the disempowering silencing of persons and cultures: "It is so important to reconceptualize discourse, as Foucault recommends, as an *event*, which includes speaker, words, hearers, location, language, and so on" (Alcoff 26). Such reinscriptions of ethnographic texts through postcolonial reading strategies that problematize the texts' discursive productions will enable readers to avoid the dictatorial impositions of scholarly authority and power that represent the indigenous "other" according to preconceived colonialist expectations. As Gerald Vizenor (Ojibwe) points out, "The various translations, interpretations, and representations of the absence of tribal realities have been posed as the verities of certain cultural traditions" (*Manifest Manners* 17). These presumptive "verities" about the Navajo require discursive interrogation and conversive engagement as a means toward the reinscription of the truths of tribal culture, traditions, history, and lives.

For well over two decades, anthropologists have been grappling with the imperialist legacy of their work and arguing for categorically new orientations and methodologies to move beyond the remaining traces of those origins. McGrane urges new directions for the field, away from what he describes as "the conventionally presumed realism of anthropology and ethnographic description" (2). In the construction of the presumably objective life-history narrative *Son of Old Man Hat*, egregious results occurred due to "one of the tacit rules of classic ethnography...[namely] the 'neutrality' of the author in the pursuit of a 'value-free science,'" which disappeared the integral intersubjective roles of the Navajo storyteller-informant Left Handed and his anthropologist Walter Dyk, participant within the co-creative storytelling circle of their ethnographic encounter (Callaway 31). Clifford Geertz pointed out thirty years ago the extent to which ethnographic description is an inherently interpretive activity, and the analysis of fieldwork data is the process of "sorting out the structures of signification—...much like that of the literary critic—and determining their social ground and import" (*Interpretation of Cultures* 20, 9). The illusion of a value-free and unbiased neutrality blinded generations of ethnographers to their roles in the construction of the narratives they presumed to be objectively scientific. As this chapter and the next emphasize, Walter Dyk's ignorance of the extent to which his presence substantially informed the stories that his various storyteller-informants related led him to represent stories as history and creativity as fact. Even more relevant for investigations into Dyk's *Son of Old Man Hat* is Kirsten Hastrup's analysis that ethnographic structures of signification go beyond the bounds of storyteller-informants' own personal and cultural worlds to invariably include their ethnographers as well: "In the intersubjective world of fieldwork, both the ethnographer and the informants are caught up in webs of signification they themselves have spun" (119).

This chapter begins a closer interrogation into Walter Dyk's ethnographic work with Left Handed, looking specifically at the well-known volume *Son of Old Man Hat*. The effects of Dyk's editorial mediation are discussed in relation to the challenges of translating oral stories into written text. In this process, the strong voice of the accomplished storyteller Left Handed is seen to have wielded far more control in the face of a colonizing scholarly agenda. Several actual examples from Left Handed's metaphoric tales are analyzed through conversive means, including stories about Navajo trading, the personification of animals, and the objectification of people. The chapter concludes by noting the power of Left Handed's coded stories, which prove to be scarcely self-referential even though related in the first-person voice required by Dyk.

The Editorial Misrepresentations
of Left Handed's Stories

In his work with Left Handed, Walter Dyk elicited particular stories from his storyteller-informant, whose words and stories were then

translated by an interpreter since the ethnographer Walter Dyk did
not know the Navajo language. Later, Dyk reworked the translated
text, editing out those passages he considered minor or unnecessar-
ily repetitive; then he reorganized the selected translated stories to
fit into a chronological life-history narrative. Determinations
regarding the inclusion and exclusion of stories, vignettes, and
statements all served the larger purpose of a constructed autobiographical text. In the deletions, Dyk imposed his own editorial axiology in deciding that some stories (deemed significant to relate by
Left Handed) were actually unimportant, or at least unimportant to
the published narrative. In his introduction to the volume, Dyk
contends that these changes do not affect the substance of Left
Handed's life story:

> As it is set down here it differs in no essentials from that
> first telling. I have tried to add nothing and have left out
> only some few minor experiences and repetitious episodes,
> besides recurring passages, such as the details of moving
> from day to day, when it seemed to me these would only
> burden the reader and add neither to his knowledge nor
> his pleasure. (xii)

In other words, according to Dyk, the published book faithfully
retells the story that he heard during the oral translations of Left
Handed's storytelling. Dyk was looking for the grand master narrative of a Navajo life history, and regardless of what Left Handed did
indeed relate, Dyk heard and then published through his editorial
control that which his preconceptions had led him to expect in the
first place. To do so, episodes that were recounted more than once
were excised, due to his editorial precision that removed the
emphatic force and significance of storytelling repetition. Within a
textually discursive framework, repetition may be devalued as
unnecessary and distracting to the progress of a narrative, for
repeated stories and vignettes would not be perceived as contributing new information; however, within the oral tradition, repetition
is often a crucial element of the telling. The episodic and associational structures of oral stories utilize repetition in such key ele-

ments as plot, theme, character, language, and image to link apparently disjointed stories and vignettes in a much larger, symbolically intricate, and meaningful interweaving. It is through such repetition that particular meanings are emphasized; events are retold (often with a slightly different, and thereby additionally significant, twist); and the range of meanings within and between events are thereby deepened, clarified, and at times changed. Through Dyk's own editorial alterations, these meaningful interconnections are diminished and obscured, if not altogether lost. Interwoven stories about particular themes and concerns relevant to Left Handed's telling, once cut up and reorganized, require conversive reading skills to co-creatively stitch together the torn fabric of the larger telling.

Additionally, Dyk assumed that what he perceived as "burdensome" and unnecessary to his narrative would be equally problematic for any (presumably white and male) reader. As Dyk relates regarding the effect of his editorial changes on the reader, they will "add neither to his knowledge nor his pleasure" (xii). Here it is important to point out that Dyk's editorial decisions were not unique among ethnographers of his time; they reflect the larger colonialist and androcentric biases that have, in fact, pervaded so much of the history of scientific inquiry. One short play by Susan Glaspell depicts poignantly the ineffectual consequences that arise when objective investigations fail to discern the underlying truths of a story. Glaspell's play "Trifles" centers around the investigation into the murder of a husband, and yet in the male search for a cause-and-effect linear facticity, those elements that are presumably irrelevant insofar as logocentric and ratiocinative thinking are concerned are, thereby, ignored as inconsequential to the inquiry. At the same time, it is the women in the home who discover the truth of the crime through their conversive interweaving of otherwise apparently unrelated "trifles" (e.g., a dead canary in a box, an unfinished quilt, preserves that had spoiled, their memories of the widow prior to her marriage and thereafter), which they piece together like the patches of the quilt that the murdered man's wife had been working on before her arrest. Like the sheriff whose own interpretive blinders obscure that which he seeks, Dyk, too, rejected the meaningful importance of what appeared to him as trifles, namely, "the details of moving from day to day," which he said would either burden a reader or add nothing to the reader's "knowledge nor his pleasure" (*Son of Old Man Hat* xii).

Dyk's incapacity to understand the diverse semiologies that underlie diverse cultures and lives is evident in his editorial reconstruction that imposed arbitrary paragraphing and chapter divisions, which establish particular narrative breaks and emphases while concomitantly ignoring and eliminating the important punctuating elements of the original telling. Although the editorial changes may fit the constraints of the literary text, in the process of doing so, the meaningful interrelationships in and between Left Handed's stories are lost. The pauses, silences, repetitions, and other interconnective links that would have been invested with substantive semiotic significance within the domain of Left Handed's oral telling are largely lost due to the translation from telling to text: "I contend that however many the direct quotations, the informants' voices cannot penetrate the discursive speech of the ethnographer" (Hastrup 121). Regarding his editing of the stories, Dyk writes, "Likewise it seemed advisable to rearrange the episodes of early childhood into what would appear to be a more chronological order from that in which they were originally given" (xii). *Son of Old Man Hat* provides us with the *appearance* of a life-history narrative, but it remains to be shown to what extent Left Handed's stories were indeed so self-referential.

The artificial reorganization of the stories into the chronological narrative yields two major areas of loss. The first involves the semiotic interrelatedness of Left Handed's stories: stories and events whose tellings would have been interwoven through a range of oral storytelling strategies (e.g., parallelism, juxtaposition, conjunction, repetition) were rearranged into the more narrow thread of chronology—thereby losing the telling through the effects of editorial literariness. In relation to Leslie Marmon Silko's autobiographical collection of stories *Storyteller*, in which she interweaves many diverse stories (historical, imaginative, literary), Bernard A. Hirsch points out the crucial importance of the links that exist between and within the stories and vignettes: "Silko, by juxtaposing different kinds of narratives and subjects, helps us to see vital, rewarding connections that might otherwise go unnoticed" (22–23)—namely, the sorts of connections and associations that are otherwise lost in the ethnographic rearrangement of orally told stories. Second, the resultant narrative chronology with which the reader is left is, as Dyk notes, "what would *appear* to be a more chronological order" (xii, my emphasis). Albeit a most assuredly unintended allusion, Dyk correctly intimates that his editing leaves us with little beyond the mere appearance or trace of a chronological life story. Ironically, the preconceived expectations of Dyk and his readers for a Navajo life history permit the approach, but never the arrival to that end.

To discover more accurately the topics of Left Handed's stories, we must deconstruct the ethnographic text to access the actual stories; to understand the stories, then we must participate in them as co-creative listener-readers, like the women in the Glaspell play who weave together the meaningfully related pieces of the larger, unfolding story. As Thomas Owen Eisemon, Martin Hallett, and John Maundu point out about stories from the African oral tradition, "Plot development in oral tradition, and perhaps in verbal discourse generally, does not require the formal logical structure of written text" (243). What is required are readers capable of responding to the episodic and conversive manner of oral storytelling, for below the surface of the skeletal text are stories waiting for listener-readers to co-creatively breathe life back into them.

Son of Old Man Hat masquerades as a Navajo autobiography when it is more accurately Dyk's own translated, interpreted, and edited Euro-American bildungsroman built upon Left Handed's stories. Interestingly, the cover of the text not only identifies the work as "A Navaho Autobiography," but references Dyk as follows: "Recorded by Walter Dyk." Dyk is neither identified as interviewer nor as editor. In his identification as "recorder," his intrusion upon Left Handed's story is hidden, thereby giving the text its spurious identity as an autobiography when it is more accurately an interpretive biography based upon the various stories and events recounted by the old Navajo man. Gerald Vizenor (Ojibwe) describes Native literatures as "the eternal shadows of the heard"—a reference that illuminates the very complexities inherent in works such as *Son of*

Old Man Hat in which stories and words struggle against their imposed narrative limits (*Manifest Manners* 68). As Stephen A. Tyler notes, "The post-modern trope of resistance and recovery tells a different tale. It speaks of the irony of representation, of that inescapable difference between appearance and reality, and exposes writing as the means that makes reality accessible only by occulting it in a simulacrum that substitutes itself for the reality it pretends to represent" (131). Underlying this process is the assumption that "the other society is weak and 'needs' to be represented by an outsider" (Clifford, "Ethnographic Allegory" 113). However, as this chapter and book clarify, the indigenous peoples of the world have wielded far more control in the ethnographic process since the beginning of European and Euro-American colonialist representations of the indigenous other. We scholars and our readers have deluded ourselves when we have not sufficiently interrogated the reliability of such ethnographic representations.

Regarding *Son of Old Man Hat*, rather than telling us the life story of Left Handed, the text tells us more about the modern era of psychoanalytically informed anthropological fieldwork and ethnographic textualization. Vizenor tells us, "Moreover, anthropologists have used the inventions of ethnic cultures and the representations of the tribes as tropes to academic power in institutions. . . . Native American Indian imagination and the pleasures of language games are disheartened in the manifest manners of documentation and the imposition of cultural representation" (*Manifest Manners* 75–76). Dyk's *Son of Old Man Hat* is no more strictly one person's monologic autobiographical telling than is Gertrude Stein's *The Autobiography of Alice B. Toklas*. Vizenor further asserts that "tribal testimonies are unheard, and tricksters, the wild ironies of survivance, transformation, natural reason, and liberation in stories, are marooned as obscure moral simulations in translations" (76). The very ethnographic process that constructed the presumed autobiography ends up being "a de facto disruption of the conventions which have long been the professional common sense of readers and writers of ethnography" (Marcus and Cushman 66). As Hastrup points out, "While the grand Master Narratives lose their authority because of their single-mindedness, anthropology flourishes as the postmodern narrative par excellence: multivocal, heteroglot and essentially inexhaustive" (129). The discursively oppositional nature of Dyk's ethnographic layerings belies any presumption of a monologic self-referential voice, regardless of the volume's presentation as a straight autobiographical narrative.

The Oral Complexities of
the Ethnographic Encounter

Son of Old Man Hat needs to be read as the heteroglossic text that it is; but to assume that the heteroglossia is merely the product of the mediation of translator and ethnographer is to miss the heteroglossia of Left Handed's original telling. The oral storytelling event manifests a conversive realm in which tellers and listeners co-create and co-participate in the story and its telling. Tellers, listeners, and characters in the story overlap and interrelate throughout the telling. The teller is not the sole creator or owner of his (or her) own story, nor is the listener an external and passive observer. James Clifford explains this in relation to Marjorie Shostak's ethnographic work *Nisa* about a !Kung woman, noting that the work reveals the intersubjective collaboration of Shostak and Nisa: "Nisa's story is revealed as a joint production, the outcome of an encounter that cannot be rewritten as a subject-object dichotomy. Something more than explaining or representing the life and words of another is going on—something more open-ended. The book is part of a new interest in revaluing subjective (more accurately, intersubjective) aspects of research" ("Ethnographic Allegory" 107). While a number of contemporary anthropologists are struggling to make their work more consciously collaborative,[1] this was not the standard methodology at all during the time of Walter Dyk's ethnographic work. As Clifford explains, "Ethnography's disappearing object is, then in significant degree, a rhetorical construct legitimating a representational practice: 'salvage' ethnography in its widest sense. The other is lost, in disintegrating time and space, but saved in the text" ("Ethnographic Allegory" 112). In contrast to Clifford's assessment regarding the colonialist disappearance of the indigenous "other," the storyteller-informants are indeed lost, but it is in the text that they are lost. The textual narratives all too often bespeak realities quite different from those that are lived and articulated by the storytellers themselves. Saved in the text are the ethnographic representations of those worlds and lives perceived as and depicted as "other." As this chapter and volume emphasize, the voices and articulations of the storyteller-informants endure within the texts, even when most problematically edited away from the originating stories, and are recoverable through conversively informed reading methods.

Anthropologists' Native informants are storytellers who employ a range of rhetorical strategies that facilitate their listeners' (and readers') entrance into the worlds of their stories (e.g., voice shifts to second person, local referents, temporal shifts, characters and events familiar to listeners, pauses for listener/reader responses, etc.). These conversive strategies demonstrate the intersubjective and inclusive relationality that is the hallmark of oral tellings. Monologic, discursive, and dialogic structures might be included within conversive tellings, but such logocentric tools would be used strategically where an argument, a position, or a linguistic distancing is sought. For example, a trickster character's self-privileging would serve as an important and valued, yet negative, example demonstrating the greater importance of the community. As Franchot Ballinger explains, "In spite of himself, Trickster encourages us to see the world through the collective social eye and thus to see beyond the individual self" (28). In fact, any privileging of an individual's or even a group's identity and subjectivity at the expense of some other's marginalization and disempowerment reflects the absence of a conversive inclusivity in which all are equally, yet diversely, empowered as subjects in the world (be that the real world or a story world as equal members in, or points on, a storytelling circle). Within a conversive domain, each assertion of self is concomitantly an assertion of the other's self and personhood such that "the individual [is] ... subordinate[d] ... to the communal and cultural" (Hirsch 2–3). Such a strategy is categorically distinct from the op/positional structures of discourse and dialogue—both of which signify even in their prefixes the idea of separation and division, of individual selves dividing up the linguistic space through their assertions of individual or collective subjectivity.

In his storytelling, Left Handed speaks to his diverse listeners—interpreters, ethnographer Dyk, any other Navajos present during the session—and beyond the originating telling event, to us, his reader-listeners. Over the course of his interactions with Dyk and their interpreter, Left Handed relates a conversive tale, while Dyk responds within his own discursive framework, scarcely perceiving himself as a part of Left Handed's telling, and positioning himself in the role of a passive and distanced scientist observer. Even so, in the process of Left Handed's storytelling, Dyk as listener is invariably part of the telling. For one thing, the stories are told in response to Dyk's inquiries. It is hardly mere coincidence that Left Handed tells an unusual number of stories emphasizing sexual behaviors and beliefs to his psychoanalytically trained ethnographer. Whereas a poststructural response might correctly note the extent to which Left Handed is lost in the ethnographic process—what David Murray describes as "a situation of dominance....[in which] the cultural translation is all one-way, and the penalty to the subordinate group for not adapting to the demands of the dominant group is to cease to exist" (6)—Vizenor reminds us that "Performance and human silence are strategies of survivance" (*Manifest Manners* 16). The very notion that Left Handed's voice is lost due to the textualization of the ethnographic work overlooks the actual controlling voice of Left Handed that undercuts and interweaves itself throughout the edited text. What is needed is a literary criticism and "a social science that [are] conceptually informed and intimately and rigorously grounded in the (intersubjective) world of human lived experience (and practical accomplishment)," so that we as listener-readers can directly engage with and within Left Handed's stories (Prus xviii). As Stephen A. Tyler writes, "Our recovery of orality is our recovery from a kind of writing that more and more gets in the way of what we want to say" (136). The conversive approach taken in this and the next chapter clarifies that the life-history narrative of the text has gotten in the way of reader access to Left Handed's voice, which is, and has always been, the controlling voice throughout *Son of Old Man Hat*.

Son of Old Man Hat's Conversive Resistance
to Ethnographic Colonization

The volume *Son of Old Man Hat: A Navaho Autobiography* was published in 1938 and based on fieldwork conducted on the Navajo Reservation by Walter Dyk during much of 1933–1935. The volume has long been recognized as a "classic" work in American Indian ethnography, as "a revelation of the real life of the tribe" (*New Yorker* 67), as "a transcript, completely unromanticized" (Walton 100), and as "a totally honest autobiography by a man to whom it is simply natural to be honest, without any exhibitionism or muscle-flexing urge to startle, an entirely unselfconscious telling" (LaFarge 6). Equally enthusiastic was a 1938 review by Clyde Kluckhohn, regarded at the time as one of the foremost authorities on Navajo culture. Giving the volume its highest legitimization at the time, Kluckhohn asserted that *Son of Old Man Hat* "could very properly be subtitled 'The Navaho as He Really Is'...[consisting of] magnificent material [that] Dr. Dyk has handled...with restraint and with rare skill" (Kluckhohn 3). Continuing the praise, a 1974 obituary entry on Dyk in the *American Anthropologist* lauded him for producing "the finest single account of the Navajo life and culture" (Eggan and Silverstein 86). Yet, as much as *Son of Old Man Hat* does indeed provide invaluable insights into Navajo culture, the story being told proves to be quite different from the narrative presented in the text.

Close conversive readings of several actual passages from *Son of Old Man Hat* demonstrate the extent to which the work cannot be read as an autobiography, and that instead, the text contains Left Handed's stories that comment very strongly on the colonization (academic and otherwise) of Navajo (and other Native) people's lives, cultures, traditions, and stories. Scholars and readers of this text bear the responsibility of engaging conversively within informed interpretive and epistemological frameworks that shed new light on the origins and substance of this and other ethnographically produced autobiographies of Native people. As Stanley Diamond advises, "History is a landscape whose unity exists only in the mind of the beholder. In a sense then, the past is always waiting to be recognized and completed by us. To grasp the meaning of any happening anywhere, any time, requires a reconstructive act of the imagination" (341). This is the very process of conversive literary and oral engagement.

All three of the Navajo "autobiographies" recorded and edited by Walter Dyk communicate much about diverse perceptions of the world and the ways by which those perceptions are understood and communicated to others. The two published ethnographies wholly based on the stories of the Navajo man Left Handed (*Son of Old Man Hat: A Navaho Autobiography* [1938] and *Left Handed: A Navajo Autobiography* [1980]) take the form of life-history narratives constructed by Dyk (and his wife, who co-edited *Left Handed*). The former volume follows the main character from birth to young adulthood, while the latter focuses on the events of three years as a young adult.² The third and briefest of Dyk's published volumes, *A Navaho Autobiography* (1947), retells stories produced from Dyk's work with an earlier informant referred to as "Old Mexican." All three of the volumes purport to tell the life stories of their respective informants through chronologically structured first-person narratives.

Although Left Handed used a first-person voice in the stories he related to Dyk, it is significant that the main character of his tellings (the son of Old Man Hat) is never personally named, nor is he identified by any Navajo clan affiliations through his own parentage—two markers that immediately call into question the autobiographical status of these works. Thus, while the context for the stories is the Navajo world clearly familiar to Left Handed, and while his tales are significant for what they tell us about his times and about his storytelling encounters with Walter Dyk, they do not constitute what has long been regarded as his autobiography, regardless of Left Handed's first-person narration in the voice and persona of the son of Old Man Hat. Far from being a life-history narrative by or about Left Handed, *Son of Old Man Hat* is instead a collection of the stories and vignettes that he deliberately chose to relate to his ethnographer. Crick tells us that it is crucial to understand the motivations of any informant. The decision of any "informant" to work with an anthropologist is much more involved than the mere financial transaction that pays for that work. As Crick points out, there is a "large range of pragmatic motives that might attract an informant to such a strange identity as an anthropologist; we need to be aware, in other words, of how the informant is 'reading' the anthropologist" ("Ali and Me" 180).

Until recently, the unbalanced power relations between anthropologist and informant were such that the actual informant's intentions were largely discounted in the search for objective scientific data—but in so doing, we lose the actual foundations upon which the ethnographic texts are constructed. Additionally obscured are the interwoven layers of meaning that exist in any human communications, and much more so within the intentionally symbolic complexities of storytelling. In an analysis of conversational inference in everyday communications, linguist John J. Gumperz addresses the interpretive challenges that are present even in apparently straightforward talk. He notes, for example, that "Interpretation in turn requires, first of all, judgments of expectedness and then a search for an interpretation that makes sense in terms of what we know and what we have perceived. We can never be certain of the ultimate meaning of any message" (204). From study in the field of social psychology, A. I. Hallowell reminded us over a half century ago of the extent to which human perception, communication, and behavior are informed by the respective cultures in which they develop (170). By means of a conversive approach to ethnography that builds upon relevant scholarship from the fields of linguistics, sociology, folklore, Native studies, women's studies, literary criticism and theory, and anthropology, a clearer picture of how we might proceed begins to emerge.

New directions in interdisciplinary scholarship demonstrate the extent to which the insights of one field (say, linguistics or Native studies) can meaningfully inform work in others (say, anthropology or literary studies), but this was not the case during those early years of the twentieth century that were Dyk's era of study, when anthropologists based their work solely on the social-scientific theories and methodologies of the day. Critical theorist Edward W. Said points out in *Culture and Imperialism* that, due to their perceptual blinders, scholars and writers have perpetuated colonialist hierarchies of power through their discourse: "The power to narrate, or to block other narratives from forming and emerging, is very important to culture and imperialism, and constitutes one of the main connections between them" (xiii). It is significant that many of the stories that Left Handed chose to relate to his ethnographer center around the themes of colonization, specifically focusing on the ways that individuals objectify, misperceive, and misunderstand peoples and cultures that they misconstrue as fundamentally different from themselves. Said notes that this strategy is common globally, as the subaltern articulates the truth that they are not "other," but in fact are fellow persons in the world, with intentionality, subjectivity, and history: "[Stories] become the method colonized people use to assert their own identity and the existence of their own history" (Culture and Imperialism xii). We see this poignantly in the stories that Left Handed chose to relate to Dyk.

In Left Handed's stories, we are told about a young man who is depicted as ignorant of Navajo culture and language, obsessed with sexual matters, and disconnected from the Navajo people around him. Such a person would certainly not be considered a typical Navajo of the first half of the twentieth century (or, most probably, of any time period); but when comprehended within the oral storytelling context that included Left Handed's young, psychoanalytically trained anthropologist, unfamiliar with either the Navajo language or culture, the ignorant, bumbling, sexually obsessed, and out-of-place young male character makes much more sense. Commenting on the role of listeners within the oral storytelling of her Laguna Pueblo people, Silko observes, "The storytelling always includes the audience and the listeners, and, in fact, a great deal of the story is believed to be inside the listener," which the storyteller picks up on and develops in the co-creation of the story ("Language" 57). As Diamond explains about the conversive communications of indigenous peoples who "live in a personal, corporate world, a world that tends to be a 'thou' to the subjective 'I' rather than an 'I' impinging upon an objectively separate and divided self" (145), interactions and relationships take the form of the "I/Thou" relationship described by Martin Buber.

Hastrup concurs, noting that "Once we realise that 'othering' is part of the anthropological practice, and that the identity of the others, *as such*, is relational, we are ready to acknowledge that they have their own self-referential discourse" (121, emphasis in original). As Richard Handler describes the human response to those perceived as other, "We act upon objects, but do not interact with them" (172).

Dyk neither understood his inevitable role within the storytelling circles during his ethnographic fieldwork, nor did he understand the processes of conversive communications and intersubjective relationality—what Robert Prus advocates as crucial to responsible ethnographic inquiry: "It is only through conversing with the other and attempting to experience the situation of the other through extended role-taking activity that one may tap into the life-worlds of the other on a more adequate (accurate, sustained, and comprehensive) basis" (23). In many of his stories, Left Handed held up a mirror to his young ethnographer as the Navajo storyteller-informant related stories that depicted the colonial attitudes and behaviors enacted against Native peoples for over five hundred years. Left Handed's own name points to his own inverted stories that prove to show much about the imperial impositions of the academy in Navajo country. Left Handed and many others who served as "informants" struggled against the externally imposed constraints of their ethnographers' demands to communicate Navajo worlds and worldviews, which included their storied responses to the asymmetrical "dialectic of world power" as manifested by generations of outside researchers (Asad 17). Literary scholar Mark Wallace points out that another well-known Native American autobiography, *Black Hawk: An Autobiography*, was in fact "intended as a story of white and Indian interaction" (488), and artist Jimmie Durham clarifies in an essay on American Indian art and literature that "Those of us who have considered ourselves militant or traditional—in the real Indian sense of that term—have often relied upon some strategy or another for presenting the 'plight of the Indian,' that is, using art to attempt to show our situation to people in the United States or to show our view of the United States to itself" (435). In many cases, indigenous informants maintained their conversive powers as co-creative storytellers, even while relating stories critical of the ethnographic objectification to which they were often subjected.

The Character of the Son of Old Man Hat
as a Storytelling Device

In *Son of Old Man Hat*, we see Left Handed's efforts to subvert Dyk's life-history agenda. For example, we are told very little about the person who is referred to as the son of Old Man Hat. As Dyk relates, Left Handed "hurriedly passed over the first twenty years of his life.... After working several weeks with Left Handed, I asked him to retrace his steps and begin with his childhood again, covering those years with the same minuteness and detail. After two days of discussion, during which Phillip Davis, interpreter, and I assured him he had told practically nothing of his youth and childhood, he offered to try" (*A Navaho Autobiography* 6). Thereafter, Left Handed related many extensively detailed stories about the childhood of the son of Old Man Hat. It is significant that the majority of Left Handed's stories focus on a young male character around the same age as the young postdoctoral researcher Walter Dyk. It is also important that Dyk arrived in Navajo country with relatively little knowledge of Navajo people, culture, or language. Dyk's doctoral studies had focused on the Wishram language. Thereafter, Dyk was sent to do fieldwork on the Navajo Reservation with a fellowship from the National Research Council, later receiving several fellowships at the Harvard Psychological Clinic. The shift from Wishram studies to Navajo ethnography would be analogous to studying Swedish and then going to Greece to do ethnographic work without having learned Greek. While there are similarities between Indian tribes, as there are between diverse European peoples, the differences are substantial. Dyk's training in psychoanalysis and linguistics (studying under the supervision of Edward Sapir first at the University of Chicago and then at Yale) provided him with a particular interpretive framework for his ethnographic work, but with insufficient prior knowledge about the Navajo people, tribe, or language. Dyk completed his doctoral work on Wishram grammar in 1933 and set off to the Navajo Nation later that year.

What we do know about Dyk's work among the Navajo includes the discomfiting fact that his Navajo informants found working with him to be emotionally taxing. It appears that Dyk's relationship with Left Handed was fraught with similar difficulties, which Dyk interprets as the result of the intensity of the "psychoanalytic treatment" (e.g., the psychoanalytically informed ethnographic fieldwork methodology). He writes, "Left Handed was even more profoundly affected. At times he became so disturbed and so worn out that he would have to take four or five days off, going away to his home or to visit relatives" (*Navaho* 6). Yet Dyk appears to have been unconcerned about the stress felt by his informants. As he explains specifically about his work with another Navajo man referred to as Old Mexican, "Once having embarked upon his life story, so intimate, so personal and detailed, the informant soon becomes as engrossed and involved as a patient in psychoanalytic treatment" (*Navaho* 6). I find this assertion quite remarkable, especially in light of the fact that Dyk's work with Old Mexican extended only for a period of several weeks, at which point Old Mexican "concluded abruptly" the paid relationship (5). From the vantage point of the early twenty-first century, one wonders what the Navajo people of the 1930s thought of Dyk's psychoanalytically oriented questioning (and, for that matter, the similar lines of questioning brought to other parts of the world by the generations of ethnographers so trained). It is hardly a mere coincidence that Left Handed tells an unusual number of stories emphasizing sexual behaviors and beliefs to his psychoanalytically oriented ethnographer.

Over and over again throughout Left Handed's stories in *Son of Old Man Hat* and *Left Handed*, we read stories about a naive, uneducated, and unnamed boy/man who repeatedly demonstrates his ignorance of even basic matters that would have been common knowledge among the reservation-reared Navajos of his time. Left Handed makes this poignantly clear in his depictions of the extent to which the main character of his stories, both as a boy and as a young man, behaves inappropriately and awkwardly around animals. In one story, Left Handed relates that his main character does not know how to put a saddle on a horse properly; that when he tries to do so, he ends up putting it on the horse's neck instead of on the horse's back; and that even when the other men show him how to saddle a horse, he still cannot do it, needing another man to saddle his horse for him (55). We know that the main character in this vignette is not a young child, but a young man big enough and old enough to saddle a horse on his own, for the other men try to instruct him to no avail ("'You'd better put it on the back of the horse.' But I just couldn't" [55]). The ignorance and incapacity of the young man is decidedly unusual for a character presented in the text as a younger version of Left Handed, or, for that matter, for any reservation-raised Navajo male of the time.

In another story, we are told that the grown son of Old Man Hat goes hunting with some Navajo men, but he confuses fresh (and hence unmistakable) deer tracks with sheep tracks (especially odd in light of the fact that the son of Old Man Hat, we are told, grew up herding sheep): "In this wash were a lot of tracks. I thought it was a herd of sheep. One of the fellows said, 'There are some deer tracks. They are all new. They must have been around here last night.' It was still early in the morning. I had never seen a deer track before, and I was wondering what kind of tracks they were" (*Left Handed* 26). One wonders what manner of young man in Navajo country would have "never seen a deer track before." Here, Left Handed uses the conversive tool of repetition to emphasize that the tracks were clearly distinguishable, first telling us that "They are all new" (26). Then he repeats that point in an associational manner by noting that it was "early in the morning" and that the deer had just been there "last night" (26). Left Handed then throws his listener-readers a curve ball, noting that his main character "had never seen a deer track before"—clearly alerting us to the fact that his main character, in all likelihood, was not a Navajo at all (26). It is highly unlikely that virtually any Navajo of that time would not recognize deer tracks, but that fact might certainly be the case for a young academic outsider with no prior hunting experience. Left Handed's hunting story proceeds in even more intriguing directions, relating that when the men do encounter the deer, the main character of the story is depicted as being afraid of the deer! "They were right close to me; I was kind of scared...I never had taken a shot at them" (27). Later, when the young man does attempt to shoot a deer, he misses—even though, as we are told, "It was standing close by me when I took a shot" (31).

In another story, Left Handed tells us about the time the son of Old Man Hat went out shooting jackrabbits, and how when one ran in the middle of a herd of sheep, he continued to shoot—ending up killing a prize ram. Then, to emphasize the extent to which this act was wholly avoidable, we are told that enough rabbits had already been killed and they did not need any more (*Left Handed* 57). Left Handed repeatedly depicts the main character of his stories as a bumbling young man who never quite seems to fit in. After he shoots the ram, an older woman chastises him: "You ought to have better sense than that, shooting in the middle of the sheep...." (57). Over and over again, we learn of a young man who never seems to find his footing in Navajo country. In the ram-shooting story, the older woman looks at the awkward young man, telling him, "A man like you not having sense enough.... So you must think. Use your head. That is what your head is for" (57)—here using a voice shift to the second-person "you," speaking directly to Dyk, and repeating several times that he is not using his head as he ought ("not having sense enough...you must think. Use your head."). Might this story be a backhanded (or left-handed) representation of a highly educated, outsider academic who appears to demonstrate his ignorance of matters that most Navajos of the time would consider fairly basic knowledge? Complicating even more the depiction of his main character, Left Handed relates how the young man disrespects his elders, even the women! Given the traditional stature of women and elders among the Navajo, one would expect a young Navajo man of Left Handed's time to have listened to the older woman's words with great respect, but, as Left Handed recounts, the son of Old Man Hat neither listened nor responded to her words of guidance. Instead, he tells us, "I just let her talk" (59).

We are told that as a boy and youth, the son of Old Man Hat had not been taught in the proper way, and that therefore as a young man, he is disobedient and stubborn, and he refuses to learn from the various Navajo people who offer him their advice. In the very first chapter of *Son of Old Man Hat*, the young boy in Left Handed's stories is shown ignoring the advice of his elders and lying to them (8), playing sexual games with girls (10–14), choking his own goat to death (15–16), lying about his mother to his father and getting his mother in trouble (18–19), and terrorizing a younger child (19–20). In the very next chapter, Left Handed relates a story in which the older boy sees two bears but says they are bucks. The very notion of a Navajo boy who does not know the difference between a buck and a bear signals the very questionable Navajo identity of the main character. Throughout these stories and others, Left Handed provides us with ample markers indicating that there is much more going on than a presumptive life-history narrative.

Stories about Bucks, Bears, Animal Hides, and "Other" Objects

To read through Dyk's constructed ethnographies as a means of accessing Left Handed's underlying stories requires the skills of conversive listening to recognize and decode the storytelling markers that remain within the text. In the actual storytelling event, listeners have the benefit of the gestures, facial expressions, and intonation of the storyteller, as well as the contributory visual and aural cues of the other listeners. The relational interactions among participants in the oral storytelling event are immediate and evident to skilled listeners. To provide the needed background information for an unfolding story, conversive courtesy and inclusiveness will lead storytellers to include occasional informational detours that contextualize the story for everyone's interpretive benefit. Such inclusive wholeness presumes the integrity of the storytelling circle in which all present are fully co-participative in the co-creation of the story. The artificiality of the ethnographic storytelling event, combined with the relational distance constructed between the objective researcher and his "informant" generate substantive ruptures that preclude the holism and inclusive openness of the storytelling circle. Such fissures lead to the discursive closures of protectively encoded texts, which are conversively open to conversive listeners, but inaccessible to a discursively distanced fieldworker. Regardless of one's interpretive positionality, or the story's oral or textual presentation, to fully engage with and within the story, individuals need conversive story-listening skills.

For example, in the story in which the main character confuses bucks and bears, Left Handed crafts the story within a larger story of dysfunctional patterns of communication: 1) a communications clash between an older woman (who speaks conversively both with humans and animals) and a boy or young man (who responds in a discursively argumentative manner); 2) the young man's objectification of the older woman he refers to as his mother; and 3) even more disturbingly, the boy's perceptual and psychological distancing from the story-events, speaking directly to his listener-readers via a second-person voice shift and telling us not to listen to the woman, asserting that he knows better than the more experienced, older Navajo woman. Left Handed's presentation of these problematic communications is especially significant for the understanding of what turns out to be a telling communications breakdown in the identification of bears and bucks.

Left Handed begins this particular story with the main character pointing out several animals that he misidentifies as "bucks" to the Navajo mother. Seeing that the young man's "bucks" are actually bears, she corrects him, saying that the animals are bears and that he should stay away from them. This confusion of bucks (male deer) is interesting for a number of reasons. First of all, both the boy and the woman see the bears, yet he erroneously calls them "bucks." While it is possible that the boy actually does not understand the difference between bucks and bears, this is pretty unlikely. Children learn to differentiate animals at a fairly young age. During Left Handed's lifetime, seeing deer (both alive and having been brought home from a hunt) would have been a part of most Navajos' ordinary lives, and young people would have grown up with stories about bears, not unlike the traditional stories told in Europe about wolves (e.g., Little Red Riding Hood); so a story in which a young male in Navajo country mistakes bears for bucks would alert listeners to something quite out of the ordinary. There is just no confusing bucks with their racks of horns with bears. It is incomprehensible that any sighted person would not be able to see the difference between three bears versus three bucks. So, if the error is not in seeing the difference, where might the young man's mistake lie?

Is it possible that the boy/young man merely misspoke? Might the confusion of bucks and bears reflect a linguistic error, with the son of Old Man Hat not knowing the correct word for bear? If this is the case, then we have a story about a boy or young man who perceives animals that are common in Navajo life and lore (here, bears) and yet who calls them by the wrong Navajo name (bucks)—an unlikely scenario for a Navajo. I remember a visit I paid back around 1990 to a Navajo kindergarten classroom. During my visit, I asked about the extent of the children's knowledge of the Navajo and English languages upon their arrival as brand-new students. Back then, I was told that all but a few of the children came to kindergarten fluent in Navajo, necessitating that the kindergarten teachers (Navajo and non-Navajo) know basic Navajo words such as *shash* for bear and *shimá* for my mother. Even though now (2005) in that same school district, relatively few of the kindergartners arrive fully fluent in Navajo (most having grown up primarily with English as the language of their early years), it is still the case that some of the earliest vocabulary words used with Navajo children include words such as bear, deer, and other culturally and regionally meaningful terms. So when Left Handed tells us a story about a boy old enough to have complex and developed thoughts and conversations (so in this story he is an older boy, or possibly a young man), it does not make sense that such a young Navajo man seventy or more years ago would not have been able to tell the difference between deer and bears, nor have known the correct Navajo words to refer to those animals.

Whereas one could imagine someone mistaking one animal for another with similar appearance, Left Handed's choice of bears and bucks leaves little room for the plausibility of such an actual visual mistake. Additionally, he says there are three bears, and therefore the animals are that much more obviously recognizable. The communications frame provides the guidepost needed to make sense of this story. The confusion of animals turns out to be not a problem of visual perception, but rather a linguistic error misattributing the word "buck" to the bears—the sort of error an outsider anthropologist largely unfamiliar with the Navajo language might make. Might Dyk have erroneously used the word for "buck" when he saw a bear, or vice versa, and might the Navajos perceive Dyk's linguistic error as perhaps an actual inability to differentiate among animals? Seeing deer yet referring to them as bears might have given Dyk's storyteller-informant Left Handed pause for thought, perhaps considering the actual implications of such confusions beyond the textual realm of language. Might such a linguistic error be sufficiently notable that Left Handed deftly crafted a story around it, including the disrespect shown to a Navajo elder who tries to correct the young man's error?

In an episodically related vignette that appears in the book just two pages later, Left Handed has his main character speak directly about his linguistic problems: "I said all kinds of things that I shouldn't have said. . . . Every time I said something that I shouldn't have said they'd tell me I shouldn't say it. From there on I wouldn't say it any more. . . . That's the way to be when you are young, and that's the way I was" (27). Might the subtle voice shift to second person ("That's the way to be when you are young") indicate a direct reference to Dyk, with Left Handed speaking directly to him and identifying him as the young man who makes mistakes in speaking Navajo? Continuing with other stories that focus on the main character's linguistic problems in Navajo, Left Handed tells a story in which the main character has a meal with a group of (other) Navajos. In the first-person narrative, the young man laments that, not knowing the language, he was not able to converse with the others. Another man arrives who speaks with him in his language:

> After a while a man came in from another house. I shook
> hands with him, and he said, "Well, my friend, you came
> again, and we're all glad to see you." This man knew our
> language. I asked him, "What are all these people talking
> about?" He said, "Why?" "Well, because I just don't know,
> because I can't understand them. I thought to myself, 'I
> wish I knew their language. If I did I could talk with
> them.'" He turned to the crowd and said something. They

all looked at one another and laughed and began to talk
with him. While they were talking they looked and pointed
their lips at me, or pointed at me with their fingers. (290)

Within the narrative framework of a life-history text, the first per-
son plural "our language" would be understood to refer to the
Navajo language, the presumed language of the main character
(assuming that the main character is Left Handed). However, this
interpretation leads to the logical impossibility of a group of
Navajos eating together and conversing in a language other than
Navajo such that the main character cannot understand them.
Today, most Navajos speak English and conceivably might speak
English around a monolingual Navajo speaking elder, but this situation would almost certainly not have been found during the late
nineteenth century when Left Handed was a young man (even if the
language at the meal were, say, Spanish). With the episodic shifts
between stories, meaningful voice shifts within them, and paralinguistic indicators (such as the characteristic Navajo lip-pointing in
the direction of the young man who does not know the Navajo language), Left Handed presents a vignette within a larger story whose
broader and deeper meaningfulness speaks to the awkward impositions of outsiders in Navajo country, having not learned the language and thereby being incapable of speaking with anyone unless
there is an interpreter present who speaks both languages.

Here again, we are told about the hapless and decidedly out-of-
place son of Old Man Hat, who demonstrates his incapacities with
the Navajo language, and who is repeatedly depicted as demonstrating an attitude of superiority, often asserting that his knowledge about the Navajos is more correct than that of the Navajos
around him. Left Handed shows him obstinately refusing to be corrected by Navajo elders, whom he judges to be wrong and foolish—
as in the case of the older woman who communicates with animals
in the buck/bear incident. After the boy points out the bears that
he says are bucks, the older woman turns away from him and then
speaks directly to the bears in an intersubjective manner, "telling
them not to come out again, telling them to watch over us and take
care of us and help us along, 'so that no danger will come to pass,

so that we'll live long and be safe all the time. Be sure and be on our side, and watch and take care of us, grandparents'" (*Son of Old Man Hat* 23). The boy, hearing her words, again responds disrespectfully, perceiving her interaction with the bears as strange: "I was looking at her and thought, 'She doesn't know what she's saying. She's just talking to herself.' It was kind of funny to me, the way she'd talked to these animals" (23).

In this vignette describing the continuing woeful—and, I might add, strange—saga of the oddly behaving boy, Left Handed provides a commentary on those who do not interact conversively with other people, but who instead observe and evaluate others from a perspective that is distanced, objectifying, oppositional, and discursively objective. Left Handed depicts a situation in which one individual observes another's behavior and interprets it in a negatively judgmental manner: "She doesn't know what she's saying" (23). In all fairness to Walter Dyk and the generations of twentieth-century ethnographers, it is important that we do not lose sight of the fact that scholars of their times were trained to work within the scholarly framework of scientific objectivity. If errors were made, and there were many, the vast majority of researchers of the time were indoctrinated into the grand master narratives of the academy that defined the colonialist methods and objectives of their work. Dyk and many of the other scholars of the time lived and worked within that framework of imperial blinders, and their subsequent lack of a more expansive vision often reduced their work to little beyond the mere replication of their initial presuppositions and theoretical assumptions. As Bernard McGrane explains, "In terms of the politics and grammar of its universe of discourse and at its very inception as an institution unconsciously geared to re-produce Western society, anthropological discourse speaks *of* the Other but never *to* the Other" (96).

In conversive communications, people speak *with* each other, not at each other. In Left Handed's story about the bears, the Navajo woman speaks conversively to and with the bears, and to and with the boy. In contrast, the boy takes a discursively distancing stance toward the woman, perceiving her as "just talking to herself" (23). It is he who responds op/positionally, objectifying his own mother—a fact that poignantly underscores the severity of the boy's attitude. It is the boy who does not speak *with* anyone else, instead talking about them to others and speaking *at* them. Furthermore, in light of the importance of the mother in Navajo culture, the boy's impertinence to, and criticism of, the older Navajo woman depicted as his mother immediately cues Left Handed's listener-readers to the un-Navajolike behaviors and attitudes of the young man. Back during Left Handed's time, most younger Navajos were taught to respect their elders. I remember that even back in the 1980s when I lived in Gallup, many of the Tribal Council members of the Navajo Nation would go and speak with the older women and men about current tribal deliberations so that the elders could help the Council members view the issues with the benefit of their wisdom, especially that of the women elders. For Left Handed to relate a story of a young man/boy who disrespects older Navajo women, this depiction is atypical of Navajo tribal life of the time.

The boy's objectification of the older woman and the articulation of his private thoughts about her ignorance alert us to the boy's odd character and his inability to relate to Navajo elders. Left Handed's subtle shifts in voice and other pronoun use demonstrate this. When the older woman uses the first-person plural pronoun "us" in asking the bears to "watch over us and take care of us," she inclusively involves the boy, even when she turns and speaks directly to the bears; nevertheless, the boy continues to perceive himself as outside and distinct from the worlds of the Navajos around him. While the Navajos in the story speak directly to him, it is the boy who repeatedly distances himself from the "others," whom he misunderstands and judges as strange and incomprehensible. Thus, when Left Handed ends the story by noting that the boy found it funny the way the older woman "talked to *these* animals" (23, my emphasis), Left Handed makes a subtle, yet very astute, commentary on the ethnographic colonial encounter. It is important to note that his words were not translated into English as "the way she'd talked to *those* animals" (23, my emphasis). In the Navajo language, one does differentiate between present and distant positionality, so that Left Handed's choice of adjective ("these") very directly relates his commentary to his immediate storytelling circle. Moreover, in Navajo, third-person pronouns are not differentiated in terms of gender, so that Left Handed's statement, "It was kind of funny to me, the way she talked to these animals," in Navajo would have the sort of ambiguity that is one of the trademarks of oral storytelling, and that would literally state "the way s/he talked to these animals." Therefore, the longer passage in Navajo could very well have indicated a male subject, translated as follows: "I was looking at him and thought, 'He doesn't know what he's saying. He's just talking to himself.' It was kind of funny to me, the way he'd talked to these animals."

Is this story a subtle commentary on the perspectives of scholarly outsiders who objectify Native peoples in colonizing ways that disrespect their humanity and view them as creatures ("animals") for analysis? Were we in Left Handed's storytelling presence, we would have had the additional benefit of his paralinguistic cues that could have guided our interpretations of the pronoun ambiguity in one direction or the other. As conversive listener-readers, we can move beyond the textual fixity of the female pronoun to the indeterminacy of the Navajo pronoun's gender to open up Left Handed's stories and commentaries that previously were hidden behind the text. The equalization of persons within a conversive mode of communication enables listener-reader access to Left Handed's coded speech, initially available to his fellow Navajos present during his sessions with Dyk. This is what James C. Scott refers to as the "realm of relative discursive freedom, outside the earshot of powerholders, where the hidden transcript is to be sought" (25). What Scott sees as "relative" freedom is a function of the inevitable oppositionality of discursive power relations. Within conversive relationality, there is more freedom, for the interrelationality inherent in conversivity reflects an inter-*subjective* engagement that affirms others' subjectivity in the affirmation of one's own, and where no one's subjective position is dependent on a denial of another's subjectivity. Through Left Handed's stories, we see Navajo and other Native people interacting in conversive ways that empower themselves and others as fellow persons in the world; in contrast, the character of the son of

Old Man Hat speaks, listens, and interacts in a discursively distancing manner.

There are many stories in *Son of Old Man Hat* that depict the main character's disrespect of Navajo elders and his insistence that he understands what he sees more accurately than they do. In another story, the young main character and his father Old Man Hat (perhaps in this case representing Left Handed or another older Navajo who brings Dyk to different places on or near the reservation) go to Hopi land, where the young man sees a blanket made up of animal skins. Left Handed tells us that the young man had never seen an animal hide before. We are told that he "thought it was a coyote hide" (52). Here we have another storytelling indicator valuable for listeners with sufficient contextual knowledge to pick up on the odd thought that a blanket would be made from coyote hides. The Navajo have many stories about the irregular and ugly fur that coyotes have (e.g., how they got such fur, how they desire better fur coats, etc.). We are told that the young man went up close to the hide to get a better look, but that he was afraid of it: "I got kind of scared and stepped away from it. I asked my father, 'What kind of skin is that?'" (52). The older man explains that what the young man has seen is a blanket made up of rabbit skins sewed together. Left Handed portrays his main character as being afraid of a fur blanket, of not recognizing rabbit pelts, and as confusing sewn rabbit pelts with a coyote hide. Later, as the two men are leaving Oraibi, the young man turns to the older Navajo man and obstinately contradicts what he has just been taught, saying, "I think it's a coyote hide. It looked like it to me" (52). The old man's response to the young man's statement is laughter. Then he corrects the error, restating that the blanket or quilt was indeed made from rabbit pelts. Here and elsewhere in the two ethnographic volumes based on his stories, Left Handed tells tales about a young man who is repeatedly sure that he knows more than do the Indian elders who try to guide him, and this attitude of superiority is depicted in the persona of a young man who cannot recognize sewn rabbit fur, is afraid of the fur blanket, and who cannot discriminate between rabbit and coyote fur.

Indigenous Trading Relationships vs.
the Ethnographic Trade Encounter

Left Handed's story about Old Man Hat, his son, and some of the Hopi people they encounter at Oraibi takes some unusual turns that offer a commentary, albeit a coded one, that reflects on the potentially colonizing relationships between ethnographers and their objectified human objects of study (perhaps pointing to a visit to Hopi made by an older Navajo storyteller and his young anthropologist?). At this point, it is necessary to note that traditionally among the Navajo, elders who guide a younger person are commonly referred to as "my mother" or "my father," and they in turn refer to the younger individuals they take under their wings as "my son" or "my daughter." When Left Handed relates a story about Old Man Hat traveling to Oraibi with his son, the filial referent needs to be understood relationally, but not necessarily in a genetic sense. This being said, this story is also shown to directly contrast the conversive relationality of the traditional indigenous barter, instead depicting the more distanced and objectified interaction of the more sterile, and alienating, economic trade encounter. In Left Handed's story, the young man accompanies the older man on a trip to the Hopi village of Oraibi to trade his Navajo mutton for Hopi corn and dried peaches. The two are not only welcomed into the village but also into the people's homes. After a large meal, Old Man Hat trades his goods for Hopi food, and as the old man and his "son" leave, the Hopis point out that now they are all friends, having eaten together and traded with each other. For the older Navajo man and the Hopi, their trading of goods is not merely an abstract and objective material exchange, but more importantly is the symbol of their new friendship and the Hopi hospitality and gifts of corn, peaches, and other foods. The Navajo's gift of mutton, the visit, and expected return visits represent far more than a material trade encounter: the exchange of goods represents a transformative act that interweaves people together into each others' worlds.

As the boy and older man get ready to leave Oraibi, they are told by the Hopis, "You must always come here to our place. Whenever you come stop at this one place, because we've become acquainted and are friends now. That's why you should come here. Now you know where to stop. We'll have everything ready for you, so you must come again, my friends" (*Son of Old Man Hat* 52). Within cultures and lives more defined in terms of conversive engagements, trade is not merely an objective and economic act, even though material goods are exchanged and even though the primary impetus for a trip is the exchange of goods. What is most important is the evolving relationship. The commodities themselves, rather than being privileged as the ends of the exchange, serve as the signs of the relationship. Diamond explains such divergent approaches to trade interactions:

> While civilized money tends to alienate man from his labor by transforming his labor into an abstract commodity, by detaching it from him and by transferring considerations of "worth" and "value" from a human to a marketing context, primitive exchange has the contrary effect: social value and social effort are always directly expressed and understood; they strengthen the sense of community. Indeed, the major emphasis in most forms of primitive exchange seems to be on *giving* ... (133–34, emphasis in original)

Although Diamond's reference to such interpersonal trading relationships as "primitive exchanges" clearly reflects the colonialist views of the time that placed indigeneity within a past and exoticized realm of simplicity, he importantly identifies the relational emphasis evidenced in Left Handed's Navajo-Hopi trading story. Rather than a purely material trade situation in which one receives something that one wants in exchange for something else (a situation in which the focus of the exchange is on the fulfillment of wants, desires, and needs), Left Handed communicates a trading experience in which the importance of individual needs and desires are defined in relational terms. The older Navajo man and his Hopi hosts demonstrate a primary focus on the needs and desires of the other person(s) involved, and the development of relational interconnections of persons, families, and tribes.

In contrast to the relationally conversive manner in which Old Man Hat and the Hopi people interact, in Left Handed's story he portrays the young man's thoughts and behaviors as atypical of what one would expect from a young Navajo of the time. Presented as an outsider who discursively distances himself from the Hopis, the young man behaves as an ostensive outside observer who adamantly insists on perceiving the Hopis as oddities. Noticing one woman with her hair "twisted into a bundle on each side of her head," he turns to Old Man Hat and asks, "Have these Indians horns?"— whereupon the old man laughs and explains that what appears to be horns is simply the hair worn differently, adding, "They're just like us" (Son of Old Man Hat 50). The young man ethnocentrically misperceives the Hopi as fundamentally different from his own definition of normal people by virtue of looking at a superficial difference and misconstruing that as an essential difference. The old man's response to the boy offers a factual correction to the boy's observation about horns and hair, and yet, in his words, Left Handed conveys much more than a mere informational correction. In saying, "They're just like us," Old Man Hat also addresses the boy's unstated assumption of Hopi subalterity (which is, perhaps, also a relegation to the demonic, with the comment about horns alluding to Christian vilifications of Native peoples as pagan).

Regarding similar objectifying preconceptions that anthropologists often brought to their work, Talal Asad explains that "the cultural heritage, education and socialisation of the anthropologist as a member of a human group which has developed certain images of 'natives' must have carried some of these images with him to the field" (270). While this helps us to understand the colonialist objectification of Native peoples by non-Native outsiders, how do we explain the same sort of objectifying attitudes and behaviors on the part of a young man/boy whose surrounding Navajo world reflected a much more inclusively conversive worldview and culture? It is true that colonial powers impose a perceptual subjugation that all too often infects those who have been reduced to the subaltern. As Ngũgĩ wa Thiong'o asserts, colonialism's "most important area of domination was the mental universe of the colonised, the control, through culture, of how people perceived themselves and their relationship to the world" (*Decolonising the Mind* 16). Such discursive, psychological, and ratiocinative manipulation and control infect both the colonized and the colonizer, for each is indoctrinated through what Althusser refers to as "the ideological state apparatus" (ISA), wielded via the educational, religious, and governmental institutions of the imperial powers that be. However, in Left Handed's stories, he does not present his main character as a Navajo who has developed his disturbing ways of thinking and acting due to the ISA's of a Euro-American imperialism (such as the Navajo children who during Left Handed's lifetime were already being subjected to impositions of Indian boarding schools), so we must look to Left Handed's storytelling for additional conversive cues.

In the story at Oraibi, as in the story about bucks and bears, Left Handed portrays the young man's disregard for his Navajo elders and his self-aggrandizing attitude. After having been corrected by the older man regarding the traditional Hopi hairstyle, Left Handed depicts the young man turning away from the older Navajo man and again speaking directly to his listeners and listener-readers: "I thought, 'Sure they've got horns all right.' But I didn't ask my father about it any more" (50). Even though the boy's prejudicial assertion is corrected by the old man, the boy refuses to listen to his elders, who affirm that the Hopi are people just like himself. Much as a colonial outsider might, the boy continues to cling to his own preconceived biases and misconceptions about Indian people, thereby remaining ignorant of their traditions, beliefs, and culture. The boy's attitude of superiority over Navajo elders and other Native people replicates the colonial devaluation of indigenous knowledge and culture that has been part and parcel of the ethnographic endeavor in Indian country. Regarding the attitudinal divergences that have existed between colonialist anthropologists and their "informants," Paul Riesman states explicitly, "The belief that all people are human has not saved Western anthropologists from feeling superior to the people they study and write about" (7). Perhaps a young anthropologist's own sense of superiority as evidenced to his elder Navajo storyteller-informant might have encouraged Left Handed to relate stories about a boy or young man who obstinately chooses to maintain his own preconceived prejudices that the Navajo and other Native people around him are somehow fundamentally different from him, despite the older man's explanations to the contrary. Left Handed's story offers a profound commentary about diverse ways of perceiving, knowing, and interacting with people. We see the old man interacting intersubjectively and relationally with the Hopi people. In contrast, we see the boy reacting to the Hopi and others in an op/positionally distancing manner that Bernard McGrane describes as "that egocentric tendency of our Western mind to identify itself as separate from what it perceives as external to itself" (5).

For well over a thousand years, one of the more well-known racist comments made about non-Christians (Jews and others maligned as "pagan") by European and Euro-American Christians has been the assertion that they have horns—an image that defines groups of people and individuals as more akin to animals than to humans (with clearly pejorative connotations). Even more disturbingly, the image of humans with horns identifies human persons in terms of the demonic (with the reference being to the Christian belief in a horned devil or Satan figure). When I mentioned this vignette about Hopis having horns to various Navajos, the invariable response was a clear recognition of the satanic allusion. One Navajo elder immediately responded, "Horns and pointy tails, too!" Even bracketing out whether or not Left Handed is explicitly referring to the tradition of racist Christian imagery of the demonic, the image nevertheless bespeaks the various biases inherent in the colonizing encounters with the "other."

Left Handed ends his story about the trading trip with an odd shift in tone. Throughout the story, Left Handed has his character Old Man Hat speak in an appreciative and gracious voice to and about the Hopi, and yet Left Handed concludes the trading story with Old Man Hat making what appears to be a harsh derogation regarding a past massacre of Hopi old people by the Navajo. Up to this point, Old Man Hat has emphasized the friendly relations between the Navajo and Hopi, who have lived in close proximity with each other for centuries. Left Handed begins his mention of a massacre by telling Dyk and his interpreter, "Years ago many Oraibi

Indians used to live right here" (*Son of Old Man Hat* 52). He then says in Navajo that other people (*dine'*) "came and killed almost all of them," in a statement that gives sympathy for a possible colonial atrocity committed against the Hopi (by the Spanish, the Mexicans, or the Euro-Americans), perhaps with Left Handed pursing his lips and pointing to Dyk to emphasize the colonizing effects of white people in that place. Within the framework of the trading story that emphasizes Old Man Hat's and the Navajos' relationships with the Hopi people, such sympathies make complete sense, but what is relayed to Dyk in the English translation of Left Handed's words is the following: "The Navaho came and killed almost all of them. They killed all the older ones and let only the younger go" (*Son of Old Man Hat* 52). The Navajo word *dine'* literally means "people," but the word is usually used with a referent that specifies which group of people is intended. Without the added referent, the ambiguity of the term is avoided by its most common usage as a specific referent for Navajo people. So the translation that Dyk's interpreter gives him is that it was "The Navaho [who] came and killed almost all of them" (52).

Regardless of whether or not Left Handed's comment is a factual account of a Hopi massacre at the hands of the Navajo, European, or Euro-American peoples, within the context of the larger trade story it becomes a lesson about one people coming into another people's land and being received with kindness, generosity, and friendship, even though years before the outsiders' ancestors had come into the land persecuting and killing those Indian people. Might such an event pertain to the way that, prior to Dyk's arrival in Navajo country, the United States Army had come into the lands of the Navajo; destroyed their crops and killed their sheep, starving the people into submission; and removed the Navajo to Fort Sumner on what has come to be known as the Navajo Long Walk? Writer Luci Tapahonso (Navajo) tells about this time in her poem "In 1864," in which she, like Left Handed, particularly notes the deaths of the old people: "We had such a long distance to cover. / Some old people fell behind, and they wouldn't let us go back to help them. / It was the saddest thing to see—my heart hurts to remember that. / ...When we crossed the Rio Grande, many people drowned. / ... Some babies, children, and some of the older men and women were swept away by the river current" (*Sáanii Dahataał* 9–10). Or, as noted above, might Left Handed's story point to what anthropologist Alfonso Ortiz (San Juan Pueblo) has described as the "destructive rampage" of the Spanish conquistadors in Hopi and other Pueblo communities (*Surviving Columbus*)? Since the Navajo word for "Navajo" is *dine'* (or people), this opens up ambiguously coded signification of people who came into the region and killed Indians. While the next chapter looks more closely at the main character of Left Handed's stories, relevant to this discussion is the fact that Left Handed begins his stories about the son of Old Man Hat by noting that he was born during the Long Walk, a clear referent that frames his stories and work with Dyk within the historical context of the colonizing internment of the Navajo.

Left Handed's Coded Stories
Told in a First-Person Voice

Over the course of Left Handed's work with Dyk, he related many stories that touch on various aspects of actual Navajo life, but the told stories lie below the descriptive surface levels of the text. Storytelling, like literature, offers deep stories rich with meanings accessible to interactive, conversive listeners and listener-readers. Elizabeth Cook-Lynn (Crow Creek Sioux) has lamented "the failure of metaphor in the modern world" (xiv). This is acutely the case when the complexities of oral storytelling are simplified to the point of absence by the reductive ends of textual mediation. At symbolic levels, a story that comes to light over and over again in Left Handed's telling addresses the confusing and divisive colonial encounters in Indian country by the presence of outsiders, be they objectifying ethnographers or other colonizing Euro-Americans. Instead of providing factual information about his own personal life, or even the life story of any other Navajo, Left Handed relates stories that function "like a code which, the more it is listened to over the years, the more it reveals.... Events that happen, creatures that are encountered, characters that appear, may be symbolic of something besides just what they appear to be or do" (Beck,

Walters, and Francisco 59, 60). Factual information about Left Handed's own life may be found in *The Trouble at Round Rock*, an account of events that occurred on the Navajo Reservation in the 1890s as recounted by three men (one identified as Left Handed) for a Navajo history project. In this narrative, the three men, including Left Handed, speak directly about their experiences from their lives. Here, Left Handed explicitly states that, as an older man, he remembers very little of his early years (*The Trouble at Round Rock* 23)—a statement that contrasts significantly with the very extensive (and unusual) levels of specificity in the "autobiographical" stories from childhood told to Dyk by the old man.

From start to finish, Left Handed portrays the son of Old Man Hat in stories that are some of the more absurd and unbelievable tales in the volume—stories in which the young man is declared a liar; a man who is ignorant about Navajo culture and traditions; a person who is intrigued by others' sexuality and appears to be sexually obsessed; and a boy/man who repeatedly ridicules and objectifies "other" Indian people (even his own mother), refuses to learn from Navajo elders (thinking he knows Navajo ways better than they do), and is disrespectful of Navajo ceremonial practices (falling asleep in a ceremony shortly after arriving, and leaving another ceremony prematurely: "I was scared, for they were all making so much noise" [61]). In short, the portrayal of the young man depicted in Left Handed's stories frequently seems to suggest the ways that the young, psychoanalytically trained anthropologist might have appeared to his Navajo storyteller-informants. Indeed, one early reviewer in the *New Republic* back in 1938 described *Son of Old Man Hat* as "a serious anthropological study that reads like a combination of 'Tobacco Road' with two parts of 'Studs Lonigan'" (Review of *Son of Old Man Hat* 28).

Since Left Handed's immediate storytelling audience always included at least one or more Navajos working as translators, the strange behaviors/tellings in the stories would have certainly signaled his listeners to be wary of the straight facticity of his stories—especially with the additional behavioral and other paralinguistic cues from Left Handed's performative telling, which would have signaled shifts between factually reliable and unreliable narratives and between a personally factual self-reference and a non-self-referential first-person voice in which the first-person subject is merely a story-telling device adopted to accord with Dyk's demand for personal life-history stories. Sherry Ortner notes this as a tool of resistance where "the cultures of dominant groups and of subalterns... speak to, even while speaking against, one another" (190). While many of Left Handed's conversive storytelling cues would have been understand-able to his Navajo translators and any other Navajos present during the particular working sessions, for an anthropologist who did not know the Navajo language and who was unfamiliar with Navajo sto-rytelling traditions, Left Handed's tales could easily have been sim-plistically misconstrued as the materials for constructing a factual Navajo autobiography. In *Language and Art in the Navajo Universe,* Gary Witherspoon explains, "Insights into another culture do not come from idle contemplation or superficial fieldwork based on questions *about* and observations *of* it; they come from intensive and extensive, serious and humorous, involvement *in* it" (6, empha-sis in original), and James Kale McNeley emphasizes how important it is for non-Navajo scholars to "assure that the Navajo point of view would be discerned and faithfully presented" in any scholarship on the Navajo (xi). As long as we continue to "think under the hege-mony of the ethnological response to the alienness of the Other; we are, today, contained within an anthropological concept of the Other" (McGrane x). When readers of ethnographies like *Son of Old Man Hat* accept the textualized narratives of academe at their repre-sented face values, the colonizing discourse of otherness is perpetu-ated, and the marginalized indigenous storytelling voice recedes from reader access.

Among the reviewers of *Son of Old Man Hat,* Wilson Follett stands out with his fairly extensive review in the *New York Times Book Review.* Follett repeatedly expresses his mystification regarding what is supposed to be a Navajo autobiography. Follett was suffi-ciently well-versed in Navajo culture to recognize what appear to be highly questionable aspects of the ethnography. In his review, he raises his concerns regarding the uncharacteristic diction of the work ("four-letter colloquialisms," "sniggering associations... convention-ally unprintable in English... [and] conventionally inadmissable in

Navaho" [33]). Interestingly, Follett also notes the apparent absence of Left Handed from a text that purports to be his autobiography. He writes, "What it leaves hopelessly baffling and obscure—to readers who are not Mr. Sapir [who provides the foreword to the volume]—is the individual quality of the man whose autobiography these chapters constitute" (33). Follett begins his review by describing *Son of Old Man Hat* as a "candid and curious document," and ends by referring to it as "so problematic a document" that it actually tells us little if anything about Left Handed (33). Follett's response to the volume is a rare gem among the generally adulatory reviews. Follett concludes his review with a remarkably direct and scathing critique of Dyk's work, and the work of those who consider *Son of Old Man Hat* to be a legitimate and trustworthy Navajo life-history narrative:

> That men of ostensible science—ethnologists, anthropologists, psychologists—can so readily detect all manner of profound, subtle significance in so problematic a document is to the layman a matter for chronic amazement.... For the veritable scientist of race, culture, mind— the scientist who derives his generalizations from fixed data through a funnel of generalization—the pertinent attitude would seem to be that of the dying Goethe's unfulfillable demand, "More light." (33)

H. David Brumble importantly notes that "It is perhaps fitting that, even embedded as we see [stories] in written words, in books, these oral traditions have still the power to struggle against the conventions of the dominant cultures" (47). Edward Said affirmed the articulative capacity of the colonized: "the subaltern *can* speak, as the history of liberation movements in the twentieth century eloquently attests" (*Orientalism* 335). He correctly elucidates the powers of the academy to discursively silence the "formerly colonized, enslaved, suppressed" (348); what we must now recognize is the extent to which "subaltern" peoples have conversively expressed their presence, their subjectivity, and their realities, notwithstanding the academy's past intransigent refusals and inabilities to listen, to see, and thereby to understand. As was evident to Follett, Left

Handed's stories speak through Dyk's text powerfully and clearly, if readers will take the responsibility to decode the text and access the stories lying within. Follett correctly points to many of the problems that pervade *Son of Old Man Hat*; nevertheless, through discursive means alone, it is not possible to discern the underlying stories that Left Handed related. Follett's critique deconstructs the text, but more is needed to conversively reconstruct the storytelling and thereby enter Left Handed's story-worlds. Thus we will understand why it is that, as Brumble points out, "many of the Indian autobiographers [from the ethnographic eras] are known to us only by their pseudonyms—and sometimes more than one pseudonym" (ix–x). The next chapter (chapter 5) continues our discussion of the *Son of Old Man Hat*, with close interrogations into the mysteriously elusive, unnamed, and clanless main character of Left Handed's stories.

Chapter Five

Trickster Storytellers and the Elusive Identity of the Son of Old Man Hat

Walter Dyk's ethnographically constructed volumes of stories that were related to him by the old Navajo man Left Handed have been explicitly presented as chronological life-history narratives in the books entitled *Son of Old Man Hat* and *Left Handed*. As this chapter and the previous one indicate, interpretive assumptions that read these texts as little more than straightforward autobiographies obscure the meaningfulness of Left Handed's symbolically coded stories by disappearing the complexities of those stories under the textual overlay defined in terms of the conceptual and definitional limits of life history. While it is true that Left Handed is the storyteller behind and within the published texts, he is clearly not an autobiographer relating his own self-referential life history. Left Handed is a turn-of-the-century (nineteenth to twentieth century CE) Navajo man who spoke Navajo, not English. His worldview is a Navajo-informed worldview, not the Euro-American perspective of those who might privilege literary romanticizations of the self. Perhaps the trickster Coyote might demonstrate such self-privileging, but then Coyote is hardly the example most Navajos would have traditionally chosen to emulate. As a conversive approach to

Dyk's volumes demonstrates, when Left Handed steps into his expected *role* of autobiographer, he does so in the role of a trickster figure telling tall tales and pulling our legs in ways that demonstrate the foolishness of such self-privileging. In fact, when Left Handed singles out the son of Old Man Hat in his stories, he goes to great lengths to emphasize the boy's/young man's lack of worthiness and his unreliability as a narrator of facts. As Gerald Vizenor (Anishinaabe) tells us, "Native American Indians are the storiers of presence, the chroniclers in the histories of this continent" (*Fugitive Poses* 1). Left Handed (or Lefty) indeed chronicles the history of his times, both in the regional and tribal descriptions of turn-of-the-century Navajo life—and also, and perhaps more significantly, in his depictions of objectifying outsiders in Navajo country. The challenge for us is to learn how to listen to "Lefty's" quite remarkable coded stories in order to make sense of a book whose textual narrative presentation may be quite far afield from its original storytelling base. In Left Handed's stories, he tells us much about his times and about his interactions with his anthropologist Walter Dyk, but as this chapter shows, Left Handed relates symbolically complex stories that go far beyond the mere textual presumptions of autobiography.

Left Handed tells us an interwoven story of events that he experienced, observed, or heard of; stories that he fabricates, skews, or exaggerates; and perhaps most significantly, stories that reflect his interaction with his German-American ethnographer Walter Dyk. The stories reinscribed through Dyk's mediation tell the very real story of Left Handed's objectification as the anthropologist's "informant." It is in this larger story that we see not only the mediating layers of Dyk's ethnographic and editorial control over his informant's telling, but more importantly, the very real control wielded by Left Handed as the guiding directives and markers of his conversive storytelling endure in their pervasive presence throughout the reinscribed and edited text. Rejecting the colonialist assumptions of utter Native disempowerment, Native American writer and scholar Craig Womack asserts,

> I reject, in other words, the supremacist notion that assimilation can only go in one direction, that white culture

always overpowers Indian culture, that white is inherently more powerful than red, that Indian resistance has never occurred in such a fashion that things European have been radically subverted by Indians. (12)

Malcolm Crick raises this very point in his discussion of ethnographic fieldwork relationships, which he describes as "mutual exploitation.... While the ethnographer clearly has the accomplishment of professional work as a central motivation, in the case of informants a range of motivations is possible" ("Ali and Me" 176–77). Throughout *Son of Old Man Hat* and its sequel volume *Left Handed*, we can see Left Handed's own repeated efforts to subvert Dyk's intended goal of "A Navaho Autobiography" through stories that range from blatant fabrications or exaggerations of actual events, to tales that only include the son of Old Man Hat as a minor or even absent character, and that never involve any character named Left Handed at all.

As the previous chapters have emphasized, a thorough reading of *Son of Old Man Hat* must not only take into account the discursive effects of the anthropological encounter as they are evidenced in the textual production of an ostensive ethnographic autobiography of a Native "informant," but even more importantly must consider deeply the inevitable communications clash that arises between conversive and discursive worlds. Whereas a modernist approach to the text as autobiographical monologue might read the text as a "Navaho Autobiography" produced by Walter Dyk, a postmodern and postcolonial response might correct this reading through an interrogation into the anthropological encounter that colonized Left Handed's words and life. Such a discursive approach would emphasize the op/positional nature of the interaction between Dyk and his informant by means of privileging Dyk as the controlling subjective voice that disempowers Left Handed through his relegation to simply the Native informant. Such an approach offers helpful insights into the colonialist ethnographic process through the recognition of Dyk's primacy and subjective position at the expense of Left Handed's objectification as the never named son of Old Man Hat. Poststructural awareness serves to decenter Dyk's primacy and ruptures his control of Left Handed's ethnographical colonization—but more is needed, for in such a reading Left Handed is still hidden behind Dyk's objectification of the old Navajo man as informant and as the son of Old Man Hat. Here we see the degree to which the textualization of Left Handed's stories disappears him as a living storyteller as his stories are silenced behind the purported life-history text. In our perception of the silencing of Left Handed and his stories, we recognize the objectifying process of objective science, but we nevertheless critically perpetuate the myth of Left Handed's disempowerment through our own critical inability to access, hear, and understand his stories.

As literary scholars and social scientists begin to differentiate the distinctive language games of conversive and discursive communications involved in orally informed work, the mediation of the text will prove to be less of a barrier to the orality otherwise obscured through the apparent primacy of the text. Then will readers be able to find Left Handed, his stories and worlds (real and fictional), behind the text of *Son of Old Man Hat*. As Michael M. J. Fischer emphasizes about the cross-cultural complexities of such texts, "This bifocality, or reciprocity of perspectives, has become increasingly important in a world of growing interdependence between societies: members of cultures described are increasingly critical readers of ethnography" ("Ethnicity" 199). The intersubjectivity of conversive approaches permits us to recognize and respond to the storytelling presence, voice, and power of Left Handed's telling, even though many of the connective links, rhetorical markers, and emphatic pauses of the oral telling are lost due to Dyk's ignorance about their semiotic importance. As Clifford Geertz explains, "The whole point of a semiotic approach to culture is, as I have said, to aid us in gaining access to the conceptual world in which our subjects live so that we can in some extended sense of the term, converse with them" (*Interpretation of Cultures* 24). Regardless of the barriers of colonialist mediation (textual and otherwise), interactively conversive responses are possible, not only in person-to-person communications but also in relation to textualized storytelling. This is especially important in relation to a text that presents itself as categorically other from what the original stories appear to have actually been about. As Gelya Frank explains in an essay that offers a phenomenological critique of traditional life-history methods,

> Especially in taped narratives, which tend toward longer documents, the conversational elements are edited out along with repetitions and other passages deemed unimportant, ambiguous, or contradictory to some general pattern that the author [ethnographer or editor] perceives. Thus the life history has usually been produced in an archival manner, as a primary document of a life, and for this reason has frequently been treated as an autobiography rather than as a document produced by collaboration. (76)

While the current generation of ethnographers are working with decidedly more conversive methods, there is over one hundred years of important storytelling that has been textualized into a discursive form categorically different from its conversive origins. Scholars trained in conversive orality will need to work with not only published ethnographies but also, where possible, field notes and recordings to differentiate the wheat from the chaff.

This chapter interrogates the extent to which the stories in the volumes *Son of Old Man Hat* and *Left Handed* are, in fact, autobiographical stories about Left Handed's own life experiences as a young man, for as James C. Scott points out in a discussion of "oral culture as popular disguise," such orally told stories, "due simply to their means of transmission, offer a kind of seclusion, control, and even anonymity that make them ideal vehicles for cultural resistance" (160). After interrogations into the lack of self-referentiality in conversive storytelling, this chapter will turn to specific examples from Left Handed's stories and experiences, concluding with attention given to the significance of naming among the Navajo, the particular meaningfulness of Left Handed's name, and parallels with other Navajo informants also named "Left Handed" or "Lefty."

The Absence of Self-Referentiality
in Conversive Storytelling

Left Handed tells us that the early years of his main character's life were deformed by neglect, abandonment, and isolation—all of which explain the origins of a young man who is depicted as being disrespectful to Navajo elders, ignorant of Navajo culture and language (evidenced in his confusions of appropriate kinship terms), unfaithful to his wife, a liar, and a person who repeatedly objectifies other people. We are told that as a boy, he lived with an older Navajo couple, neither of whom are his biological parents nor grandparents; that he did not want to learn everyday skills from them; and that they did not teach him sacred songs and rituals important to the Navajo [perhaps a veiled assurance to others that Left Handed did not share sacred knowledge with Dyk?]. Speaking in the person of the son of Old Man Hat, Left Handed relates the following about the young man's relationship to the two Navajo elders: "My mother [an older clan sister of his birth mother] and her husband were the only ones who took care of me" (4). Within the extended family and clan network common among the Navajo, the boy's relative isolation from other relatives is highly irregular, as is his apparent incapacity regarding very basic skills. For example, when he is asked to grind up corn, he complains that he cannot even figure out how to hold the grinding stone: "My mother never did show me how to hold the rock, and how to use it. She'd just say, 'Go ahead and grind up the corn,' that was all, and then she'd go out with the herd" (9). The very idea of a person complaining about something so basic as how to hold a stone for grinding grain bespeaks much about the distinct oddity of Left Handed's main character.

Left Handed explains that the young man lives in the home of the older Navajo couple, and that in return, he is given food and shelter. Left Handed makes it very clear that he is neither their biological son, nor has he received the rudimentary education that would be expected for Navajo males of that time. Might the described living arrangement reflect the relationship of an outside researcher living temporarily among the Navajo? It is crucial that we consider how Left Handed chose to portray the main character of his stories—the majority of which take place over a three-year period in the young man's life [paralleling Dyk's visits to the Navajo Nation over the course of three years], with no related stories about the young man's later years and only a few told about the young man's childhood. Readers must interrogate the past ethnographic record about the Navajo and other peoples worldwide, bringing conversively informed engagements to generations of stories, opening them up through new insights and understandings. In a paper describing her work with/about Pentecostal women preachers, Elaine J. Lawless writes that "The final phase of the hermeneutic circle, then, demands that we subject our interpretations to the interpretations of our subjects" (313). This is the ideal, providing an invaluable corrective measure, but even when it is impossible to speak directly with past storytelling-informants ("subjects") to gain their responses to the scholarly presentation of their lives and words, it is nevertheless possible to discern the underlying directions inherent in the stories within fieldwork "data." Whereas literary scholars have long understood the errors that occur when the persona of a poem or character in prose fiction is confused with the author, such distinctions that are also the rule in oral storytelling need to be recognized both in the field and by readers of published ethnographic "autobiographies."

Within traditional Native cultures, even when individuals do share experiences from their own lives, the stories are rarely autobiographical in the romantic sense of privileging the storyteller. In a discussion of American Indian autobiography, David H. Brumble explains, "The preliterate autobiographies especially put before us conceptions of the self that are foreign to modern, individualistic societies" (3). Insofar as ethnographically induced Navajo storytelling is concerned, Clyde Kluckhohn reported his frustrations regarding this fact, noting the utter lack of personal life-history referents in the stories told him by one Navajo informant who was engaged to relate his life history:

> The first thing we notice, I think, in this story is that it
> is hardly even a meager autobiography in our sense. He

mentions very few particular events and no persons
except his father enter more than casually into history.
What he says constitutes much more a kind of philo-
sophic homily than a proper life history. In part, this is to
be understood in the context that the man had been a
chief for many years and was accustomed to have people
come to him for advice of a general nature. It may be also
that to another person or under other circumstances he
might have given a more chronologically ordered account
of particular happenings in his life. All of my experience,
however, gives me grounds to doubt this. ("A Navaho
Personal Document" 273)

Perhaps Clyde Kluckhohn's personal experience having summered
near the Navajo during his early years helped him to pick up on this
man's personally evasive storytelling (although insufficient to procure what he sought). Walter Dyk's greater unfamiliarity with, and
apparent objectification of, the Navajo prevented him from recognizing the degree to which his informants related largely non-self-
referential stories. Such confusions arise when the creative license
in storytelling is overlooked due to the scientific desires for historical information.

Albert Yava's work with his ethnographer Harold Courlander
forthrightly discusses these sorts of interpretive errors. As Yava
(Tewa/Hopi) points out regarding his own ethnographic stories,
his recounting of his times is not about himself, but more accurately about particular events and situations that he has lived or
heard about. He relates stories that strike him as significant to
retell, explaining, "I am going to recall some of the things I know,
the way I say them or heard them, or the way they were taught to
me. Maybe our young people will get an inkling of what life was
like on this mesa when I was a boy, or how it was in the time of
our fathers and grandfathers" (Courlander 4). Unlike Dyk's more
imperialist encounters with Left Handed, Harold Courlander
worked collaboratively with Albert Yava, enabling Yava to tell his
stories in his own way without forcing their reconstruction into
an artificial life-history narrative. Yava was also able to offer his

own interpretive guidance concerning the extent to which his stories are not autobiographical in the sense of being *about* him and his own life. He further explains that his presence in his stories provides his knowledge about the events of the stories, but that the stories are not about him—rather, they are about the larger storied events that he relates (4). In Yava's storytelling, he does relate many historically factual and verifiable occurrences in which he was literally present (including degrees of specificity indicative of this). However this is not the case in Left Handed's stories, for he never explicitly identifies himself as the son of Old Man Hat or as any of the characters in his stories, and his stories demonstrate consistently remarkable levels of ambiguity and indeterminate specificity. Were *Son of Old Man Hat* about Left Handed himself, one would expect some sort of personal identification in the text: most important for a Navajo would be his respective clan affiliations. In *Big Falling Snow*, Albert Yava begins his stories with his identification of his own lineage. In *Son of Old Man Hat*, however, we learn neither Left Handed's true parentage and lineage nor his clan affiliations through either his parents or his grandparents, even though such identification is traditionally given primacy in a Navajo's introduction. Even today, most Navajo children learn their clan affiliations very early. Recently, when I was invited to speak with students at one of the high schools on the Navajo Reservation, as I asked the students to introduce themselves at the beginning of each class, all but a very few began by identifying themselves through their clan affiliations. It is telling to have such a significant absence in stories that are purported to be about a Navajo. Fortunately, we have other sources of information about Left Handed to help direct us away from the misinterpretation of Dyk's volumes as autobiographical narratives.

Left Handed's Storytelling Ethnographic Work: Trade Encounters

Left Handed, like a number of other Native informants, worked with other anthropologists and scholars. For example, in the 1940s he served as one of the Navajo informants for W. W. Hill. In Hill's article "Navaho Trading and Trading Ritual: A Study of Cultural Dynamics," he not only lists the names of his informants but also includes the locations on the reservation where they lived: "The following informants were used. Their locations give indication of the territory covered in the work. Where important divergences occur in the accounts, the initials of the informants have been appended" (373). What is especially helpful in these choices is that throughout Hill's essay, certain pieces of information (including some actual quotations) are explicitly identified with particular informants. Additionally, Hill's footnote identification of his informants by name and location makes it easier for readers today to connect certain informants with some of their work with other anthropologists, such as Left Handed from the Round Rock/Lukachukai area. Since Hill's article focuses specifically on Navajo trading practices and not autobiography, he provides little other information about his informants beyond their names and home locations. Nevertheless, he does quote from several of his informants fairly extensively, including a number of very interesting statements from Left Handed. In some cases, Left Handed's comments appear to be fairly straightforward descriptions of Navajo/Pueblo trading relationships; in other cases, some of his comments appear to be less straightforward and deserving of greater interpretive understanding.

In a discussion of intertribal trading relationships between the Navajo and their neighboring Ute and Pueblo tribes, Hill notes that such relationships often proved long-lasting, with Navajo individuals and families continuing to trade with particular Ute or Pueblo individuals and families for many years. Such intertribal connections are evidenced in the previous chapter's discussion about Old Man Hat's trip to Oraibi to trade with the Hopi. Oddly, Hill undercuts the substantive nature of these relationships by reporting that "such 'friendships,' once established, continued until one or the other died, or in some cases relationships were maintained in the two families for several generations" (389). By putting the term "friendships" in quotation marks, Hill calls into question the authenticity of those trading relationships. While trade encounters within a capitalist context rarely create such enduring relationships, within the conversive realms of the indigenous peoples of the world, those interrelations that were solidified through gifting often reflect deep friendships. In Leslie Marmon Silko's volume *Storyteller* (an interwoven collection of poetry, fiction, traditional stories, photographs, and autobiographical stories), she includes a pertinent vignette from her grandfather's life. She relates that for many years, during certain special Feast Days at the Pueblo, one old Navajo man would always come and visit with her grandfather at his store. They would give each other certain items, presents, and trade goods. The Navajo man would come every year; but one year when he came, her grandfather was not there. When the old Navajo man learned that her grandfather had passed on, the Navajo man began to cry. Silko notes that "He never came back anymore after that" (*Storyteller* 187). Although the two men traded goods with each other on a regular basis, the most important aspect of the Navajo man's visits was his friendship with Silko's grandfather. Were primacy given to the trade, then the trips to and trading at that store would have continued after her grandfather's death with whoever else ran the store, but that Navajo man never came back. The cessation of his visits demonstrates the primacy of the interpersonal relationship and depicts one representative example of the enduring relationships, initiated through trade, that developed among the Navajo and Pueblo people.

Even though many such relationships that include trade activities might appear to outsiders to be based on the material exchange of various items, in fact those items (with material value in and of themselves) serve a larger purpose as signs of the developing relationships. On this specific aspect of the trade, the Navajos Left Handed and Kinipai affirm for Hill the enduring character of those relationships (389). Several of Hill's "informants" expressly complained to him about relationships that were solely based on the economic exchange, stressing that those relations that were superficially based on a monetary payment were "resented and deplored by the Navaho" (389). While this might be a veiled commentary on the contractually based ethnographic-fieldwork relationships, Hill interprets the comments as specific to trade relations between the Navajo and the Pueblo people. Hill writes that his informants criticized what they described as those "uncongenial" relationships that were "on a hard and fast commercial basis" (389). Might these comments made to an anthropologist whose relationship with the Navajo was temporary and based on the exchange of money and information serve as coded commentaries about the ethnographic trade encounter rather than about what Hill understands as the "uncongenial atmosphere pervading Navaho-Pueblo trade relations" (389)?

Regardless of our possible answers to this question, we do know that in Hill's reference to Left Handed's and Kinipai's comments about the relationships that develop through trade, Hill calls into question the legitimacy of those relationships by placing the word "friendships" in quotes. Hill offers no explanation either in the text of his article or in a footnote (of an otherwise extensively footnoted essay) clarifying his decision to question indigenous trade relationships as true friendships. While these relationships may not take the form that Hill might recognize as "friendship" in his own culture, for many Navajo, Pueblo, and other Native peoples such intertribal friendships were taken very seriously indeed. Certainly the old Navajo man who stopped by Silko's grandfather's store took their friendship pretty seriously. The old Navajo man's tears clearly indicate the depth of his caring for Silko's Laguna Pueblo grandfather, and they bear out Left Handed's statement regarding the relational centrality of traditional Navajo trading. Other comments made by Left Handed to Hill regarding Navajo "trading rituals" invite a deeper conversive engagement, especially insofar as what they reveal about the intentionality, deliberation, and facticity of Left Handed's work with his various anthropologists.

In Hill's article, he delineates a range of activities that he presents as typical practices in Navajo trading journeys. Some of these seem fairly representative of similar practices of conversively informed indigenous cultures—namely, the establishment of relationships upon which the trade activity is based (388–90), the greater frequency of trade among peoples in closer geographic proximity to each other (374–75), and the variability of "trading parties" based on the reasons for the journeys (382–83). Notably, it is only Hill's storytelling-informant Left Handed who emphasizes one of the more intriguing parts of what is presented as a traditional Navajo trading "ritual," which, tellingly, none of Hill's other informants mention. I leave it to my own readers to consider why it might be that no other Navajo mentioned what Left Handed describes as a crucial element of Navajo trading expeditions; being named Left Handed or Lefty (which in Navajo often connotes a shifty or tricky individual who does not necessarily always speak or deal in a direct or right manner), even his name is a forewarning to his listeners and readers regarding the manner of approaching some of his stories.

Since within a conversive storytelling framework what is important is the larger unfolding story, the specific facts, details, and information (whether persons, places, times, events—the who, what, when, and where) are less consequential before the greater importance of the underlying meaningfulness (the why) of the story. In Hill's essay, we are given what he has gleaned to be "data" from the range of responses and stories told by his informants. Without more complete accounts of his informants' comments, it is much harder to get a sense of the directions of their words. In this respect, the larger ethnographic monographs like *Son of Old Man Hat* offer listener-readers far greater opportunities to bring to bear corrective conversive understandings of various storyteller-informants' words. Nevertheless, even in Hill's much shorter essay, sufficient story-telling markers can be found in Left Handed's quoted words to con-versively open up the larger stories behind the veneer of textual data. With this in mind, Hill points out that Left Handed related certain Navajo trading-ritual practices that he portrayed as tradi-tional and common among the Navajo. Left Handed told Hill that when Navajo people travel to trade with other people, the Navajos all must sleep at night lying in the same direction with "members lying with their heads toward the home, their feet in the direction they were traveling" (387). Hill writes that Left Handed explained this ritual, telling Hill that "This was to insure the success of your trip" (387). The voice shift to second person is a typical storytelling device that serves to bring the listeners into the story. Might Left Handed have been relating this questionably factual ritual in the second person as a means of suggesting this practice for Hill? Were

Left Handed speaking of Navajo practices, one would imagine that he would have phrased his statement in the third-person plural, as he did in the previous sentence.

Left Handed then expands on this directional trading "ritual"— telling Hill that travelers must also urinate in the same direction as they sleep. As Hill writes, "A somewhat similar observance was associated with urinating; the individual always faced toward home" (387). As Left Handed pointed toward home, directing Hill in that direction, one might wonder about the direction from which the wind was blowing. I sincerely hope that Hill did not try this practice himself outdoors when the wind was against him. Even so, it is remarkable that Hill does not question the veracity of this practice, even though he identifies Left Handed as the only informant who described these required "ritual" behaviors. In Left Handed's turn to the scatological (from trade to urination), he alerts his conversive listeners and listener-readers to the dubious veracity of his entire trading-rituals report. A conversive listening-reading response to Left Handed's comments (picking up on particular storytelling cues such as meaningful voice shifts or story twists that tend toward the absurd) indicates that there might be some very good reasons why Left Handed was the only person who related purportedly "traditional" practices.

These bits and pieces from Left Handed's work with Hill shows us that much more is going on in Left Handed's storytelling than purely factual information. As Arnold Krupat advocates for our understandings of the "bicultural composite composition" of ethnographically produced autobiographies, our "reading [of these works] must be centrally a *literary* reading" (*For Those* 31, xxvii). Krupat points us in crucial conversive directions, moving our interpretations of these constructed texts beyond the more simplistic and reductive surface readings of historical data, cultural facticity, and personal information. Left Handed and many of the other indigenous "informants" of the past hundred-plus years functioned as intentional subjects in control of their own storytelling deliberations, in some cases relating historically factual events, and in other cases relating stories whose truths reside at the deeper symbolic levels of conversive storytelling. We see both strategies in Left

Handed's storytelling. As one would expect due to the co-creative nature of storytelling in which "the storyteller's role is to draw the story out of the listeners" (Silko, "Language" 57), Left Handed's modus operandi appears to have varied based on his relationships and work with different anthropologists; yet throughout his work, Left Handed's craft as a storyteller is evident, even in work that is presumably reportorial and factual.

Boarding-School Resistance at Round Rock

Just a few years after Left Handed's work with Hill, another Navajo named Left Handed (from the same Round Rock/Lukachukai region of the reservation and of roughly the same age) and two other Navajo men worked with the anthropologist William Morgan and the linguist Robert W. Young (compiler of the first extensive Navajo/English dictionary). The history that Left Handed relates to Morgan and Young demonstrates both his craft as a creative story-teller and also his commitment to the factual recording of a colonial-ist situation that occurred during the institutional intensification of the education of Navajo children. Even though the name "Lefty" among the Navajo does and did connote a "left-handed' or "back-handed" way of communicating, this fact nowise means that indi-viduals so named never spoke factually or only communicated as tricksters. The other two Navajo men related fairly straightforward historical accounts; it is notable that Left Handed's account is the one of the three that is the longest and most creatively depicted. The work of the three Navajo men with Morgan and Young con-sisted of recording and documenting Navajo views of the historical events of 1892–1894 that led up to and included a serious alterca-tion that occurred between a number of Navajos and the Indian Affairs agent of the time. The specific difficulties in the Round Rock area of the Navajo Reservation concerned the requirement of compulsory boarding-school attendance for Navajo children. In other parts of the Navajo Reservation, many of the children were already being sent to the Indian boarding schools; however, in Round Rock and the other areas that were supposed to send their children to the boarding school at Ft. Defiance, the adults were resisting this externally imposed requirement.

When Lt. Edwin H. Plummer took over as the Indian agent in Ft. Defiance in 1893, he decided that the hesitancy on the part of the Navajo in the remote northern and northwestern parts of the reservation was due to their relative geographic isolation and ignorance of the importance of Western-style education. Plummer decided to get funding to bring a number of the Navajo to Chicago and the World's Columbian Exposition of 1893. "There were eleven men, one school girl, and two school boys in the group.... They visited all the exhibits, and everything they saw was carefully explained to them. They were also shown about the city and visited many large industries there.... Two of the Navajo leaders were said to have spoken out strongly urging the people to place their children in school" (Young and Morgan 20). Subsequent to this visit and during Agent Plummer's tenure, more Navajo children were sent to the boarding schools, which at the time were overcrowded, disease-ridden, understaffed, underfunded, and in disrepair.

The event that precipitated Lt. Plummer's arrival and the Chicago trip was an attack by a number of Navajos against the previous Indian agent in 1892. The people had been complaining about the treatment of their children in the regional boarding school at Ft. Defiance for a number of years. There were reports of boys who had been handcuffed and locked in the cellar, and others who had been confined for days without food. The agent for the Navajo in 1892 was Dana L. Shipley, who served in that post for only a year and half before resigning. The stories recorded by Left Handed, Howard Gorman, and the nephew of Former Big Man focus on a fight that occurred between the Navajo and Agent Shipley. In Shipley's brief tenure on the Navajo Reservation, his strong-armed tactics created such animosity among the Navajo that he resigned out of fear. Young and Morgan write that "Almost as soon as he became the Agent he began to have trouble with the Navajos because he tried to force them to put their children in school. He would take policemen to get the children" (Left-Handed 1). A man named Black Horse spoke out strongly against the schools. "The Agent, Mr. Shipley, insisted on taking the children, so Black Horse attacked him" (1). Young and

Morgan sought to record the circumstances of the time from close relatives of some of those who had been present and involved in the altercation. The oldest of the three Navajo men, Left Handed, had actually been present at the events when he was a young man.

Unlike Hill in his objectifying work on Navajo trading and trade "rituals," or Dyk in his efforts to record a "typical" Navajo life-history narrative, Young (who was conversant in Navajo) and Morgan were simply interested in documenting the historical events of that time. They had the formal report that had been presented to the commissioner of Indian Affairs, and the letters of the Navajo agents from those years. As Young and Morgan declare at the end of their own introduction, which recounts the prior written record of the event, their interest was in providing a balanced view of the situation: "Now we will present the stories of three Navajos, one of whom [Left Handed] was present at Round Rock when the fight with Black Horse occurred. You have read the white man's account of what happened. Now to make the story complete you should also read the Navajo account. In that way you can learn both sides of the story" (Left-Handed 22). *The Trouble at Round Rock* includes three first-person accounts of the events that led up to and transpired when Agent Shipley was beaten up by Black Horse and the others, then rescued by one large Navajo who carried the wounded agent into the flour storage room of the trading post, where he and a few others stayed blockaded in and later "defecated all around in the flour" (29). Of the three accounts, Left Handed's is by far the longest and most developed. The other two Navajos, who were not present during the events, related brief accounts as they had heard the story from relatives who were involved. In contrast to the objectified "informant" status to which Left Handed of *Son of Old Man Hat* fame was relegated, in the work with Young and Morgan, all three of the Navajo men were respected coworkers in the collaborative project. And all five of the men involved were committed to re-membering the Navajo side of the historical event for future generations. Each of the accounts faithfully relate the main events, including comments about the agent's ignorant and aggressive behaviors and how the flour that was to be distributed to the Navajos was ruined (29, 34).

Left Handed relates the longest and most embellished account,
which demonstrates his storytelling craft. In the tradition of Navajo
storytelling, Left Handed begins by introducing himself, identifying
his clan membership and how his family came to live in the
Lukachukai area. In contrast to the extensively detailed childhood
stories that were related to Walter Dyk, this Left Handed explicitly
states that since he is an older man, he remembers little specifically
about his early childhood (Left-Handed 23). He does note that after
his birth, his grandfather and others held a feast "with great joy,"
celebrating the baby's birth and the people's return from Ft. Sumner
(23–24). Left Handed relates a few details from his childhood and
young adult years, such as the care given to him by his grandfather,
the chores he learned as a teenager working for an uncle, the epi-
demic of 1887 ("the time when the throat killed many" [24]). The
few specifics that Left Handed as an old man says he remembers
contrast with the remarkably detailed events in the stories that
appear in the ethnographic volumes *Son of Old Man Hat* and *Left
Handed*. Both Left Handeds are skilled and creative storytellers, of
roughly the same age and from the same locale. Although Robert
Young has said that he does not believe that the Left Handed with
whom he worked was the same Left Handed as Walter Dyk's
"informant," he related that he could not say so with absolute cer-
tainty.[1] Perhaps future historians could research this connection
and possible identification further.

In *The Trouble at Round Rock*, we see Left Handed drawing on
a number of traditional conversive storytelling strategies, including voice shifts, repetition and pauses for emphasis and reflection,
episodic and associational narrative, intersubjective relationality,
first-person storytelling beginning and ending frames, and humor
throughout. The repeated mention of the flour demonstrates the
conversive tool of associational signification with the dirty flour
emblematic of the disastrous agent. By defecating "all around" the
storage room, the agent ruins the flour destined for distribution to
the Navajos, and thereby demonstrates his attitude toward the
Navajos. Notwithstanding individual needs to relieve themselves,
surely that could have been accomplished in one specific location
of the room so as to not contaminate the rest of the flour. The

agent's behavior reflects his lack of control, his disregard for wastefulness, and his antagonistic attitude and aggressive behaviors toward the people he had been charged to serve—made even more emphatic by the fact that each of the men who related the historical event made it a point to mention the agent's actions in the storage room.

In another example of Left Handed's conversive skill, he uses symbolism, allusion, and minimalism to emphasize the incapacity of one white agent. He does so in order to show the problematic origins of the trading post at Round Rock where the altercation occurred. The two men who founded the trading post were a white man and a Navajo interpreter. In his chronicle, Left Handed refers to the Navajo interpreter by his name, but when he refers to the white man, Aldrich, it is only by the descriptive and symbolic name that some of the Navajos used: "Big Lump Setting Up" (Left-Handed 24). Left Handed clearly seems to enjoy the white trader's descriptive name (which I doubt people used in his presence). Left Handed certainly could have referred to the trader simply as "the white trader," much as he references one Navajo policeman whom he refers to simply as "the policeman" in his narrative (28), but instead, the individual references to the white trader at Round Rock use the funny, if rather rude, descriptive name "Big Lump Setting Up" (24). An additional pejorative joke is levied in the direction of another trader that the Navajos called "The Bat" (31). We are told that this man used to brag about his bravery on the soldiers' side at Round Rock:

> The white man called The Bat used to say that he was on
> the soldiers' side.
> "I too had my gun ready like this,"
> he used to say. [showing the people how he'd hold a gun]
> People would laugh at him when he told about this.
> He was a trader. (31)

To help convey the orality of Left Handed's words, I have put the explanatory statement in brackets and added additional line spacing to demonstrate the emphatic pauses in Left Handed's speech, otherwise noted by punctuation. Left Handed's final two sentences are especially telling, including the pauses that precede and succeed them. The first pause provides emphatic space for the listener (listener-reader) to consider the statement about how the Navajos would laugh at "The Bat" when he would brag about his bravery—including a possible storytelling demonstration to show how oddly the trader would hold a gun, proving that he could not have been a soldier—which the Navajos did not believe, "laugh[ing] at him" (31). To underscore their disbelief even further, Left Handed then adds his final (seemingly digressive) comment about The Bat, clarifying that he was not a fighter: "He was a trader" (31). In a conversive listening-reading, the final sentence, "He was a trader," is less descriptive and more conclusive regarding certain types of persons who would not be perceived as fighters, such as "traders." Left Handed's behavioral comment (perhaps with a paralinguistic visual demonstration) regarding the trader's gun-holding stance; his comment about the Navajos' laughter, possibly combined with his own during the telling; and his final conclusion regarding the man's bravery are all very funny. Throughout the storytelling, regardless of the degree of factuality and reliability, the stories are spiced up with humor, both direct and indirect (e.g., wry asides, funny vignettes, and unusual and unlikely descriptions and events).

The Descriptive Meaningfulness of Naming

In his version of *The Trouble at Round Rock* (23–31), Left Handed gives us clear examples that demonstrate the weight that Navajos traditionally placed on the meaningfulness of persons' names. Generally, he refers to the others involved in the altercation by their descriptive Navajo names (as in the case of the trader Aldrich, referring to him by the descriptive name that the Navajos called him). In those other cases where Left Handed does not remember the name, he clarifies that explicitly: "There were three Navajo policemen there in that connection. One of them turned out to be Bead Clan Gambler, one was Singed Man from Fort Defiance.... Another...was killed recently at St. Michael's at a rodeo....I can't think what his name was—I merely knew him by sight. He was merely called Interpreter's brother-in-law" (26). Here Left Handed communicates to us that he might not remember a person's name if it was someone he did not know well, so he refers to the third policeman by telling us how he was related to the interpreter Chee Dodge. This offers an intriguing parallel to the storyteller-informant Left Handed's work with Walter Dyk. In all of the stories this Left Handed related to Dyk, he never named the main character, and—unlike the work with Young and Morgan—in the published volumes *Son of Old Man Hat* and *Left Handed*, we are given no explanation for the main character's namelessness throughout the weeks and months of storytelling work with Dyk. The fact that the main character is unnamed is especially significant within a cultural framework (Navajo) in which great attention is given to naming (whether that be of a sacred or secular orientation, serious, whimsical, or humorous). In one of the novels of Native writer James Welch (Blackfeet), *Winter in the Blood*, his main character is never named. In an interview with Kay Bonetti, Welch relates that after thirty or so pages into the novel, he realized that he had not yet named the young male protagonist. Over the course of the novel, Welch notes that his main character really had not done anything sufficiently significant to merit a name, so he subsequently decided to leave the young man nameless. As Welch makes very clear, the absence of a name can signify the importance of naming, perhaps even more powerfully than by the nominal presence. Language poet and scholar Joan Retallack has noted that whereas Derrida asserts that in presence there is absence, John Cage has profoundly reminded us that in absence there is presence ("Poethics of Words and/as Music" 1991). Also, while the nature of a person's name has been traditionally significant among the Navajo, the unusual absence of a name would be most significant. Left Handed emphasizes this sort of signification in naming by its obvious absence in the stories he told Dyk. While this strategy may signify a person's inherent deficiencies, as in the case of the main character in Welch's novel, the lack of naming may also serve as a protective form of coding. In *From the Glittering World: A Navajo Novel* by Irvin Morris (Navajo), Morris includes a cryptic story, "Meat and the Man," that centers around a bumbling white man obsessed with all things and persons Navajo. As in Left Handed's stories with Dyk, in this story Morris never names his main Euro-American character; however, he intersperses the story with Navajos who repeatedly ask, "What was that man's name?" This conversive interrogative signals Morris's listener-readers to consider what might be his name, perhaps even thinking of an actual person. This sort of identity coding parallels Left Handed's stories about another bumbling man in Navajo country: the son of Old Man Hat. Left Handed's unnamed main character and the absence of markers that would identify Left Handed as an actual character in both *Son of Old Man Hat* and *Left Handed* (e.g., clan affiliation, family lineage, etc.) point to the unlikely identity of Left Handed as an autobiographical storyteller in his work with Dyk.

Without substantive information about Left Handed in these narratives, we can never really approach him in terms of narrative facticity, but merely circle around him as the absent center of an elusive and illusory autobiographical narrative whose subject matter is never really the teller, and whose teller absents himself from the telling as a trickster figure telling first-person-voiced stories that are not really about him at all. This is further called into question by the lack of particular familial, clan, and geographic markers that would reference the stories more firmly in Left Handed's personal world—although there are some stories in which the character Old Man Hat seems to be a reference to the older Navajo man Left Handed, with the younger man in the stories emblematic of Left Handed's young anthropologist. The absence of the real Left Handed as the main character of his stories alerts his readers to the fact that we should not approach the stories about the son of Old Man Hat as Left Handed's autobiography. His absence also raises very real questions about past readings of the text, and specifically about the symbolic significance and identity of his main character.

In Left Handed's stories, we are continually presented, essentially, with a bildungsroman about the childhood and young adulthood of a young man. Left Handed's stories never show the son of Old Man Hat beyond young adulthood. We never see the son of Old Man Hat as an older man. Left Handed's stories primarily focus on the son of Old Man Hat as a grown but still young man. Tellingly, there are relatively few stories about the main character's early years. As Dyk has explained elsewhere, Left Handed resisted telling stories about his childhood and youth, preferring to only tell stories about his main character as a young adult (*A Navaho Autobiography* 6). When Walter Dyk conducted his research on the Navajo Reservation, he was in his early thirties, certainly a young man in Left Handed's eyes—and perhaps emblematic of a character much like the son of Old Man Hat who is never named, who is depicted as sexually obsessed, who is ignorant of Navajo ways, who disrespects "other" Indian people (including elders), and who neither understands nor respects Navajo ceremonies. Left Handed tells us that his main character was conspicuous in his close observations of the people around him, including any possible sexual intimacies: "When a man and a woman were around together I used to watch them closely, but I never saw a man get on a woman" (48). He reminds us repeatedly that his main character is a liar—perhaps advice that we are not to take Left Handed's stories literally, perhaps guidance that the actual main character (Dyk?) misrepresents the Navajo: "I'd already told lots of lies. . . . So I'd told them a lie lots of times. I didn't steal or cheat anybody, but I kept telling lies. That's the way I was" (254). Left Handed's repeated emphasis on the lack of veracity on the part of his main character obfuscates the already complicated interrogations into what is a clearly ambiguous and potentially shifting identity.

The volume *Son of Old Man Hat* is bereft of markers that might indicate that it is Left Handed's autobiography, other than those textual markers added by Dyk that identify the constructed narrative text as a life history. The ethnography may not even consist of stories about a young Navajo man's life at all (if the main character was indeed based on Dyk's behavior among the Navajo), even though the storytelling context for the stories is the Navajo world familiar to Left Handed. *Son of Old Man Hat* appears to consist of Left Handed's made-up stories about the formative years of the sort of person who would become his psychoanalytically trained anthropologist Walter Dyk. Was Left Handed repeatedly holding up a mirror for his young ethnographer, telling stories

about the objectification of Native peoples by young outsiders disrespectful of the knowledge and wisdom of his elders? Even though
I believe that many of the stories that Left Handed told his ethnographer refract back to Dyk's own behavior in Navajo country, I
really do not believe that the older Navajo man was necessarily
ridiculing or otherwise disrespecting the young Dyk. In the number of weeks and months that Left Handed worked with Walter
Dyk, there really is the sense that he came to care for the young
anthropologist. Even though Dyk did not maintain contact with
his informant beyond their working relationship, Dyk does refer to
Left Handed as his friend; and unlike the other Navajos who
worked with Walter Dyk for brief periods, some of whom ended up
breaking off their working relationships quite abruptly, Left
Handed returned to his work with Dyk over and over again.
Repeatedly in his stories, Left Handed tells us that his main character, the son of Old Man Hat, is a man who likes to make up stories about Navajos, is sexually obsessed, but who is otherwise an
honest man. Perhaps he hoped that at some point Dyk would stop
perceiving the old man's stories as little more than ethnographic
facts and life-history data. Perhaps, if the stories became recent
enough in their reflexivity and increasingly more specific (as is the
case of some of the stories in the subsequent volume *Left Handed*),
Left Handed hoped that Dyk might begin to listen to and learn
from the older man's stories as complexly crafted stories, rich in
meaning and invaluable in their insights not only into the ethnographic process but also into the racist, colonialist, and hegemonic
intrusions of outsiders (academic and otherwise) into Navajo country—which are decidedly unhelpful insofar as Left Handed's personal life history is concerned.

In a manner analogous to Gertrude Stein's *Autobiography of
Alice B. Toklas*, through his first-person storytelling voice Left
Handed steps into the role of the metaphoric son of Old Man Hat
and tells us the autobiographical stories (imagined and real) of a
character who is not himself, but instead representative of colonizing academics, government officials, and other outsiders who
intrude upon the Navajo. It is especially telling that in his foreword to the book, Edward Sapir writes, "Nor is this book a heavily

documented contribution to individual psychology. It is in no sense the study of a personality. It is a sequence of memories that need an extraordinarily well-defined personality to hold them together, yet nowhere is this unique consciousness obtruded upon us" (viii). Might it be the case that the "well-defined personality" who holds the stories together is Dyk, while the missing individual psychology and unique consciousness are due to Left Handed's personal absence in the text? By freeing up Left Handed's stories from the textually constraining life-history narrative into which they were forced, we are also freed to engage directly with the told stories. In such manner, we can see how Left Handed's stories fit together: stories that reflect his interactions with Walter Dyk, stories specifically told for his immediate audience, and stories which have been misread for almost sixty years.

In contradistinction to the textual primacy emphasized by twentieth-century literary criticism (whether in the formalism of the modernist era or the various poststructural critical practices of postmodernity), a conversive approach decenters and, thereby, de-emphasizes the text as the restorative means that returns the storytelling to its fitting center of the conversively co-creative storytelling circle. As linguist John J. Gumperz reminds us, "Meaning in conversations is usually jointly produced" (195). Therefore, our epistemological interpretive responses must needs take on a conversive orientation if we hope to approach orally related stories in a meaningful and accurate way. By not privileging the text as such, the text is no longer ostensibly read as the autobiographical narrative it purports to be, and Left Handed is no longer foregrounded in a way that distracts our attention from the range of issues and concerns that are at the heart of his telling. By means of conversive reading strategies, Left Handed's stories (not Dyk's ethnographic narrative) are foregrounded in the co-creative and interwoven interactions of listener-readers, story characters, and storyteller—thereby, neither text, writer, nor reader are given primacy. If there is any privileging involved, precedence is given to the unfolding story. Malcolm Crick points out that, in effect, "ethnography is a kind of storytelling" (35). In Left Handed's case, as a storyteller-informant, he crafted symbolically complex stories

that require vastly different interpretive strategies from those critical methods that interact primarily with the surface level of the
text (whether that interaction is in concord with the text or an
interrogation of it). The ambiguity embedded in Left Handed's
choice to neither name the main character in *Son of Old Man Hat*
nor to explicitly identify that character as himself demands conversive reader interrogations into the very autobiographical nature of
the constructed narrative and its underlying stories.

Stories Defined by American Empire-Building: The Son of Old Man Hat and the Long Walk

In order to read Left Handed's stories, we have seen that we need to
move away from the preconceived expectations of a "Navaho autobiography." The importance of such a strategy can be further seen in
the extent to which Left Handed de-emphasizes his main character
(the son of Old Man Hat) when he (Left Handed) has larger points to
make in his telling—a fact that is evident at the very outset of the
book, which begins with a notably brief recounting of the main character's birth. Dyk's choice to place the birth story first fits with his
commitment to a chronological narrative. As he explains in the
introduction to the volume, he had to reorganize Left Handed's stories from their initial episodic connections in order to put them in
the shape of a chronological narrative: "Likewise it seemed advisable to rearrange the episodes of early childhood into what would
appear to be a more exact chronological order from that in which
they were originally given" (xii, my emphasis). In this way, Dyk begs
the question of the authenticity of the stories as autobiographical,
thereby leading his readers to approach the text primarily as a source
of information about Navajo cultural anthropology and ethnographic autobiography. Dyk gives the first few paragraphs a textual
primacy by their insertion at the beginning of the narrative, but
their ostensive focus on the main character as a young boy elides the
broader realities that lie behind their telling. Even though the asso-
ciative connections between the told stories are largely lost due to
their reorganization, a conversive ear brought to these paragraphs
can nevertheless reveal a story that is much larger than that of one

person's birth: namely, the story of the Long Walk and its profound and enduring effects on the Navajo people.

Son of Old Man Hat begins with a couple of pages that point out the title character's time and place of birth, and his early struggles to survive. While this beginning story gives us some information about the newborn child, we are actually told much more about the historical context and times surrounding that birth and early life. Left Handed tells us that the child was born at Ft. Sumner (where the Navajo were imprisoned during the time of the Long Walk), and that he was a sickly baby born prematurely—an aberrant and danger-ous situation that immediately alerts his listener-readers to the hor-rors of that period for the Navajo. As Left Handed explains, "Something had happened to my mother, she'd hurt herself, that was why I was born before my time. I was just a tiny baby, and my feet and fingers weren't strong, they were like water. My mother thought I wasn't going to live" (3). Even in these few lines, we see the boy less as the primary topic and instead as a conversive sign pointing outward to other persons and events. Instead of telling us specifically about the baby, in Left Handed's stories about the begin-ning life of the son of Old Man Hat, he focuses largely on the boy's mother. Her centrality in his stories parallels the Navajo respect given to the mother, but in the stories about the son of Old Man Hat, we learn extensively about the boy's mother, both in her presence and in her later absence.[2] We read about her untimely delivery, her hurt condition, and her fears about her premature baby.

Immediately after noting the woman's concerns about the baby ("My mother thought I wasn't going to live"), Left Handed tells us that the boy's mother "had no milk" (3), and that her older sister struggled to find women who could nurse the baby. Notably, Left Handed relates nothing about the identity of the baby's real father. The evident silence surrounding the boy's paternity bespeaks much about the circumstances of a child fathered at Ft. Sumner, but who returns home without any mention of that father. Even ignoring the question of whether or not this a true story about Left Handed's birth, it certainly tells the story of the terrible conditions that the Navajos had to survive and endure at Ft. Sumner. Babies were born sickly. Mothers were hurt, often due to the violent rapes by the

United States soldiers. Food was in short supply, and mothers did not always produce enough milk for their babies. In his short story "The Blood Stone," Irvin Morris (Navajo) tells about a red-haired great-grandfather who was conceived through a rape at Ft. Sumner, and about a great-great-grandmother who as a young woman was raped throughout her pregnancy:

> In the spring of the fourth year, [the boy's] mother's belly begins to grow, but there is no joy. At night, she thrashes and moans. He covers his ears not to hear, but he does anyway. *"Dooda! Dooda!"* ["No! No!"] she pleads with the hairy face looming over her, straining red, breathing liquor in her face. (In Walters, *Neon Powwow* 23)

When Left Handed tells us that "something had happened to my mother," volumes of the history of that horrific period echo throughout his words. Additionally, the lack of specificity in the phrase "something had happened..." demonstrates a common storytelling tool that opens up the telling to listeners' co-creative consideration—here, regarding just what might have hurt a pregnant Navajo woman at Hwééldi (Ft. Sumner). The stories from that time have been passed down from generation to generation of Navajo families. The story Left Handed tells Dyk about his birth is the story of Hwééldi: a story of the horrifically oppressive conditions, of a hurt woman, a sickly child, a sick mother incapable of nursing her own baby because of an absence of milk, and of a mother who later rejects her child and is almost completely absent in his subsequent child-rearing. This is a story that has become all too common today, with rape being wielded as a weapon of war from Bosnia to Rwanda. One news story reported "hollow-eyed women" who arrived at clinics and hospitals to birth babies conceived from brutal rapes nine months before during the horrific genocide in Rwanda. Many of those women left the babies behind at the hospitals, being unable physically and psychologically to raise them. In Left Handed's story, he offers us a very brief glance at the Navajo Long Walk, and yet in his few lines, much is communicated about the unimaginable atrocity that was Hwééldi.

In Left Handed's stories, he also shows us the resilience of the Navajo to survive. An older clan relative of the sickly baby's mother finds women to nurse the baby to life and health, and the child survives into adulthood. A people decimated and impoverished by the effects of United States government policy against them survive their internment at Ft. Sumner and the destruction of their crops and livestock. Left Handed clearly wants us to understand the real-world effects of American colonization as he relates, "This was the year after we returned from Fort Sumner. There were no sheep, and we had nothing to live on. My mother had gone to Black Mountain, but when she got there it was the same" (4). Here, Left Handed communicates the widespread impoverishment of the Navajo people during this time. In Dyk's punctuation that presumably reflects the pauses in the oral telling, there is an emphatic pause after Left Handed's conclusion to the birth story: "This was the year after we returned from Fort Sumner." Here, he repeats the fact that the time was after the Navajo internment, so that his listeners and listener-readers can process the effects of nineteenth-century United States government policies and military actions against the Navajo, and the enduring legacy of the Long Walk. And the Navajos who survived the Long Walk returned home, but to a barren land: "There were no sheep, and we had nothing to live on" (37).

Left Handed's pauses give his listeners the time to reflect on the significance of those hard times, perhaps remembering the prior wide-scale destruction of Navajo crops and livestock in the attempt to impoverish the Navajos into submitting to the relocation to Ft. Sumner. Such emphatic pauses permit listeners and listener-readers to engage deeply with and within the story, gaining deeper empathic understandings of the dire circumstances surrounding those years. However, in Dyk's edited narrative, there is no break delineated after the mention of the Long Walk and the people's impoverishment, no space given for the listener-reader to respond. The narrative immediately moves to discuss Old Man Hat's Paiute slave, without even a paragraph break between the different topics. The paragraphing and chapter divisions within *Son of Old Man Hat* fit the constraints of the presumed autobiographical narrative, but in the process, we lose important punctuating elements of, and interconnective links in, the oral telling. The majority of the emphatic pauses, silences, repetitions that would have been invested with substantive semiotic significance within the domain of Left Handed's oral telling are lost in the translation from telling to text.

Conversive readers are needed to slow the text down to permit its underlying meaningful orality to speak forth through Dyk's mediated text. The skills of painstaking close analysis developed by formalist critics could be usefully brought to bear in opening up many of the early ethnographic works of Indian people from the nineteenth and twentieth centuries. However, such textual analyses can only go so far. The sort of close reading that is needed to open up orally originated texts is not the critical imposition of preconceived interpretive categories upon those texts, but instead, a conversive listening-reading approach that combines a slow and close reading with the listening strategies of the oral tradition. Otherwise we will continue to perpetuate misinterpretations such as the categorization of Left Handed's stories as autobiographical, when in certain cases, they are about his anthropologist, the colonial anthropological encounter, and more generally about the colonization of the Navajo people, their lives, their cultures, their traditions, and their stories. Commenting on similar empire-building efforts and colonialist relations in Africa, Kwame Anthony Appiah writes, "Most of us who were raised during and for some time after the colonial era are sharply aware of the ways in which the colonizers were never as fully in control as our elders allowed them to appear. We all experienced the persistent power of our own cognitive and moral traditions" (7). We see this quite profoundly in Left Handed's ability to relate important stories about his times, and about the continuing colonization (racist, governmental, academic) of his people. In many ways, his stories are his manner of resistance. From beyond the grave, Left Handed's stories can still speak loud and clear to us if we are willing to make the requisite conversive efforts to hear them. As Don and Terry Allen point out about Navajo linguistic resistance back during the days of Ft. Sumner, "As a body, the Navajos refused to collaborate with the enemy.... Why should they even speak to the enemy? When communication became essential, they'd subject understanding to the vagaries of two interpreters—Navaho to Spanish to English. Insisting on a Spanish-speaking go-between was a way of expressing scorn for the language of 'Wah-sheen-don'" (5, 8). Perhaps in the future, scholars will be able to work with Walter Dyk's field notes to further decipher Left Handed's stories. This chapter and the preceding one provide an opening into those stories. Even without recourse to actual field notes, readers who bring a conversive approach to orally informed texts can, nevertheless, find new ways to begin to access the underlying stories.

Left Handed and Other
Tricksters Named "Lefty"

As a means of concluding these investigations into Left Handed's storytelling, a brief interrogation into Left Handed's own name is warranted. Among the Navajo, individuals are often referred to as "Left Handed" or "Lefty" by virtue of their inclinations to lie and make up stories—connotations not unlike certain significances the name holds in English. The Webster's Unabridged International Dictionary includes "of doubtful sincerity, dubious" in one of the definitions of the terms "lefty" and "left-handed." Walter Dyk's storyteller-informant Left Handed is not the only Navajo named Left Handed or Lefty who worked as an "informant" for various ethnographers. One of the early informants who worked with Father Berard Haile, O.F.M. (a priest who was assigned to the Catholic Navajo Missions in 1900 and who remained at his post there until his stroke in 1954)[3] was also called "Left Handed" or "Lefty." It was Father Haile's informant Lefty who told him about a supposedly traditional Navajo Fire Dance ceremony that included a "smoking owl." Essentially, the (I might note, very funny) smoking owl demonstration consisted of a dead owl that Lefty had propped up with a cigarette in its mouth and tubing that ran down from the owl's mouth, then underground to where Lefty sat smoking a cigarette and sending the cigarette smoke through the tubing so it appeared that the owl was smoking the cigarette. Father Berard writes about this "ceremony" as follows: "Perhaps Lefty and other singers could explain the purpose of this exhibit and its connection with Upward-reachingway ceremonial. But natives are not over-anxious to speak about this ceremonial, because it is concerned too much with ghosts of deceased natives and nobody likes to dream or think of even deceased relatives" (*The Navaho Fire Dance* 51). Of course, as Haile continues to explain, the other Navajos with whom he spoke denied that the smoking-owl presentation was part of the larger ceremony, telling him that "the exhibit is named after Lefty and is not connected directly with Upward-reachingway, at least not among the rank in file" (51). For whatever reasons, Haile tends to discount these denials and faithfully reports the smoking-owl "ceremony" as a plausible part of traditional Navajo sacred ceremonies!

Perhaps Father Haile's informant Lefty was indeed named solely because of a physiological left-handed proficiency. After all, this is how he explained his name to Haile, but in light of his smoking-owl display, it seems that his name also reflected his own tendencies toward a highly dubious, trickster storytelling. While it is true that the names Left Handed and Lefty can certainly refer to a person's greater dexterity with his or her left hand than with the right, in Navajo country and in many other places worldwide, this name also carries significant connotative meaning. I first learned about this among the Navajo a number of years back from a Navajo friend who affirmed that "Back home [on the reservation], when someone is called Lefty or Left Handed, that usually means that he is tricky. You know, someone who tends to tell stories, a liar" (personal communication). Throughout Left Handed's stories, he repeatedly reminds us that the main character of his first-person-voice stories, the son of Old Man Hat, is a liar who tells stories that are not true. In this way, he frames and punctuates his storytelling by alerting his listeners that the stories told by the character of the son of Old Man Hat are stories whose veracity requires interrogations into their actual meaningfulness. Here, Left Handed offers us a coded way of pointing to the fact that many of the stories that he related to Dyk ought not to be taken as historically factual. If indeed many of the stories are indirectly about his anthropologist's behaviors and knowledge of Navajos (as evidenced in the storytelling depictions of the main character as ignorant of Navajo culture and traditions), then Left Handed is further warning us about the extent to which we should trust the levels of autobiographical facticity in Dyk's three published Navajo "autobiographies." Even in Left Handed's own name, we are further alerted to the trickster manners of stretching the truth and telling stories that are tellingly implicated throughout *Son of Old Man Hat*.

As Gelya Frank asked over twenty years ago, "What is it that has led investigators and readers to expect that a life history speaks for itself and that the material is self-evident?" (71). Of course, the larger answer lies in the colonialist blinders that prevented scholars from seeing beyond their own interpretive rubrics, and as Ann Laura Stoler notes, "even where we have probed the nature of colonial discourse and the politics of its language, the texts are often assumed to express a shared European mentality, the sentiments of a unified, conquering elite" ("Rethinking" 135), the narratives of western literary categories, and the tendency "to homogenize the subaltern subject" (Pathak and Rajan 565). These chapters on *Son of Old Man Hat* show us the pitfalls of our preconceived expectations of autobiographical facticity that obscure the originating arenas of Navajo storytelling. John Mandell Barrett offers a helpful clarification regarding the differences between autobiography and fiction, explaining that "The world of autobiography is dependent on the real world of the author, and the writer who creates a totally self-sufficient and self-contained world and cuts off the rhetorical signals which reveal that the book is an imitation of a real world has crossed the thin line and created fiction" (220). It is crucial that scholars of orally informed ethnographies bring to bear on their work a sophisticated sense of those rhetorical signals that indicate the conversive nature of a text. In such manner, we will be able to avoid the serious errors of confusing imaginative and symbolic stories with historical fact—complexities that led Clifford Geertz to write that "Understanding the form and pressure of...[indigenous people's] inner lives is more like grasping a proverb, catching an allusion, seeing a joke—or, as I have suggested, reading a poem" (*Local Knowledge* 70). For too many years, *Son of Old Man Hat* has been widely read as the literal autobiography of one Navajo man. As this chapter and the preceding ones stress, the boundaries between autobiography and fiction are far less clear-cut than have often been realized.

Throughout *Son of Old Man Hat* and *Left Handed*, we are offered highly crafted (and crafty) stories that invite us to engage with them on a conversive basis. In so doing, as listener-readers of Left Handed's stories, we can become co-creative story-listeners and join Left Handed (and Walter Dyk) in the storytelling circle of the storied worlds of Old Man Hat, his son, and all the others who populate those storied worlds with them. To do so means to hear very different stories from the presumed life-history narratives of the published texts. If we are truly interested in the facts about Left Handed's own life, we will have to go elsewhere than these purported autobiographies. There are many factual life histories of the Navajo, but readers must distinguish between these and those other spurious and questionable texts like *Son of Old Man Hat*. The next chapter provides a survey of much of the exemplary ethnography conducted in Navajo country. As the next chapter demonstrates, the Navajo ethnographies that are consistently reliable, accurate, and factual are those works that invariably originate from within the community (solely or in collaboration with nontribal members), are explicitly directed toward an audience that consists of Navajo people (either entirely or in part), are intended to be of value to the tribe and its members, and are constructed with substantive tribal input (work either produced wholly by Navajos, collaboratively produced by Navajos and non-Navajos together, or largely produced by outsiders who have subjected the work to review by relevant tribal members). This is seen in the next chapter's presentation of the range of solid ethnography about the Navajo.

Chapter Six

Postcolonial Navajo Ethnography

Writing the People's Own Stories from within Tribal Culture

I n contrast to the earlier generations of ethnographic work produced about the Navajo during the twentieth century, the past
few decades have seen a radical transformation in the ethnographic
process as the more traditional forms of academic and scientific
objectivity and distance have been rejected in favor of more intersubjectively collaborative and interpersonally conversive working
relationships. In each of the examples explored in this chapter, real
lived relationships were developed between the ethnographers
(working in the diverse fields of anthropology, folklore, weaving, and
photography) and their Navajo storyteller-colleagues, thereby yielding storytelling texts that in fact tell us much more about the lives
of various Navajo elders, their tribal culture and beliefs, and Navajo
history than is the case in the ivory tower's colonialist scholarship
about the Navajo, which has been all too often misleading at best,
and at worst altogether spurious. The Navajo ethnography that is

the most reliable is invariably that which has been substantially informed and guided by Navajos (either in the role of storytellers or ethnographers)—following the sort of relational model that in the past was ascribed to women (Belenky; Sidonie Smith; Stanton; Underhill). As Sandra Harding has pointed out, "Conventionally, what it means to be scientific is to be dispassionate, disinterested, impartial, concerned with abstract principles and rules; but what it means to be a woman is to be emotional, interested in and partial to the welfare of family and friends, concerned with concrete practices and contextual relations" (47). The academy's demands for objective science ostensibly served to absent the Navajo voice, as scholars spoke for the Navajo rather than engaging in intersubjective and consultative converse with them. It is profoundly ironic that in its exhaustive efforts to document the tribe, the academy's colonialist presumptions to "know" the Navajo better than the Navajo know themselves prevented scholars from actually achieving that which they sought.

In practice, an overview of those ethnographically produced texts that have been built upon enduring interpersonal relationships between Navajo storytellers and their anthropologists demonstrates that such intersubjectively created work produces more reliable and meaningful records of indigenous knowledge and information (both in terms of their historical facticity and storytelling depth). The turn toward a relational model in research has been described and advocated by various feminist scholars in a range of disciplines, including Nel Noddings in her introduction to care ethics (*Caring*) and Susan Stanford Friedman in her literary critical discussions of relational epistemology (247–61). Interrogating what would be involved in "the possibility of doing meaningful ethnography," Daniel Bradburd notes the crucial need for new fieldwork practices (159). As this chapter clarifies, truly meaningful ethnography is that which is centered in those relationships out of which people's stories arise and are shared (Lawless, "'Reciprocal' Ethnography"; O'Connor; Prus). This is what Bernard McGrane points to when he advocates scholars "engaging in dialogue" with those we seek to understand as fellow "subject[s], comparable to what I am myself" (127). In such wise, both Navajo storytellers and their ethnographers

(Navajo and non-Navajo) work together intersubjectively and inter-personally as fellow subjects and persons co-creating and co-constructing their ethnographic productions.

In contrast to the short-lived communications between an ethnographer and informant that cease upon the conclusion of the specific project, in the examples introduced in this chapter, enduring working relationships were established. Key here is that the work is substantially informed by the Navajos who are involved in these ethnographic projects. Often their ethnographers serve in the capacity of textual catalysts, initiating and carrying through the responsibilities involved in bringing the various people's stories to print. Noting the repercussions that can arise from work that is insufficiently tribally guided, literary scholar Paul Zolbrod acknowledges the tribal outcry that he faced when he desired to publish a print version of the Navajo Blessingway along with a translation in English (Dine' bahane). Zolbrod explains that, at the time, he did not understand the implications of taking a sacred oral story that is traditionally told in the co-creative manner of Navajo sacred healing processes and fixing a sacred process into a static textualized document. As Zolbrod relates, "If I did not fully appreciate that complexity when I began this work, I came to realize it as I asked various Navajos for help. While most of them cooperated, many were hostile to the idea of having it written down" (21–22). The conflictual aspects of his work that Zolbrod had to address are often reduced or avoided in those projects whose originating conceptions are more relationally based within the tribal community. Akhil Gupta and James Ferguson echo Zolbrod's concerns, noting that ethnography requires a "decolonized anthropology" that renounces "the distancing and exoticization of the conventional anthropological 'field,'" while "foregrounding the ways in which we anthropologists are historically and socially (not just biographically) linked with the areas we study" (38). In light of the requirements for objectivity, it is not surprising that much of the earlier generations of conversively informed ethnography among the Navajo is to be found in the more collaborative ethnographic productions of women anthropologists and other ethnographers who lived among the Navajo and became actual and integral parts of Navajo community life on and around the reservation.

Feminist scholars have noted the extent to which women's interactions with each other in the world demonstrate greater degrees of interpersonal cooperation and intimacy than is generally the case within the bounds of traditional androcentric relations (Belenky; Friedman; Noddings; Underhill). Mary C. Raugust comments that such women's experiences represent a more "feminist ethical discourse [that] attends to values of cooperation, relationship, and interdependent nurturance...[while being] rooted in practical, everyday realities" (125). This is the very essence of interpersonal conversive relationships (O'Connor). Within the dominant culture of white America, such relations have tended to be fairly stratified across gender lines, with women engaging in conversive relationships more comfortably than men. We can see this even in the manner by which scholars have acknowledged those Navajos who have assisted their work. In contrast to earlier generations of ethnographers who rarely identified their various informants, John R. Farella thanks those he refers to as his "Navajo teachers" (ix). In the preface to *The Main Stalk: A Synthesis of Navajo Philosophy*, Farella thanks many scholars by name, but he does not do so for any of the Navajos with whom he worked, writing that "for a variety of reasons, I have not used the names by which I knew them. Many other Navajos also deserve my gratitude, but again, not by name" (ix). A decade later, in *Language Shift among the Navajos*, Deborah House goes much further in acknowledging the importance of those Navajos who assisted her work, naming each and every one, as well as describing the manner of their assistance: "Some of these people let me interview them; others were instructors in my Navajo and Indian studies classes; still others taught me through their conversations and actions.... *Ahe'hee*" (here concluding with the Navajo word for thanks, xii). In House's acknowledgments, she emphasizes her relationships with all those who worked with her on her Navajo language study. In her trenchant article "Feminism, Postmodernism, and Gender-Skepticism," Susan Bordo reminds us of the complex relations inherent in all aspects of a culture: "intellectual, psychological, institutional, and sociological" (135). The conversive elements of indigenous cultural communications have proved more accessible and comprehensible to generations of women scholars for whom such communications patterns were more the norm.

Within those cultures that are still varyingly close to their oral roots, conversive relations are still widely practiced and valued, regardless of gender. This is true throughout much of Indian country, and especially so in the Navajo Nation, where the more recent ethnographic work has been driven by Navajo ethical concerns regarding fieldwork methodology and fieldworker responsibilities to the Navajo storyteller-informants and the tribe. In such a turn toward the postcolonial conversive, male folklore scholar Barre Toelken pioneered an academically deferent position to the Navajos with whom he worked. Toelken made a striking shift away from the standard colonialist model of academic empire-building, choosing to publish less work from his field notes and recordings than would have been otherwise possible, and taking the extraordinary step several years ago of returning "60-plus hours of original field recording tapes" per the request of his informant's widow ("The Yellowman Tapes" 385). Toelken explains that his successful work over the years with the Little Wagon and Yellowman families was largely due to the relationship that was established between them and him: "My ability to record—or, more properly, Navajo permission for me to record—was made possible by my promise that I would play the tapes only during the season in which they could properly be performed. Because my Navajo friends trusted my word in this matter, they were quite willing to record anything I asked for" (381). Toelken struggled with his responsibilities to his scholarly work, his students, and the Navajo families with whom he worked. Over the years, he learned that his folklore studies of/with the Navajo would be largely determined by the values and customs of all involved. As he writes elsewhere, "Ideas about right and wrong are rooted in ancient custom, but they are acted out where the tire meets the road: in contemporary life" ("End of Folklore" 96).

Among the many anthropologists who have worked among the Navajo, Charlotte J. Frisbie's work has stood out in her enduring commitment to the tribe and her collaborative work with tribal members. Frisbie and David P. McAllester edited the volume *Navajo Blessingway Singer: The Autobiography of Frank Mitchell:*

1881–1967, which came out in 1978 and was reissued recently with an updated introduction, and Frisbie later brought out the related volume *Tall Woman: The Life Story of Rose Mitchell, a Navajo Woman, c. 1874–1978*. The published autobiographies about the Mitchells frame their stories within the textual narrative of a life history. In the future, it would be helpful to have such volumes foreground more substantially the broader dimensions of their conversively told stories as a means toward assisting readers' deeper understandings. The presumptive facticity surrounding the life-history information in ethnographically constructed autobiographies all too often predetermines readers' inclinations away from the semiotic complexities inherent in conversively episodic and associational storytelling. While readers need to bring conversively informed interpretive skills to bear on the entire range of Navajo ethnographies to access their symbolic richness, those volumes produced by non-Navajo scholars such as Toelken and Frisbie are to be commended for their authenticity, reliability, and historical accuracy. Frisbie's volume about Frank Mitchell communicates much about the life and world of a Navajo singer (a spiritual and physical healer). A conversive parallel study that looked at Frisbie's book in conjunction with interrogations into an earlier volume that purports to be about another such healer, *Lucky the Navajo Singer*, would be most illuminating. *Lucky the Navajo Singer* is based on stories that were told to and recorded by Alexander H. Leighton and Dorothea C. Leighton. While it is documented that "Lucky" was a shiftless drunk, gambler, and thief; an unfaithful and neglectful husband and father; an unreliable worker; and an all-around trickster, it remains to be shown whether "Lucky" was indeed a Navajo ceremonial singer or merely a singer of tall tales.

Photographer John Pack

As is evident in this chapter's overview of Navajo ethnography, the ethnographic work done in Navajo country that is by far the most reliable, accurate, and meaningful is that which is conversively postcolonial, with ethnographers (non-Navajo and/or Navajo) working collaboratively with tribal members. To help clarify the

importance of strongly conversive work in relation to the recording and interpretation of oral storytelling, the pictorial example of
the work of a non-Navajo photographer who lived and worked in
the Navajo Nation provides a powerful model of the success that
comes from a co-creative commitment to the conversive. John
Pack is a Euro-American photographer who in the early 1980s had
recently completed a series of photos of the Navajo. I had just
moved into Gallup, New Mexico, and was informed about a private
showing of Pack's work in someone's home. Later that day, I found
myself in that home looking at pictures that were unlike any professional photographs I had ever seen of Native peoples (or of any
people, for that matter). Most of the photographs I had seen of the
various indigenous peoples of the world were static and reportorial
in their exoticized subalterity, like many of the ethnographic photos I had grown up seeing in magazines like the *National
Geographic*. However in Pack's work, the Navajo people he photographed were alive; they were fully there in his pictures. As we
looked at the photographs and the people in them, it felt as if the
photographed Navajos were right in front of us, in full control of
their own subjective status, looking right back at us.

Pack's photographs brought stories to life through the actual
presences, lives, and worlds of those Navajos. This was not the
realm of the voyeuristic gaze discussed by Theresa de Lauretis
(*Alice Doesn't*). Such an objectifying gaze presumes the existence
of an objectifying text upon which that gaze is directed. Of course,
the very textualizing mediation of a photograph or a work of literature opens up the realm of storytelling to textual objectification.
This was very much the effect of the great era of twentieth-century
criticism and theory (formalist and postmodern, structuralist and
poststructuralist) that struggled to constrict literature and other
art forms into texts, stories into narratives, lives into (auto)biogra-
phies, and cultures into historical "artifactions." Derrida correctly
elucidated the tenor of the twentieth century when he asserted
that "Il n'y a pas de hors-texte." What he did not explain was that
these texts, the results of our own interpretive constructions,
obscured the very real realities lying underneath their respective
textualized facades. This was definitely not the case with Pack's

photographs of various Navajo people who lived in the Ganado, Arizona, region of the Navajo Reservation. These were living photographic stories, not representations.

When I first encountered John Pack's work, it was clear that what I was seeing was unusual. In no way did I have the sense of being a voyeuristic observer looking at a world (Navajo), a community (Ganado, Arizona), and persons' lives. I had the distinct sense that I was being offered a story co-creatively related by Pack and the Navajo people he had come to know. The storytelling opportunity presented before me included the chance to step into the worlds of those photographs and become a part of the offered stories as a listener-viewer. In one of the photos taken by Pack, an old Navajo grandma sits at her loom, turning around to face John Pack and the viewers of her photo directly. There is a twinkle in her eyes and a small smile registering her amusement as she watches Pack take her picture. This photograph and the others in the Ganado Series are all co-created through the collaborative relationships between people who clearly cared about each other, and who enjoyed their time watching each other in the production of their (the Navajo subjects and their photographer) photos. There is no sense of objectification, nor of a disempowering gaze robbing the photographed of their presence and subjectivity in the world and in their photos. Looking at the Pack photos that I have in my home, I really feel as if I, like Pack, am in relationship with the people who grace my home. It is as if Pack, as the storyteller, enables me and anyone else to begin to get to know his subjects, much as a story-listener comes to be in relationship to the storyteller and the characters in the story as the listener actually enters and becomes a part of the story. This is the difference between the hierarchized power relationships within discursively constructed narrative texts and the collaboratively balanced intersubjective relationships within conversively informed stories (lived and related). John Pack's Ganado Series is a story, as is each photograph in that series, and through his collaborative storytelling/story-showing, he assists his viewers to become story-viewers of the worlds of his photographic stories.

In order to achieve the successful, living storytelling in those photographs, Pack very consciously understood the importance of intersubjective relationships in producing a visual presentation of people's lives and stories. I was fortunate not only to be able to purchase a few of Pack's photographs, but also to talk with him about his work. Shortly before the private Gallup showing, Pack had just returned from a major show of his work in New York, and when I met him, he was about to leave for a prestigious position as a photography professor in Europe. The day after the Gallup showing, I met Pack in his home to pick up the photos I had purchased, their having been matted and signed by the photographer. I had a definite sense that it was important for me to talk with Pack about his work, to hear his story and the story of his Ganado Series photographs. I made a date to have lunch with him before he left town. We met at Earl's Two, the short-lived sister restaurant to the well-known Earl's restaurant in Gallup, and over lunch I asked John about his photography and his Ganado Series. As we sat there, he began to tell me his story, which I have come to understand as one storytelling of the story that is also told by the photographs themselves.

Pack explained that he had wanted to do a photographic series of the Navajo, but that he learned quickly upon his arrival in Navajo country that one does not receive without first giving to the community. So, Pack got work as an EMT (emergency medical technician) and firefighter, and became a part of the world in which he eventually hoped to create his photographs. If my memory serves me correctly, I believe that Pack said that he lived and worked on the reservation for five or so years, and then taught photography to Navajo students at a regional community college. Pack related that he was willing to wait however long it took to produce the photographs he dreamed of making. Over the course of his time in Navajo country, he became a part of the lives of the individuals who came to be in his photographs, as those people too became part of his life and world. As Pack explained it to me, the success of his project was the direct result of the collaborative nature of his work. He pointed out that he was only able to produce his Ganado Series photographs by being in relation to the individuals he photographed. In other words, the photographs came out of the deep relationships that developed between Pack and some of the people he had gotten to know. Pack did not approach the Navajo people in the Ganado region of the Navajo Reservation as objectified "subjects" for photographic study. From start to finish, the people were fellow people to Pack, and through his relationships with them, they were able to co-create these remarkable photographs.

Over the last two decades or so, a number of anthropologists have called for more of a dialogic approach in their ethnographic fieldwork (Dwyer, "Dialogic of Field Work" and "Dialogic of Ethnology"; Scholte, "Literary Turn"; Whiteley), but the real-world relationships that Pack established with the people who populate his photos goes substantially beyond the "establishment of intersubjective objectivity *between the ethnographer and his subjects*" as advocated by Johannes Fabian ("Language" 32, emphasis in original). Such discursively based "language-oriented anthropology" privileges people's linguistic communications, rather than placing at the center of the engagement the lived interrelationships among those involved (Fabian 23). Anthropologists like Fabian have struggled to move anthropology away from the more strictly controlled mediation of ethnographer and editor through discursively constructed dialogue, but far more can be achieved by taking a conversive turn (Alcoff; Fabian, "Culture"; Marcus, *Ethnography*). As Pack learned, at the center of conversive relations are the relationships themselves.

Leslie Marmon Silko (Laguna Pueblo) states quite explicitly what she tries to convey to others in her own writing: "relationships...That's all there really is" ("Stories and their Tellers" 22). Julie Cruikshank relates that her work with Yukon Native women elders taught her about the relational nature of stories: "Stories connect people" (*Social Life* 46). As George E. Marcus asserts, "If there is anything left to discover by ethnography it is relationships, connections, and indeed cultures of connection, association, and circulation that are completely missed through the use and naming of the object of study in terms of categories 'natural' to subjects' preexisting discourses about them" (*Ethnography* 16). Whether this is through the extensive years of lived interaction between a trader on the Navajo Reservation and local Navajo friends (Newcomb), or whether this involves anthropologists who develop lifelong relationships with tribal members (Frisbie), invariably the ethnographic work I have encountered that is the most reliable, informative, substantive, trustworthy, and rich with meaning is that which is based upon lived and enduring relationships among the individuals involved in the respective ethnographic projects (Crick; Watkins). The rest of this chapter introduces the relational focus of a number of women (and, in a few cases, men) whose work in Navajo country was developed upon the framework of long-lasting interpersonal and intersubjective connections with the people whose stories they recorded. There are more than can be mentioned in one chapter, but a few stand out for their high levels of reliability, trust, and care.

Franc Johnson Newcomb

In 1964, Franc Johnson Newcomb published an exemplary and unequivocally non-colonialist biography of her neighbor, family friend, and mentor Hosteen Klah, "noted medicine man, wealthy stockman, and unsurpassed weaver" (*Hosteen Klah* xv). Newcomb was not an academic seeking a subject for academic study, nor was Newcomb a non-Navajo outsider with a romanticized fascination with the Navajo people and their culture. Franc Johnson Newcomb was a woman who lived on the Navajo Reservation where she and her husband ran the Pesh-do-clish trading post, and where they raised their children during the first half of the twentieth century. As Newcomb explains, "Our post was not only the center of community trade, but also the center of information concerning social functions and the exigencies of family life. We were always aware of family, clan, or community activities and were generally invited to participate. We were asked to weddings, rodeos, horse races and barbecues. It was not a far step from these forms of entertainment to their religious rites and ceremonials" (xxi). The fact that Newcomb and her family were invited to such a range of personal, familial, clan, and tribal events, and that the Newcombs made the effort to attend these doings, bespeaks a great deal about the extent to which the Newcombs truly became interactive members of the Navajo community in which they lived.

Regarding the Navajo medicine man Hosteen Klah, with whom Newcomb worked in compiling Navajo stories, she writes that he and "his clan family were our neighbors, our helpers, and our best friends. It was through his influence that I was able to attend Navajo religious ceremonies, and it was with his permission that I started making sketches of his sacred sand paintings" (xv). In this very important passage, Newcomb communicates much about her relationships with Hosteen Klah and the other Navajo people with whom she produced her various books, such as *Hosteen Klah: Navaho Medicine Man and Sand Painter*, and *Navaho Folk Tales*. Newcomb makes it very clear that her work was done with the express permission of Hosteen Klah (and other Navajos), whether regarding her very accurate depictions of the sand paintings Klah created during particular ceremonies, or her recording of his stories.[1] Newcomb recounts:

> I have pleasant memories of long winter evenings before the huge open fireplace, sometimes with a baby in my lap or perhaps with my hands busy sewing some small garment while I listened to the deep voice of Hosteen Klah recounting traditions of his people or tribal events that took place long before he was born. Often he would pause to say, "I may not be telling this again; why do you not write it down?" But generally there was something else I wished to do, and often I was weary at the close of day. (xxii)

While Newcomb became deeply interested in her ethnographic work on the reservation, it is crucial to emphasize that her studies came out of her own and her Navajo neighbors' everyday lives and experience. Regardless of the Newcombs' privileged socioeconomic positions as traders on the reservation, they worked hard, lived simply, and were committed to interacting as full members (albeit non-Navajo members) of their community, including their immediate and rigorous study and successful learning of the Navajo language. As Newcomb makes very clear in the passage quoted above, much of her recorded ethnography was not even initiated by her, but by Hosteen Klah and other Navajos who were interested in having their stories and traditions recorded for future generations by a faithful community ethnographer.

Over their many years running the trading post on the Navajo Reservation at what is now called Newcomb, Arizona, Franc Johnson Newcomb and her husband Arthur became very close friends with many of their Navajo neighbors. Newcomb relates that when Hosteen Klah became seriously ill with pneumonia at the end of his life, the Newcombs were the ones who made all the arrangements to get him to the Indian hospital in Gallup. Then Franc Newcomb arranged to have a woman stay with her daughters so that she could travel to Gallup to be with Hosteen Klah. At the Rehoboth Mission hospital, the staff even made space in a linen room for a cot so that Newcomb could stay at the hospital near the old man. Not long thereafter, with his own family present, Klah asked Newcomb's husband to oversee arrangements for a "white" burial, while his own family would take care of the appropriate Navajo burial traditions. Newcomb relates that her husband mourned Klah greatly, saying, "He was the best friend I ever had" (212). Franc Johnson Newcomb lived her relationships with the people whose stories she published in her various books. For her, the Navajo people she got to know were simply "our neighbors, our helpers, and our best friends" (xv).

Photographer Kenji Kawano

Just as Franc Johnson Newcomb was deeply integrated into her surrounding Navajo world, so too was Kenji Kawano, "a native-born Japanese who came to America in 1973 and was drawn to the mystery and beauty of the Navajo Reservation" (Kawano n.p., back cover). Kawano was a photographer who came to the Navajo Reservation in 1974, oblivious of the important connections that he would discover between his own life and that of many Navajo men. As the Navajo artist Carl N. Gorman relates, "It was about fifteen years ago that I saw a man walking along the road in Window Rock, Arizona. He was carrying a big camera bag over his shoulder. I stopped my car and asked if he'd like a lift" (Kawano ix).[2] That man was Kawano, the son of a Japanese veteran who fought against the United States in World War II. Instead of taking Kawano to Ganado, where he was living, the Gormans brought him along with them to a traditional Navajo Enemy Way Ceremony (or Squaw Dance). The significance of this event was portentous for both men. Gorman was one of the original Navajo Code Talkers who served as marines during World War II, with responsibilities to communicate secret codes based on the Navajo language. Their codes were the only ones that Japanese cryptographers could never break, and have been hailed as crucial to the American success in the Pacific during the war. Kawano's father was one of the Japanese servicemen who fought for his country against the Americans.

In many ways, Kawano's developing relationships with Gorman and, later, with the other Navajo Code Talkers were personally healing for many of the men (Navajo and the Japanese-American Kawano) in the ways that conversively informed relationships can be. Gorman introduced Kawano to other Navajo veterans who had served in the Marines as Code Talkers. Kawano writes that during official events, each of the men would wear "the Navajo code talker's uniform [devised since the War to reflect both their service in the Marines and the importance of their culture and language in that service]—a turquoise-colored cap, a gold Navajo shirt, well-pressed khaki-colored pants, shiny black shoes, a turquoise necklace, and other decoration—with pride. Many Navajo people were proud of them" (xiv). Later, in 1982, Kawano was designated the official Navajo Code Talkers Association photographer, taking photographs of the Code Talkers in their uniforms and at various events. Kawano became so involved in Code Talker activities and in the lives of a number of the Code Talkers that they even took the remarkable step of naming him an honorary Code Talker (xiv).

The published collection of Kawano's Code Talker photographs, *Warriors: Navajo Code Talkers*, emerged from his desire to call attention to the experiences of the Navajo veterans, and to enable the men to express their own stories (both in photographic images and in words). This work was one of many acts of service Kawano rendered to the Navajo veterans. To craft the men's official photographs for the books, he told them that he would come to their homes to take their photographs, even though this was an especially challenging and time-consuming task since the men were scattered throughout the Navajo Reservation and few had telephones (xv). One story from Kawano's experiences of taking the personal photographs tells us much about the extent to which the men had come to value Kawano's work and his efforts to include as many of the Code Talkers as possible, even in the face of great obstacles:

> David Jordan (Sweetwater, Arizona) lived an hour away
> from the paved highway, and it was hard to find his home.
> He used his tractor to fix the dirt road that had been
> washed away by rain a few days before I was scheduled to
> visit him. He did this just for me, and I was deeply moved.
> I got lost several times on the way to his house, and
> thought of giving up; when I found out how much trouble
> he'd gone to with the road, I was glad I'd persevered. (xvi).

Here, as an old man, Jordan went to great efforts to make it possible for the Japanese-American photographer to reach his home and hear his stories, this even in spite of the painful racist experiences that Jordan remembers from his service years: "An Army security guard shoved his gun in my back and took my rifle away because he thought I was Japanese. . . . He took me to camp headquarters, where another Navajo soldier recognized me. I was freed after that" (54). Even in this one brief vignette, we see the warm openness and historical accuracy that comes from Kawano's conversive efforts with the men. In Jordan's conversation, he speaks very directly and relationally to his Japanese photographer about military racism, and yet the story he chooses to relate is one whose parallelism binds him to Kawano through Kawano's Japanese ancestry and Jordan's erroneously presumed Japanese appearance.

Warriors: Navajo Code Talkers is centered in the portrait photographs of seventy-five of the over two hundred Code Talkers still living in the late 1980s. Each entry includes one man's photograph, along with his Navajo identification through his respective clans and his Marine identification through his division and the places where he served as a Code Talker (e.g., Guam, Saipan, Okinawa, Guadalcanal, Iwo Jima, Bougainville, etc.). Kawano also includes a statement from each of the represented seventy-five Code Talkers about their experiences. In these statements, the

men [and in some cases their widows] share their experiences and
memories with us all, ranging from expressions of patriotic and
tribal pride, of socioeconomic racism, of joyous humor in the face
of wartime horror, of poignant human loss and bravery, and of the
enduring psychological effects of wartime service, even after traditional tribal healing ceremonies:

> When I was inducted into the service, one of the
> commitments I made was that I was willing to die for
> my country—the U.S., the Navajo Nation, and my family.
> My language was my weapon.—David E. Patterson,
> Tachii'nii and Kinlichii'nii clans; 4th Marine Division:
> Roi Atoll, Marshall Islands, Kwajalein Atoll. (Kawano 75)

> I volunteered to serve my country.—Pahe D. Yazzie,
> Todich'ii'nii and Tachii'nii clans; 5th Marine Division:
> New Caledonia, Hawaii, Saipan. (98)

> I went to war because there were no jobs on the reserva-
> tion.—Wilson Keedah Sr., Kin yaa'aanii clan; 6th Marine
> Division: Okinawa, Guadalcanal, Iwo Jima. (56)

> On post guard duty one night, six of us were sharing one
> foxhole when we heard something coming at us through the
> underbrush. We opened fire . . . it was a wild pig!—John
> Goodluck, To'aheedliinii and Dibe lizhini clans; 3rd Marine
> Division: Guadalcanal, Bougainville, Guam, Iwo Jima. (46)

> While I was stationed in Guam, I saw a soldier step on a
> landmine. Both of his legs and one hand were destroyed.
> He asked for a smoke, saying, "I still have one hand."—
> John Kinsel Sr., Kin lichii'nii clan; 3rd Marine Division:
> Guadalcanal, Bougainville, Guam, Iwo Jima. (59)

> Navajos' main diet is mutton and goat meat. On Okinawa,
> we discovered a lot of domesticated goats running loose;
> their owners were behind the skirmishes and combat

lines. Some of us captured and butchered a few of the animals and had a feast. The non-Navajo military men were
surprised.—Samuel F. Sandoval, Naasht'ezhi dine clan; 1st
Marine Division: Guadalcanal, Bougainville, Guam, Palua
Islands, Enewetak Atoll, Okinawa. (80)

What I remember is carrying messages from headquarters
to the front line, night and day, eighty-two days. I lost
friends in Okinawa. When I came home from the war,
my family had two-day and two-night healing ceremonies,
as well as two squaw dances, to help me get well, but I
am still sick.—Deswood R. Johnson Sr., 6th Marine
Division: Okinawa. (53)

While on the hospital ship *Benevolence*, my friend and I
took liberty and went into the village of Yokusuka, which
was supposed to be off-limits to American soldiers. We
came back okay, and met some nice people in the village.—Mike Kiyaani, Ashiihi clan; 6th Marine Division:
Guadalcanal, Guam, Okinawa. (62)

In this last quotation, we see that even in the midst of wartime dangers, a Navajo young man (Mike Kiyaani) nevertheless perceives the
Japanese people in a conversively relational manner. A Japanese village that the marines were not allowed to enter becomes a place for
a simple visit to meet the people of the village who were supposed
to be enemies. The Navajo marines do not perceive the Japanese in
a distancing and objectified way, but rather as fellow human persons. Kiyaani and his friend enter Yokusuka and visit with their
enemies, who become their friends. Perhaps there was some sort of
material exchange during the visit to symbolize their relationship. . . . Be that as it may, it is certainly fitting that a Navajo marine
serving on a hospital ship named *Benevolence* would embark on
such a journey, defined in terms of the actual benevolence shown
between Japanese civilians and a young Navajo Code Talker.
    In the brief vignettes, statements, and photographs that grace
the pages of *Warriors*, these Navajo old men opened up their lives

and stories to Kawano in words and in images; in turn, Kawano opened himself up to the men's stories, even including the stories and photographs of the deceased as shared by the men's widows. Four of the photographs taken in the men's homes show their widows proudly holding service photographs of their husbands. In fact, when the Code Talkers participate in official events, they have welcomed widows, whom I have seen proudly marching along with the veterans, each woman carrying a photograph of her deceased husband to enable him to continue to march with his fellow Code Talkers. In the photograph for Harry Belone, we see Mrs. Lanabah Belone seated at a table, holding a service photograph of her husband and displaying his uniform jacket on the table (31). Kawano writes, "She told me that after he went to war, she supported their family by weaving and selling her rugs. When the children cried for their father, she cried with them, many times. She told me a lot in her own language" (xvi). This brief vignette speaks volumes about the close conversive relationships that Kawano established with the men and their families. Over and over again, we see very personal photographs, many of which include the men with their various family members (most often grandchildren and wives), and we hear their reflections and remembrances of their wartime experiences.

Kawano's book makes it possible for the men to share their stories with the world. As Carl Gorman explains, "The portrait photos in this book reflect years of contact with us as individuals as we are today, and something of who we were forty years ago when our language helped the United States defeat his [Kawano's] people.... he wanted the American people to know more about us. He decided to do a book that would honor us. Kenji Kawano's portraits speak for themselves" (x–xi). Gorman tells us that Kawano's interest in producing this book was not for himself, but as a gift to the men, a way to "honor" them. More than standard portraits, Kawano's photos open themselves up to their viewers as stories and vignettes that all come together in the larger story of the tremendous service of these Navajo men in World War II. Kawano's photographic collection as a whole tells this larger story of the Navajo Code Talkers' World War II service, while it also serves as the vehicle for the Code Talkers' own autobiographical stories from their own lives, experiences, and families. The volume is relationally co-creative throughout as Kawano relates his own story in becoming a part of Navajo country and the story of the book's origin; but most importantly, his photographic-storytelling art assists the Navajo veterans in sharing their stories with a much wider audience than would be otherwise possible. Gorman concludes his foreword to the volume, writing, "As our friendship began with a visit to a Navajo Enemy Way Ceremony, so does this book and tribute symbolize the healing of the wounds of war. To Kenji Kawano, my Japanese-Navajo friend, I say *ahéhee* (thank you)" (xi, emphasis in original). Kawano became such a part of Navajo country, the world of the Code Talkers, and Gorman's own life and family that, insofar as Carl Gorman is concerned, Kawano was not only a friend of the Navajo, but even more, a member of the community: a Japanese-Navajo. Key here in Kawano's ethnographic Navajo photography, as well as other notable works of Navajo ethnography, is the way Gorman describes Kawano...as his *friend*, with all the profundity of what that conveys within a Navajo tribal context. Over and over again, I have seen Navajo country opened up wide to those non-Navajos who, in turn, open themselves up wide to their Navajo friends in the true development of deep and lasting friendship (Begay; Forsman).

Mary Shepardson and Irene Stewart

Unlike Pack, Newcomb, and Kawano, the anthropologist Mary Shepardson never lived among the Navajo other than during her free summers or sabbatical periods. She first arrived in Navajo country in 1955 as a graduate student interested in the tribal council, tribal elections, and the campaign of one woman candidate, Mrs. Greyeyes (Irene) Stewart. Shepardson did not go to the reservation expecting to establish a lifelong relationship, and yet that is what occurred. Much of her most productive and valuable work came out of her friendship with one Navajo woman:

> My first interview with Irene Stewart in 1955 marked the
> beginning of an acquaintanceship which—over the years, as
> I returned again and again to Chinle for further studies—

grew into a deep and enduring friendship between two
women across the cultural divide. Together we attended
meetings, interviewed old medicine men and retired
judges of the Navajo Tribal Courts, visited Chapters in
other communities, observed the Tribal Council in session
at Window Rock, with Irene acting as guide, interpreter,
and friend.... My friendship with Irene grew perhaps
because we were of the same age and had both lived
through many of the same joys and disappointments,
failures and successes—the universals of human life.
Or perhaps it grew because we shared an intense interest
in the building of self-government in our country's largest
Indian society, a tribe which is at the same time a
'domestic dependent nation.' Perhaps we became fast
friends simply because we enjoyed each other" (6–7).

It was not until years later that Shepardson turned her attention
from other aspects of Navajo tribal culture and governance to her
friend's own life and experiences. Over time, the two women corresponded, and Stewart shared her life story in greater detail with
Shepardson through "a series of letters" (7). Finally, in 1980,
Shepardson published a narrative based on those letters: *A Voice
in Her Tribe: A Navajo Woman's Own Story*, by Irene Stewart,
foreword by Mary Shepardson, edited by Doris Ostrander Dawdy.
It was the editor, Dawdy, who reorganized Stewart's stories, which
"weave back and forth in time," to establish a more chronological
narrative structure (7). Had Stewart's stories been presented in
their original episodic order with the meaningful interweaving of
times and worlds, along with Shepardson's prior questions clarifying the stories' initiating contexts, such a volume would have provided Stewart's life and experiences as a lens for the broader
understanding of the larger issues interwoven throughout her stories. Nevertheless, even with the more limited autobiographical
focus of the edited volume, Shepardson's relationship with
Stewart provides a solid foundation for Stewart's open and honest
storytelling, and I can recommend the relatively unknown *A
Voice in Her Tribe* as a promising model for ethnographic work

that seeks to assist individuals in offering their stories to a broader audience of listener-readers.

Tiana Bighorse, Noël Bennett, and *Bighorse the Warrior*

The Navajo "autobiography" *Bighorse the Warrior* is a remarkable postcolonial work, both in its stories and in the manner of its construction. Although non-Navajo Noël Bennett served as the volume's editor, nowise did her role in the project impede or override Navajo Tiana Bighorse's voice. Rather, the two women developed an exemplary and egalitarian working relationship. The book consists of Bighorse's stories about his experiences and observations from the Navajo Long Walk years. One particularly intriguing aspect of this volume is that it is Bighorse's daughter Tiana Bighorse who relates her father's life stories. While this gives the volume an extra layer of mediation, it nowise creates any further distancing from the worlds of the stories. In Navajo storytelling fashion, Bighorse's daughter does not privilege herself in the telling, but rather relates the stories in her father's voice as she remembers him telling his stories to her and the family. Noël Bennett, a longtime Euro-American friend of Tiana Bighorse, edited the stories into their published form. Although Tiana Bighorse serves as the storytelling medium relating the stories to Bennett, it is crucial to reiterate that the stories are neither about her nor by her, for they are first and foremost her father's stories. As Bennett explains Tiana Bighorse's decision-making process in the crafting of her stories, "Tiana wondered who would be telling the stories, she or her father? Eventually she decided it would be her father, and moreover, he would tell the stories in the present tense because it's closest to how he told them. 'He always makes it feel like it's happening right now'" (Bighorse xvi–xvii). When I first read this, I remembered the conversively told Passover stories of my childhood, when we would hear, "When *we* were slaves of Pharaoh...," and how I would magically and powerfully become a part of the story as we all remembered ourselves back into that time of our ancestors. I also remembered Luci Tapahonso's powerful poem about the Long Walk, "In 1864," in which she, like Tiana Bighorse, relates stories of the Long Walk in the present tense, and in the voice of an older relative who had lived through those difficult and fearful years (Tapahonso, *Saanii Dahataał*).

Bighorse's Long Walk stories emerged out of the relationship that Bennett and Tiana Bighorse developed initially through Bennett's interest in Navajo weaving. At the time (1968), Bennett had arrived on the Navajo Reservation largely due to her husband's work there as a physician. Bennett learned about Navajo weaving from Tiana Bighorse, and over the years they became very close friends and collaborators, coauthoring the book *Working with the Wool: How to Weave a Navajo Rug*. One day, Tiana Bighorse asked Bennett if she would help her record her father's stories. Bennett had moved to a more remote part of the reservation, and it was not easy for the women to work together on that project. The women communicated with each other through "constant letters between us [that] shared family news and the world of color and design we wove on our loom[s]" (Bighorse xiii). Bighorse again inquired about the possibility of recording her father's stories. Due to the difficulty of transportation, Bennett suggested a writer friend of hers who lived nearer to Bighorse, and arranged for them to meet. Bighorse later wrote to Bennett saying, "I liked your friend, but no stories came out" (xiii). What Bennett had not fully understood, at that time, was the necessity of a developed relationship within which deeply held stories could conversively emerge.

Bennett's prior work with Tiana Bighorse came out of their mutual interest in weaving, and Bennett understood the importance of their collaboration in her tutelage as a weaver. The book the two women produced about Navajo weaving required the assistance of both women, a fact which they clearly understood, but Bennett did not yet understand the crucial function of friendship for such work. When she was asked to help with the collection of Bighorse's father's stories, Bennett did not immediately realize the significance of her role in that production. So, since the work did not proceed with Bennett's writer friend, she simply suggested that Bighorse write her stories down herself:

"How about your father's stories? You could write
them down."
    "My English isn't good; nobody'd understand me.
I don't spell right."
    "That doesn't matter. Just write them down. Every
time you think of a story, write it down so it won't be
forgotten. Later, maybe your kids can help you make
a book. Or when I can, I will." (xiv)

What is evident in the two women's relationship is that their
friendship was that of equals. Responding to Bighorse's interest in
recording her father's stories, Bennett encourages her friend to go
forward with that project. When Bighorse points out her weaknesses in writing, Bennett affirms Bighorse's ability in putting
the stories down on paper, telling her to not worry about any
writing errors, that it "doesn't matter," that Bighorse can still
write the stories down, and that later, there would be help to publish them as a book, mentioning the possibility of Bighorse's children when they are older. Here, Bennett not only encourages the
recording of Bighorse's father's stories, but she does so in suggesting that the project could be a completely Navajo project, with
Bighorse's own children helping her with the writing—and only
then, as a last resort, does she say that she might be able to help
when possible.

    As Bennett relates, many years went by, and the women lived
through various life changes. Bighorse's father's stories were forgotten, or so Bennett presumed. Finally, Bennett, who had moved away
from the Navajo Reservation, returned for a visit in 1986. As they
were visiting in the front room of Bighorse's home, Bennett relates
that Bighorse "pulled some papers out of a top dresser drawer and
laid them beside me on the couch—a stack of ruled binder papers an
inch high. 'Do you want to see these?'" (xiv). The stack included
Bighorse's collection of her father's stories written down over the
course of the previous twelve years. Bennett writes that she was
astounded: "*My God*, I thought, *she's been writing those stories all
these years!*" (xiv, emphasis in the original). The fact that her friend
had been patiently writing her father's stories over many years and

simply waiting until the two women could get together in person touched Bennett very deeply.

As Bennett began to read through her friend's stories, she was puzzled by their episodic organization. They seemed to jump around, seemingly without order. "The same stories appeared in different places, sometimes full and complete, sometimes segmented, fractionated" (xiv). But Bennett knew her friend and knew how deliberative she was. Bennett did not assume that Bighorse's stories were meaninglessly jumbled, nor did she presume that the stories were little more than Bighorse's father's life history in editorial need of a chronological narrative structure. Already a part of the Bighorse family through friendship, and a skilled interpreter of symbolism as a weaver, Bennett read the stories her friend had written down in a conversive manner, listening for meaningful interconnections within the associational organization. Bennett tells us about her initial experience with the written stories: "Intent on finding meaning beyond the form, . . . [Bennett] read on, collecting clues. Running, hiding, bands of warriors, Canyon de Chelly, Kit Carson—suddenly it was clear. Tiana was writing about the Long Walk!" (xv). The stories that Bennett read conveyed great tragedy, horror, "disease, starvation, brutality, . . . [and] vision and compassion, . . . courage, . . . endurance, . . . and [the people's] unmistakably deep and compelling love for [their] Land" (xv).

Committed to maintaining the interwoven Navajo voice of Tiana Bighorse and her father in the completed manuscript, Bennett was committed to compiling the stories in a format that the two women thought would best tell the story that Bighorse's father felt compelled to pass on to his daughter. They decided to keep the stories in the voice and grammar of its English-language Navajo storyteller—Tiana Bighorse. The scholarly reader who evaluated the manuscript in blind review praised the work highly, but criticized the "problematic language style" and the "bad English grammar," which would prevent readers from being able to consider the substance of Bighorse's stories (xxi). Bighorse's reservation English was perceived as an impediment for readers. Bennett writes that she grappled with how to respond to such language concerns. She thought about her own weaving work in repairing moth damage and

other worn spots and considered how she could patch up perceived
linguistic problems in ways that would not compromise Bighorse's
own voice and stories, but Bennett was torn. As she explains,

> I had started with a clear purpose: to protect the integrity
> of the Navajo voice. Then, for reader clarity, I had stan-
> dardized most verbs in present tense, edited them to agree
> with their subject, and corrected disorienting words—such
> as *man* when Tiana meant men. I had rewoven the large
> and middle-sized holes.
>
> "I got seven children," the monitor said. *A small dis-
> continuity in form*, my inner voice insisted. *A mere frayed
> edge in a timeless tapestry....*
>
> But blankets that had been restored down to their thin
> warp and frayed edges showed nothing. Pertinent cultural
> information, lost forever because the restorer didn't distin-
> guish damage from wear, didn't know what to weave and
> what to leave, didn't know when to stop.
>
> Now I wanted to preserve the storyteller's essence in
> this culturally rich manuscript. Now I needed to distin-
> guish perspicuity from formality. So I reread Tiana's sto-
> ries. They were clear and very Navajo. I switched the
> monitor off; my part was done. (xxiii, emphasis in original)

Bennett brilliantly brought her training as a weaver to bear in
editing the Bighorse stories. Understanding the harmonious
integrity of an artistically crafted weaving, Bennett applied the
process of patching and otherwise fixing a worn rug, and the
process of taking sections of a rug and stitching them together in a
coherent whole that permits the rug's larger images and stories to
emerge. In the co-creative role of a conversive listener-reader,
Bennett listened to the words of the stories, hearing the larger and
deeper stories related by Bighorse. Her diction, voice, grammar,
and rhetoric reflect the Navajo world of her stories and are part of
the very warp and woof of the stories' fabric. Thereby, listener-
readers are brought that much more closely into the Navajo world
of her father, his father, and the times of the Long Walk. Although

Bennett made some corrections throughout the manuscript to ensure a consistent and clear narrative, she made the difficult decision to keep Bighorse's stories in her own Navajo and reservation-English voice. This choice produces a storytelling voice that has the conversive closeness of an intimate storytelling; it is as if Tiana Bighorse is sitting right next to her listener-readers, relating her father's stories directly, comfortably, and perhaps most importantly, in her own Navajo voice. Through this process, the product of Bennett's collaboration with Bighorse yields a powerful depiction of Navajo history from the Long Walk and internment years of the 1860s to the later period that involved government-mandated livestock reduction during the 1930s and 1940s. As Bennett states explicitly, the success of the volume was a direct result of the inherently cooperative and conversive nature of the women's work together and Bennett's commitment to that storytelling process: "I was beginning to sense how important a twenty-year friendship and eight years of living on the reservation were going to be to this book" (xvii).

In Bennett's prior collaborative work with Bighorse on their book *Working with the Wool: How to Weave a Navajo Rug* (1971), the importance of the collaborative endeavor was obvious to Bennett—after all, Tiana Bighorse was the expert Navajo weaver and Bennett her apprentice. But *Bighorse the Warrior* was an entirely different sort of project: these were Bighorse's stories as passed down through his daughter. At the outset, Bennett perceived the project as the activity of a storytelling narrator who only needed the editorial assistance of an experienced writer. It was not until years later when she finally read her friend's stories that she learned the extent to which her interactive role as Bighorse's story-listener was crucial to the success of the entire undertaking. This was a lesson that is far less evident in two of the early ethnographic volumes on Navajo weaving: *Spiderwoman: A Story of Navajo Weavers and Chanters* (1934), and *Navajo Shepherd and Weaver* (1936), both by Gladys Reichard. Reichard, like Bennett, was interested in learning Navajo weaving. One big difference is that Bennett, as a weaver and artist, sought to learn the craft, whereas Reichard came to her studies of Navajo weaving

from the position of an outside academic whose time among the
Navajo was defined in the colonialist terms of scholarly privilege,
interest, and agenda. Bennett brought to her work the co-creativity
of a weaver's eye and a story-listener's ear. Her familiarity with the
process of interweaving divergent strands and threads into one
coherent, beautiful, and meaningful whole enabled Bennett to
understand very deeply the conversive nature and episodically
associational form of oral storytelling as a means of producing one
of the finest works of postcolonial Navajo autobiography.

Barney Blackhorse Mitchell
and *Miracle Hill*

The pioneering autobiography *Miracle Hill* grew out of a high-
school writing assignment that was given to Barney Mitchell when
he was a student at the Institute for American Indian Arts in Santa
Fe. His teacher, Mrs. Terry Allen, recognized the young man's writing ability and encouraged him to continue writing stories from his
life. As Mitchell's writing continued, Allen realized that it could
develop into a publishable book-length manuscript about a Navajo
boy's early years up to his time in boarding school. Mitchell continued to write, a publisher was found (the University of
Oklahoma Press), and in the initial publication of the book, Allen
as Mitchell's editor provided the introduction to the volume.[3]
Years later, when Mitchell was approached to bring the book back
into print, he decided to ask a scholar of Navajo literature, Paul
Zolbrod, to write an updated introduction to the new edition. In
that introduction, Zolbrod notes that Mitchell and Allen had a
falling-out regarding the new edition, with Allen feeling that her
past help was not being appreciated and Mitchell distancing himself from her as a means of affirming the centrality of his own
voice in the narrative. Even assuming that Allen's past efforts had
been well intentioned, the history of the American colonization of
the Navajo people and their lands; the racist indoctrination of
boarding-school education that negligibly valued, and in most
cases overtly devalued, the students' cultural traditions and language; and the subaltern status to which most Native peoples have

been relegated within the dominant culture of the United States—
all have served to create an environment where Navajo-white relations are invariably complicated by this historical context.

A "well-intentioned" colonialism is nevertheless paternalisti-
cally demoralizing at best, and overtly disempowering, immobiliz-
ing, culturally destructive, and genocidal at worst. Mitchell, as an
educator and faculty member at Diné College, had the resources,
knowledge, and opportunity to assert his own voice in the determi-
nation of the eventual directions his autobiographical book would
take (republished in 2004 by the University of Arizona Press). For
the vast majority of life-history narratives produced under the control of generations of past ethnographers, it will be up to faculty
and students to consider those texts anew (as Mitchell was able to
do with his own stories) and free them from the colonial control
wielded by distant and objectifying editors. Mitchell's decision to
excise Allen's introduction from his book was an act of courage,
self-affirmation, and integrity necessary to free his book from a
colonial legacy that had prevented its availability for many years.
It is a shame that Mrs. Allen could not understand this need, for
the very presence of the book and the stories within it nevertheless
affirm the importance of Mitchell's teacher in encouraging his
writing and further studies. Whereas Tiana Bighorse's book relates
her father's stories about his life and times, in Mitchell's book, he
directly relates his own stories from his childhood and the years
away from home in boarding school. In the future, it would be
wonderful to have extensive historical work about the boarding
schools attended by many of the Navajo young people analyzed in
conjunction with Mitchell's powerful stories. This is the sort of
scholarship made possible by those reliable life histories whose
Navajo authenticity is unquestioned.

Oral History Stories of The Long Walk:
Hwéeldi Baa Hané

I would like to end this chapter's discussion of Navajo autobiography by turning to the tremendous contributions of Navajo
Community College Press, the Navajo Curriculum Center Press

publisher of the Rough Rock Demonstration School materials, and other recently published stories and books that have been produced by tribal members. Most explicitly postcolonial in their predominant Navajo voice and production, these volumes demonstrate the power and accuracy of texts unmediated by alien ivory towers. *Oral History Stories of The Long Walk: Hwéeldi Baa Hané,* by The Diné of the Eastern Region of the Navajo Reservation, is an invaluable collection of stories about the Long Walk (1990). This volume includes stories about the Long Walk from thirty-eight Navajos of the Lake Valley, White Rock, Chaco Canyon, and Bisti communities. As explained in the introduction, "The stories have been passed down from grandfathers to sons and from great-grandmothers to their children's children. They are the remembered experiences of a time past that altered their existence" (Diné 1). The U.S. Department of Education funded the Lake Valley Navajo School in Crownpoint, New Mexico, with a grant that included the recording of these stories. Just as Kenji Kawano had to persevere in reaching many of the Navajo Code Talker veterans spread remotely throughout the Navajo Reservation lands, the Lake Valley Title VII bilingual staff acknowledged the challenges involved in collecting and recording these stories:

> It has not been an easy task to gather these stories.
> Navajo staff of the Title VII program spent many days
> visiting with their elders in their hogans, nudging their
> memories, tape recording what they could remember
> of words they had heard so long ago as young children.
> They worked long hours translating this material from
> Navajo to English and typing it into a word processor.
>   Some people remembered only portions of a story.
> Others moved randomly from one event to another as
> storytellers often do. (Diné 1)

The transmission of oral stories into a textual form invariably loses much of the stories' orality. The school staff explicitly noted the losses involved with meaningful digressions in the told stories that were found problematic and confusing in written form. "The richness of gesture and voice inflection, facial expressions, fluctuation in loudness and softness, and the intimacy of the storyteller's physical presence (including the many tears shed during the telling of these stories) were all necessarily lost" (Diné 1). As Dennis Tedlock and Leslie Marmon Silko have demonstrated in their textual renditions of oral stories, there are poetic and conversive tools that can be brought to bear in this process, which, while incapable of fully reproducing the oral storytelling event, can nevertheless incorporate much of the paralinguistic richness of tone, voice shifts, and emphatic pauses. Additionally, extensive notes could be included to share storyteller and listener responses. Current technology is such that the storytelling events could even be recorded, and then marketed with a compact disc of the sessions sold along with the hard-copy texts.

Also noted regarding the Long Walk stories were the inevitable variations concerning the specific facts and details in the different stories. In contrast to the recent debates about the legitimation of Rigoberta Menchú's autobiography, the Navajo staff at the Crownpoint school brought a greater sophistication and understanding to their oral-history work, demonstrating their comfort with factual differences that occur among orally told stories: "It is not uncommon in oral tradition for events to be remolded and take on new shapes with retelling" (Diné 1). The Lake Valley Navajo staff, familiar with the elders' storytelling ways, were committed to preserving the integrity of the stories as best they could on paper. The stories are printed in block-prose form. Hopefully in the future, skilled creative writers will assist such projects by bringing their own poetic and storytelling skills to bear in the process of transcription of oral stories in order to preserve as much as possible the conversive orality of the stories even in their written forms (Kroskrity; Silko, *Storyteller*; Tedlock, *Spoken Word*).

Denetsosie

The Rough Rock reservation school in Rough Rock, Arizona, has actively pioneered bilingual education for their students for many years. Not only has this included bilingual education in the classroom but also the production of bilingual Navajo/English written materials for students and the larger community. One of their publications is the Navajo autobiography of Denetsosie, an elder sheep and cattle rancher who was also an early tribal councilman and chapter officer and, toward the end of his life, a member of the board of directors of the Navajo Culture Center in Fort Defiance. The book retells Denetsosie's life in the third person, giving it the feel of a third-party-authored biography, but John Dick (member of the board of education of the Rough Rock Demonstration School) explains that "the story is largely an autobiography, as Denetsosie told it in the Navajo language" (Johnson iv). In a conversive manner, the printed stories interweave Denetsosie's direct first-person storytelling voice throughout the framing third-person narrative. In such fashion, this Rough Rock Demonstration School production redefines traditional Western categories that strictly differentiate biography from autobiography—much like Tiana Bighorse's book, which interweaves her voice with her father's in a first-person narrative. Like other exemplary Navajo ethnographies, *Denetsosie* emerged from within the tribe. As an important Navajo elder and leader, tribal members knew the importance of recording Denetsosie's stories about his life, his experiences, and his times. As John Dick states in the introductory section of the book entitled "A Talk with Navajo Students," "It is important for us to remember who we are and that we are a strong and happy people. As we learn of, and remember, our great forefathers such as Denetsosie, we will be able to face the future of change with confidence and a sense of security" (Johnson v).

The volume ends with the intimacy of an interpersonal conversation among friends or family members, with the editors (Broderick H. Johnson, Sydney M. Callaway, and others) offering a brief update on Denetsosie and his family—noting his passing in 1969; providing more recent information about how his wife, children, and grandchildren are doing; and quoting Denetsosie's wish for his relatives' and people's education in both Navajo and Euro-American ways: "'I respect all of them—Navajos, other Indians and white men.'... [Denetsosie] stood tall as a man who knew and respected both the Navajo culture and the Anglo way of life" (Johnson 46). Even while *Denetsosie* is ostensibly a book about one man's life, the conversive storytelling manner of the man and his biography tell stories that are much broader than the limited bounds of one man's life. The stories that make up Denetsosie's biography bring listener-readers into a lived and imagined Navajo world that includes the generations that precede and succeed his lifetime. Denetsosie's life is not textualized into an artificially constructed autobiography; rather, his life is storied and given life into a story-world that intertwines the mythic and the real, the historic and the storied, and one man's life and accomplishments and their inextricable interconnections with his ancestors and descendants. This contrasts with colonizing ethnographic works such as *Son of Old Man Hat* that attenuate stories into forced narrative texts. In conversive ethnography and life history, lived experiences are broadened and deepened through the larger fabric of story (creative and historical). *Denetsosie* tells us much about the man, but paralleling the conversive decentering of the individual ego and Denetsosie's own inclinations away from the hubris and self-referentiality of an autobiographical posture, Denetsosie's stories and book honor the man while articulating stories and events that are much larger than the life of one man, even one as significant as was Denetsosie.

Ruth Roessel's
Women in Navajo Society

Even within works that are ostensibly discursive treatments of specific topics, it is possible to craft the text in ways that facilitate conversive engagements across worlds and times. Arguably the most important ethnographic work to date on Navajo women is Ruth Roessel's *Women in Navajo Society*, which was published by the Navajo Resource Center at the Rough Rock Demonstration School back in 1981. Although as a whole it is not explicitly a work of ethnographic autobiography and so not a primary focus in this chapter, the volume does include one life-history story of Asdzą́ą́? Anilí (Raggedy Lady). This story parallels the storytelling pattern in *Denetsosie*, with an interweaving of third-person and first-person narrative that is based on Raggedy Lady's own stories as passed down within her family. Ruth Roessel is Raggedy Lady's great-granddaughter, and she demonstrates great love, care, and respect for Raggedy Lady and her story. As Roessel explains in the introduction, "This book not only describes the role of Navajo women in a changing Navajo society, it also reflects personal experiences and feeling of the author" (viii). The entire volume offers the most comprehensive and reliable presentation of the roles of Navajo women within tribal community life and belief. Roessel begins the volume with a fairly extensive review of the literature on Navajo women from roughly 1930 through the late 1970s.[4] As a rule, the published information that she reviews as most accurate comes from those Navajo and non-Navajo scholars and writers who demonstrated greater interpersonal connections and commitments to the Navajo people and the tribe as a whole. Interrogating the academic empire-building agendas of so many of those who came to study the Navajo and then left, Roessel raises a compelling inquiry regarding their interests in her people: "What were their objectives?" (30). Roessel's rhetorical question exemplifies one of the central tools of conversive communications in inviting her readers to consider just what might have been the motivations of generations of outside researchers. Roessel's comment is not a blanket criticism of non-Navajo scholars, for she notes that the most reliable scholarship on the Navajo comes from those writers (Navajo and non-Navajo) whose work comes full circle, originating in the tribal community (wholly or in part) and returning the work to the Navajo people. Two of the elements of scholarly integrity that Roessel notes as central to work about and with the Navajo include the responsibility of scholars to contribute to the benefit of the Navajo people (what John Pack referred to as "giving back" to those from whom one has received), and to conduct their research with the Navajo people as their primary intended audience (in toto or in part). Roessel's own ethnographic presentations about her ancestor Raggedy Lady and Roessel's own daughter (photographed for the section on Navajo girls' puberty rites) demonstrate the accurate and effective knowledge production that accrues from deeply connective conversive relations—clearly evident in her choices of Navajo women to showcase in her book: in both cases, these are females Roessel knows intimately through personal and family relationships (lived and storied). Such relations provide the conversive foundation for substantive Navajo ethnography.

Roessel raises direct challenges to those whose "writings appear to be primarily for other scholars and other university types," and even more problematically, those who "appear to be writing primarily for their professional colleagues and their individual reputations. They want to make generalizations, and the Navajos are a means to an end. They conduct fieldwork on the Reservation, publish and move on. Some publish material that should not be printed" (30). It is crucial that we all consider deeply the frustrations that so many indigenous peoples have regarding the generations of objective science that objectified human persons, exoticized tribes, and artifacted cultures. Thereby, we will be able to understand even more profoundly Pierre Bourdieu's critique that "objective relations of power tend to reproduce themselves in symbolic relations of power, in visions of the social world which contribute to ensuring the permanence of those relations of power" (*Language* 238). Scientific objectivity and objectification translate far too easily into the imperial disempowerment, marginalization, and relative invisibility of indigenous peoples, as Roessel makes explicit regarding her own people.

Contemporary Guidance for Navajo Study

Much of the ethnographic and oral-history work produced by Navajo and other Native scholars, writers, photographers, filmmakers, and artists—such as Jennifer Denetdale, Ruth Roessel, Blackhorse Mitchell, Luci Tapahonso, Irvin Morris, Tsinnajinnie—provides conversively relational models for ethnographers interested in working in Indian country. Non-Native ethnographers such as Franc Johnson Newcomb, Noël Bennett, and Kenji Kawano (who worked with traditional stories, rug-weaving, photography, and friendship) demonstrate the powerful and meaningful effects of truly intersubjective ethnography that is rooted in the lives of its respectively interrelated communities. Whether this be Newcomb's collections of Navajo stories that were written down at the invitation of Hosteen Klah, Tiana Bighorse's request of Noël Bennett to help produce an autobiography of her father, or the Navajo Code Talkers' appointment of Kenjo Kawano as their official photographer, each of these ethnographies opens itself up to us much like a storyteller who welcomes her or his listeners into the world of the story. Non-Native academics such as Charlotte Frisbie, Barre Toelken, and Mary Shepardson have pioneered intersubjective ethnographic relations that manifest their enduring commitments and ethically based responsibilities to the tribe and the individual Navajos with whom they worked.

There is a power in conversive storytelling that is mutually transforming, as well as informing (Brill de Ramírez, *Contemporary* 1–20). Thereby we will all be able to begin to listen to each other's stories and conversively share those stories with others through a methodology that is inherently collaborative, intersubjective, reciprocal, conversive, and ethical. In light of the past five hundred years of European and Euro-American colonization of Native peoples, it is important that any outside scholar interested in working with Native peoples do so from a relationally intersubjective position, and with a commitment to such a fully collaborative and conversive methodology. To this end, the Navajo Nation's Historic Preservation Department now includes a Cultural Resource Compliance section that oversees and approves all research that is conducted on the reservation. The office seeks to be informed about all research done about the Navajo, whether field-based or not—less as a means of censoring work and more as an office designed to assist scholars, writers, filmmakers, and others to ensure levels of accuracy and reliability that will ensure that the future generations of scholarship on the Navajo will endure and be of far greater value than, alas, has been the case for far too much of the earlier work.

It is crucial that we learn from the past mistakes of a colonialist academy, so that we can avoid such reifying errors of perception, awareness, judgment, and interpretation caused by the scientific blinders that prevented scholars from ever really getting to know the peoples and tribes they sought to understand. The story of the academic study of the Navajo and other indigenous peoples really has been a story of great tragedy. There have been horrific real-world consequences for the native peoples of the world due to such blindness and ignorance. This cannot be underscored enough. There has also been a great loss to the academy. Generations of researchers have produced "knowledge" whose foundations lie on the shifting sands of imperial self-delusion, only to pass on their misinterpretations, misunderstandings, and misinformation to subsequent generations of students and fellow researchers. How do we recognize, admit, and correct the extent of past errors and their effects on other scholarship, government policy, tribal progress, and individual lives? Insofar as the academy is concerned, the teaching of colonialist misinformation about the Navajo perpetuated and reinforced the very colonialist ideologies upon which the studies were based. The objectification of the Navajo and other Native peoples as fascinating and exoticized artifacts of the Western gaze has helped to create the popular success of the Tony Hillerman "Navajo" novels, while the tribal poetry and fiction of Navajo writers gain a much smaller audience despite their tribal authenticity, and perhaps because of it.

In the exemplary ethnographies presented in this chapter, we see that reliable and accurate ethnographic work about the Navajo is most often produced by those individuals who have lived and/or worked among the Navajo and established enduring intersubjective relationships with the tribe and its members. Insofar as work on the Navajo is concerned, reliability appears to cut across gender lines, with both women and men producing solid work built upon comparable relational foundations (Bighorse; Frisbie; Kawano; Newcomb; Roessel; Stewart; Toelken). Where I have noticed a gender divide is in the development of those close-working relationships and lived friendships that involve great geographic distances and limited interpersonal time together, as in the case of anthropologists whose lives and work are centered far away from the Navajo Reservation, and whose actual time with their storyteller-informants is relatively limited (Bighorse; Frisbie; Stewart). Here, the abilities of women to develop close and deep interpersonal relationships fairly quickly and to maintain those relationships over great distances and times demonstrate how such conversive interconnections can be established across worlds, times, and places.

I cannot emphasize enough the extent to which increasingly greater degrees of collaboration and relationship will continue to enrich not only the field of Native American ethnography, but more broadly, all forms of fieldwork in which the scholar establishes enduring and lived ties to the communities s/he studies. Relational examinations into the ethnographically produced autobiographies of Navajo elders demonstrate the successful production of postcolonial knowledge that has been achieved through their conversively informed work. Winnie Tomm and other feminists have criticized scholarship that has reinforced hegemonies of power over peoples and persons, identifying such problematic work in patriarchal terms: "Patriarchal morality is based on the desire for power over the other, beginning with sexual power over women and extending to political power over nations.... [In contrast,] intersubjective space is where mutual respect of interacting subjects is expressed" (105). In each of the examples foregrounded in this chapter, we see ethnographic practices that step beyond the traditionally prescribed androcentric bounds of objective science and objectifying power relations—thereby sacrificing scientific objectivity as a means of achieving substantially greater degrees of reliability, accuracy, and meaningfulness in their work (Asad; Harding; Morrison; O'Connor). Deborah E. Reed-Danahay notes that even with the recognition of "the politics of representation and of power relations inherent in traditional ethnographic accounts," there is nevertheless a "tension between creativity and restraint associated with...the act of self-narrative" (2, 3). Reed-Danahay (and, too, the New Critics of literary modernity) perceive tension in the forced conjunction of apparently opposite tendencies; yet within the conversive realm of story, such differences are more comfortably interwoven as the diverse threads, colors, and textures of the larger storied weaving. Intersubjective ethnography (grounded within the people's tribal culture and values, and developed through meaningful interpersonal relations) will yield forth the promise of storytelling insights and wisdom and the fruits of conversively informed texts whose authenticity is evident and whose value will endure. In his essay about ethnographic work among the Hopi, Peter Whiteley observes that "The most interesting 'ethnography' by, and to some extent of, Native Americans today is literary (Leslie Marmon Silko, Louise Erdrich), or cultural critique-based (Gerald Vizenor), or visual (Victor Masayesva Jr.) rather than being in a strictly anthropological frame" (143). As this volume clarifies, the ethnography that is indeed factually reliable and deeply engaging is invariably that which has been so conversively informed and tribally centered.

Epilogue

Future Directions for Interrogations into Orally Produced Ethnographies, and Specific Conversive Signposts Evidenced in Navajo Life-History Texts

The past 2,500 years of literary criticism in the West, from Plato to today, have demonstrated a continuing effort to articulate those elements and qualities that distinguish literature from other forms of communication. This work has provided various lenses through which literary texts can be opened, appreciated, and understood; yet the increasing layers of critical discourse have, over time, obscured the fact that at the center of literature and beneath narrative lie their storytelling origins, and that the process of understanding literature and story need not be as complicated as the extensive history of interpretive axiology and critical theory have led us to believe. The gradual textualization of storytelling into written literatures has progressively distanced readers and critics from the conversive relationality that is inherent in the act of storytelling and in the discernment of a story's meaningfulness. I have written this book not to complicate further our understandings of those Native American life-history narratives constructed via ethnography, but rather to remind us that autobiography (whether it be ethnographically constructed or not) is a literary genre nonetheless descended from its respective storytelling roots.

There may be no other genre of Native American literature that is more problematic than that which has been labeled "autobiography." Unlike most other ethnic/cultural bodies of American literatures whose autobiographies have, by and large, been self-authored, the canon of Native American literatures includes many presumptive autobiographical narratives whose very construction calls into question the degree to which those ethnographies are autobiographical at all. The fact that most of these artificially constructed textual narratives originated as oral and performative storytelling events compounds the difficulties invariably inherent in the mediating presence of translators, interpreters, ethnographers, and editors. Folklorist John Miles Foley explains that "Words are always situated; they cannot naturally occur but in context, and they cannot naturally recur without reference to prior occurrences and prior contexts" ("Word Power" 275). In the case of ethnographically produced Native American autobiographies, the crux of the interpretive problem is found in the two very different semiotic systems in which academically trained ethnographers and Native American storyteller-informants function: one that interprets significance based on signs and objects from an objective distance, and the other that seeks relational meaning through intersubjective proximity. A critical reluctance to work within the conversive realm of the Native storyteller has led to very serious misunderstandings of peoples and cultures. While some might castigate ethnographers like Walter Dyk for gross misrepresentations, readers (non-Native, non-Navajo, and Navajo alike) also bear responsibility for misreadings of texts like *Son of Old Man Hat* that have been, and continue to be, taught and read as factual life histories. The result is often what American Indian literature scholar and writer Sidner Larson (Grosventre) has described as "the Euramerican tendency to sacrifice truth in favor of literary closure" (65).

In all fairness, it is important to restate that a great deal of our interpretive errors and biases are the result of the interpretive frameworks in which we (scholars and other readers) have been trained. While this does not excuse any of us from our responsibilities to produce accurate and reliable scholarship and understandings of the texts we read, the production of knowledge is an evolving process, with each generation building on the work of the past, correcting past errors, and providing new work for later scholars to learn from, work with, and correct. My offering in this volume is to provide a beginning guide for a conversive revisioning of and relistening to the Navajo ethnography of the past century. Even insofar as the exemplary ethnographies are concerned (such as Kawano's work with the Navajo Code Talkers and Ruth Roessel's stories about her daughter and her ancestor Raggedy Lady), these works, too, deserve a literary eye and a conversive ear that can access the deep layers of storytelling meaning within the works. The relational nature of stories invites a relational response. As Helen Carr pointed out regarding the intersubjective construction of Native American ethnography, "These early anthropologists present the autobiographies they collected as monologic, solely the words of the Native American speaker. They are not that but they are at least dialogic, and in that their value lies" (241). In that, their meaningfulness must be engaged—conversively, intersubjectively, respectfully, familiarly—such that conversive relations define engagements both in the field and with the published scholarship: "As in a personal conversational exchange, in which the other provides information, yet also questions and challenges and affirms and criticizes my points and my point of view, so too, the subjects whom we study (dead or alive, near or far) can be envisioned as participating in our research according to this interactive dialectic" (O'Connor 9).

As this volume makes poignantly clear, mistakes have been made in the past by some of our most eminent scholars—and yet, merely pointing out those errors is of marginal utility to us now if it is not combined with the needed reconstructive efforts. Our charge, as I see it, is to offer a corrective lens and a co-creative ear to generations of textualized stories (both in their published and field-note forms). This is an issue of academic accuracy, reliability, rigor, responsibility, relationality, integrity, and ethics. As Winnie

Tomm suggests, "I see ethics to be largely about respect within a context of human interdependency. It is respect for the inner space of personal location as well as for interpersonal dialogical space. Respect for disparate interests is a matter of justice" (104). To respect disparate interests requires a prior effort to recognize those interests, their voices and worlds, and a concomitantly requisite openness to listening to those voices and stories—a process that was decidedly not the rule for the vast majority of Native American ethnography conducted during the colonialist empire-building of twentieth-century ivory towers. A half century ago, Margaret Mead lamented her difficulties in getting Native "informants" to communicate in the discursively informational forms that she desired. Instead of giving her facts about their lives, cultures, and tribes, Mead was told stories. As she complained, "This is a very discouraging job, ethnologically speaking. You find a man whose father or uncle had a vision. You go to see him four times, driving eight or ten miles with an interpreter. The first time he isn't home, the second time he's drunk, the next time his wife's sick, and the fourth time, on the advice of the interpreter, you start the interview with a $5 bill, for which he offers thanks to Wakanda, prays Wakanda to give *him* a long life, and proceeds to lie steadily for four hours" (313–14, original emphasis). Rosalie Wax describes the early twentieth-century work of Franz Boas in even more discouraging terms: "He found the uncooperative attitude of many of the Indians thoroughly exasperating, and complains that they would not talk at all, or that they would work for a few hours and then disappear, or that they demanded payment when he wished to photograph their totem poles.... An occasional remark suggests that he found conversation with Indians a waste of time—except insofar as it related to the collection of textual materials" (Wax 32–33).

As we have seen in much of the ethnography conducted in Navajo country, the disinclination of many Navajos to cooperate with various ethnographers (anthropologists, linguists, musicologists, botanists, folklorists, etc.) represents the people's efforts to resist the academic colonization that in far too many cases misrepresented the Navajo people, their culture, and their traditions to generations of students, fellow scholars, and general readers.

Historian Devon Abbott Mihesuah (Choctaw Nation of Oklahoma) speaks very directly about the colonialist legacy of the past and current scholarship about Native peoples, and the responsibilities for corrective work:

> Considering that this is a country founded by colonizers whose policies and behaviors disrupted and almost destroyed Indigenous cultures, historians of the Indigenous past have a responsibility to examine critically the effects of their historical narratives on the well-being of Natives and to also examine their stories' influence on the retention and maintenance of the colonial power structure. ("American Indian History" 157)

In his concluding essay to Mihesuah and Wilson's *Indigenizing the Academy: Transforming Scholarship and Empowering Communities*, David Anthony Tyeeme Clark (Mesquakie and Potawatomi) sums up the concerns voiced throughout the volume in his call for "Visualizing, Signifying, Counter-colonizing" (218). He writes that the "contributors to this volume propose that Indigenous academics and our non-Indigenous allies labor to reconfigure both the colonial structure of the academy and the colonizing frames of mind affecting our consciousness" (219). If what I have seen in my own research into the past one hundred years of Navajo ethnography is at all representative of the ethnographic work directed toward the other indigenous peoples of the world, then the need for corrective and accurate scholarship is paramount. As Taiaiake Alfred (Kanien'Kehaka) directly and laconically points out, "With very few exceptions, universities are sites of production of imperial values and ethics" (93). The colonialist history of the academy demonstrates that "people not only resist political domination; they resist, or anyway evade, textual domination as well" (Ortner 188). Accordingly, the ethnographic record presents far greater degrees of complexity and obfuscation than has even been realized to date. Well over a century of textualized stories produced via ethnographic scholarship lies in need of conversive clarity.

My studies of the extensive scholarship on the Navajo of the twentieth century have discerned a range of conversive storytelling strategies that are frequently evidenced in the ethnographically produced record. The ideal in decoding these texts would be to have access to the ethnographers' field notes and recordings. Thereby, listener-readers (and listeners in the case of recordings) would be able to bring conversive storytelling ears directly to the stories told by Navajos to ethnographers. When it is not possible to work with the original recordings, it is nevertheless possible to read through the published texts to engage with/in the stories and to decipher texts that may, in fact, represent themselves as quite other from what they may actually contain. Even for the increasing numbers of reliable Navajo ethnographies, a conversive response opens up the protectively coded depths and intersubjective meaningfulness integral to the stories in those texts. Perhaps in the future, the published texts will be printed with introductory sections and extensive notes to conversively guide readers through the surface levels of textuality and in/to the deeper and co-creative levels of the stories.

By means of a conclusion to this volume and a beginning guide to the conversive decoding work of twentieth-century ethnography, let me delineate some of the conversive elements encountered in the texts discussed herein. These elements serve as the entryways and signposts into the stories behind and within the texts. There is no one way of understanding these directional guides, for the nature of storytelling lies in its co-creative development. This book is a lens through which we can identify selected signposts that have often been overlooked in the process of textualization. The responsibility of conversive listener-readers is to recognize these guiding elements and to consider them seriously. As the philosopher Ludwig Wittgenstein emphasized, there is a living and interactive engagement that each person has with such indicators:

> Does the sign-post leave no doubt open about the way I have to go? Does it shew [sic] which direction I am to take when I have passed it; whether along the road or the footpath or cross-country? But where is it said which way I am to follow it; whether in the direction of its finger or (e.g.)

in the opposite one?—And if there were, not a single sign-
post, but a chain of adjacent ones or of chalk marks on the
ground—is there only *one* way of interpreting them? (85,
original emphasis)

In the autobiographical presentation of Left Handed's stories in *Son
of Old Man Hat,* we have been given one interpretive orientation to
Left Handed's stories: that they represent Left Handed's own life
history. But storytelling signs are conversively open-ended, inviting
a co-creative completion that may take as many different directions
as there are persons engaging with the stories, and each person upon
a rereading/rehearing will engage with/in a story differently, as it
should be. Sandra Harding has given us much insight regarding the
boundaries of logocentric science, including that of the social sciences, noting that "disciplinary traditions and conventions in philosophy, the social studies of science, and the sciences themselves
lead practitioners in these fields to hold primarily archaic, exces-
sively narrow, or suppressed or unconscious epistemologies and
sociologies of knowledge" (*Whose Science?* 308). Accordingly it is
time that scholars begin to listen to people's stories (even when textualized) with the conversively relational participation that is
invited of all listeners (and listener-readers). We can begin doing so
through our recognition of the conversive signposts that skilled
Navajo storytellers have placed to guide our ways. The following
section delineates and explains a number of the conversive elements that provide important keys for decoding those ethnographic
texts that are substantially orally informed.

Conversive Elements Evident in
Navajo Ethnographic Storytelling

Structure: *Episodic structures* include apparently different stories
that are told in conjunction with each other. Each of these episodes
or stories is meaningfully interrelated, with each offering a pathway
into the subsequent story. These structures are also *associational*
in that each part is meaningfully associated with each other part. In
this sort of interwoven structure, meaning is understood through

the unfolding tapestry of stories and vignettes that shed light on each other. To try to understand any one story or vignette in isolation would be to miss important interconnective links. This structure of *interconnectedness* and *interdependency* guides listener-readers in seeing the larger design and hearing the larger story that comes into being through each listener-reader's co-creative weaving together of the parts in various meaningful ways. While it is true that the storyteller places particular stories in proximity with others, it is only through each listener-reader's interpretive efforts that the storytelling circle (which requires both storyteller and listener) is completed and the stories come to meaningful fruition. This is further manifested in the *sophisticated interweaving of diverse worlds, persons, places, and times* (including even the mythic and the historic, the real and the imagined, the extraordinary and the everyday). It is important to note that structure is central to an unfolding story. The meaningful focus is rarely on a character, a place, or a time—the larger focus being on the interwoven story and its conversively interrelational meanings.

Characterization and voice: The nature of a storytelling circle is such that each person is a co-equal point on the circle, all equally important to the successful storytelling event. The geometric image of a circle also demonstrates that every point on the circle is connected to every other point, and that no one point achieves the sort of linear primacy that would be evident, say, in the three defining points of a triangle (e.g., the semiotic triangle of semiological discourse). Furthermore, in a circle, every point is equally crucial; the absence of any one point would break up the circle. In traditional indigenous storytelling, the *co-equal importance of every participant* involved in a storytelling can be seen in the relationality that pervades the event. In many ethnographic "autobiographies," the storyteller-informants go to great lengths to de-emphasize themselves as a means of underscoring that primacy neither given to their persons nor even their storytelling voices. This *de-emphasis of the storyteller* reinforces the co-creative nature of storytelling: that the story is not the product of the storyteller alone, but rather is the collaborative effort of all involved in the story. Persons are emphasized, but primarily in terms of the *intersubjective relationality* that brings together all the persons who are participant in the unfolding story-world (storyteller, listeners, characters in the story), each with subjectivity, intentionality, and importance. Each person, as part of the story, is thereby understood in terms of a *relational sense of self*—hence the absence of an abstract word for "mother" in Navajo, whereas there are multiple such relational words (e.g., *shima'* for "my mother," *nihima'* for "our mother"). The *minimalism* by which characters in the story are sketched emphasizes not only their lack of primacy but also the co-creative telling that must be fleshed out by the listeners and listener-readers.

Voice and diction: There are many strategies that storytellers use to assist listeners' participation in the story. Two of these are *voice shifts* to a *second-person direct address* in which the storyteller speaks directly to the listeners, and the inclusive *first-person plural* in which the storyteller speaks for the listeners and storyteller as a unified body. Other voice shifts suggest twists and turns in the story, and at times may represent a subtle form of coding, as in the example in *Son of Old Man Hat* where Left Handed switches from a distant third-person referent to the closer and more immediate referent "these" (chapter 5). Voice shifts and other word choices are often used for connective purposes. Such *linking words, names, phrases, and even sounds* interrelate persons, situations, places, vignettes, and stories in meaningful ways. These also include *traditional storytelling words and phrases* that need to be recognized and understood within their respective tribal contexts.

Articulation and indication: There are many different conversive tools that Navajo storyteller-informants have used to articulate and indicate meaningful directions for story-listener and listener-reader engagements with/in a story: *repetition* (both for emphasis and for learning, with a deepened and different understanding that comes from each conversive repetition); *symbolism* and *metaphor*; *coding* (especially when storyteller-informants would make allusions that they wanted their fellow Navajos to understand, but not their non-Navajo ethnographers); *ambiguity* (especially important in light of the co-creative nature of storytelling in which listeners and listener-readers complete each story for themselves); *irony*; *parallelism* (to interrelate relevant threads of a story); *defamiliarization* and *familiarization.* In contrast to the Russian formalist literary concept of defamiliarization, familiarization is the practice of making what is unfamiliar familiar, such as the mythic, the ancient, the imagined, and the distant. *Understatement, omission, minimalism, pauses,* and *silence*, with places, characters, situations de-emphasized, absented, or sketched rather than fleshed out, permit listeners' and listener-readers' participation in the co-creative aspects of conversive storytelling; these are all tools for emphatic direction, to invite the listener's own responses, and for deeper reflection that will lead to more accurate and deeper understanding.

Community: *Humor* (a lighthearted way to bring everyone participant in the storytelling together in community with each other, and a means of easing listener engagement with the more difficult or painful aspects of stories); *situational familiarity* (here the storyteller brings the story into the listeners' and listener-readers' worlds to facilitate their entries into, and participation in, the story); and *interpersonal references* to specifics from various participants' own lives and/or other connective strategies that bring all participants together within the storytelling community and thereby help bring each person further into the world of the story.[1] Here it is important to re-emphasize the centrality of the *intersubjective relationality* and *affection* that is felt and expressed by all present within any storytelling circle, and that is crucial for the holistic and cohesive integrity of the storytelling community.

Concluding Comments

All of the conversive strategies delineated above serve two overriding purposes: namely, those of relationality and learning. Stories bring people together in the intertwined physical and metaphysical act of the storytelling event, and through the mutually intertwined processes of personal growth and learning that come from deep conversive engagements with/in the stories. Conversive learning comes from empathically relational thinking that draws on heart and mind—what Nel Noddings guided us toward in her book *Caring: A Feminist Approach to Ethics and Moral Education*: "At times we must suspend [rational-objective thinking] in favor of subjective thinking and reflection, allowing time and space for seeing and feeling" (26). This describes the transforming nature of conversive communications that are at the heart of traditional oral storytelling, much of the history of literature globally, interpersonal conversations, and other orally informed texts. Iranian novelist Bahíyyíh Nakhjávaní has depicted the coldness of a world that privileges ratiocinative, logocentric thought and its resultant hierarchized imbalances in human relations: "There is a language lying all about us that we have not learned to read. There is a syntax of the spirit that we hunger for. But, accustomed to the narrow roads of grey assumption and the fierce possessive drive for resolution, it is hard for us, this desperate generation, to turn aside from the highway...and consider what we've missed....The road, its teeth clenched in grammatical assertion, has forgotten what it chased" (*Response* 6–7).

If we are interested in accessing the meaningfulness of the ethnography conducted among the Navajo, if we are interested in differentiating those works that are factually reliable from those that are not, if we are interested in learning what generations of Navajo storyteller-informants have told their ethnographers, then we need to approach the texts with literarily informed conversive strategies. There are over one hundred years of ethnography on the Navajo that desperately need and deserve skilled listener-readers to begin the process of translation into useful and meaningful texts. This is not to say that the exhaustive ethnography of the Navajo is little more than straw, as St. Thomas Aquinas tragically lamented regarding the barrenness of his *Summa Theologica* scholarship. In reviewing so much of the past scholarship on the Navajo, there are lessons to be learned here for all scholars, regardless of discipline, so that we do not end up like Aquinas, who so tragically wasted so much of his life's work on scholarship that he did not recognize as empty until the end of his life. Insofar as Navajo scholarship is concerned, there is much ethnography that is indeed reliable, as chapter 6 presents, but conversively trained researchers are needed to

work with the range of past Navajo scholarship to differentiate history and story, fact and fiction, data and creative details, historical
lives and storied characters, and information and meaning.

While many non-Navajos have made grievous mistakes in the
efforts to get to know Navajo people, culture, tribal traditions, and
practice, we must and can learn from these past efforts, no matter
how ill-composed and ill-directed, once we learn how to approach
these texts. The violence and divisiveness that is tearing apart our
planet with increasing ferocity and horror these days demands that
we all relearn conversive ways of communicating, to come to know
and understand our fellow humans—empathically and conversively,
with both mind and heart engaged. Past scholars such as Walter Dyk
acted as they had been trained: to be objective, distanced, logical,
scientific. Personally, I do not think that we are well served by
overly harsh criticism of the earlier generations of ethnographers.
Despite their egregious errors and patent biases, their work provides
not only a collected wealth of stories that we would not have otherwise, but also some of the clearest examples of the imperialism that
scholarly objectivity and phallogocentric science have used to justify
biased and erroneous theories, and both real and illusory colonialist
exigencies of power. James C. Scott points out "that even close readings of historical and archival evidence tend to favor a hegemonic
account of power relations" (xii). The editorial control wielded by
ethnographers reproduces the preconceived master narratives that in
many ways have predetermined readers' interpretations of the published texts, even while readers' own ideological and interpretive
positions have further directed their perceptions and evaluations of
those texts. Nevertheless, this in no way denies the actual storytelling power that is latent beneath the surface levels of the text,
which awaits the co-creative hermeneutical openings of conversive
listener-readers. As we see in Left Handed's storytelling (like that of
many other Navajo storyteller-informants), he effectively resisted
scholarly domination 1) by absenting himself from what so many
scholars and other readers have erroneously interpreted as a life-
history text, and 2) in his commitment to tell stories that he felt
were important for us all to hear and learn from—focused around
the topics of colonization, prejudice, and objectification. As Ortner

declares, "The notion that colonial or academic texts are able completely to distort or exclude the voices and perspectives of those being written about seems to me to endow these texts with far greater power than they have" (188). Perhaps the ethnographic past can serve as a vehicle for reconsideration of the broader ends and means of the academy as a whole. My hope is that this book's beginning studies of ethnographically constructed Navajo autobiographies will prove to be relevant to and helpful in what I see as the academy's gradual shift toward greater degrees of conversively informed methods, rigorously evaluative thought, and empathically reasoned ways of knowing in all disciplines.

Notes

Introduction

1. See William M. Clements, *Oratory in Native North America* (Tucson: University of Arizona Press, 2002), for a discussion of such early Native American accounts; and my review of the book in *Studies in American Indian Literature* 16.4 (Summer 2004): 88–92.

2. Throughout this volume, several terms and phrases will be used with some overlap to reference the indigenous peoples of the Americas: Native Americans, American Indians, Native peoples of the Americas, indigenous Americans, indigenous peoples of the Americas, First Nations peoples, and the most regionally specific Alaskan Natives. While each of these referents indicates the Native peoples of the Americas, my usage in the text will note subtle, yet meaningful differences in denotation. First Nations is used specifically to reference the indigenous peoples of Canada. Indigenous and Native American are the broadest, including under their denotative rubric any and all of the Native peoples of the Americas. American Indian embraces all the indigenous peoples and tribes of the Americas understood under the rubric of Indian. Alaskan Native, while regionally specific, is broader than Indian, for it includes both the Indian and non-Indian (e.g., Tlingit, Inuit, Yupik) Native peoples of that region.

3. For a beginning interrogation of twentieth-century Native American ethnography, see my review essay of Arnold Krupat's collection *Native American Autobiography: An Anthology* (Madison: University of Wisconsin Press, 1994), published in *Biography* 19.3 (Summer 1996): 308–12.

4. For a much more extensive discussion and analysis of the conversive (conversative and transformative) interweaving of orality within contemporary Native American literatures, see my previous volume *Contemporary American Indian Literatures and the Oral Tradition* (Tucson: University of Arizona Press, 1999).

5. Anne E. Goldman argues for the expansion of our conceptions of autobiography in "Autobiography, Ethnography, and History: A Model for Reading," in *"Take My Word": Autobiographical Innovations by Ethnic American Working Women* (Berkeley: University of California Press, 1996), xv–xxxv.

Chapter One

1. The story about Little Wagon can be found in its entirety in Barre Toelken's essay "The Pretty Language of Yellowman," which appeared in *Genre*. That article was revised and expanded as "Poetic Retranslation and the 'Pretty Languages' of Yellowman," by Barre Toelken and Tacheeni Scott, in *Traditional Literatures of the American Indian: Texts and Interpretations*, comp. and ed. Karl Kroeber (Lincoln, University of Nebraska: 1981), 65–116.

2. For a more complete discussion of a descriptive psychological approach to the status of persons, I strongly recommend James R. Holmes's article "The Status of Persons or Who Was That Masked Metaphor?"—referenced in the Works Cited section. For a good introduction to descriptive psychology (a psychological method largely, but not exclusively, informed by Wittgensteinian philosophy), see Peter Ossorio, "An Overview of Descriptive Psychology," in *The Social Construction of the Person*, ed. Kenneth J. Gergen and Keith E. Davis (New York: Springer-Verlag, 1985), 19–40; Mary Kathleen Roberts, "Worlds and World Reconstruction," *Advances in Descriptive Psychology* 4 (1985): 17–43; and Carolyn Allen Zeiger, "The Miss Marple Model of Psychological Assessment," *Advances in Descriptive Psychology* 6 (1991): 159–83.

3. For an example of just the sort of "performable script" Tedlock advocates, Leslie Marmon Silko's remarkable volume *Storyteller* is a model for the transcription and translation of oral stories via a textual medium (*Spoken Word* 62). Her brilliant use of spacing, indentation, type font, and italics assists her readers to step beyond their respective interpretive distances and invites them into the world of "Storytelling."

Chapter Two

1. The published text inserts the word "and" in the passage, which potentially changes the meaning significantly; the materials are described, ending with "the many-fringed sash, (and) the Coyote robe." The original Navajo does not include the "and." Therefore the original Navajo might very well indicate that the previously listed garments altogether constitute what the storyteller refers to as "the Coyote robe."

2. *The Navaho Door: An Introduction to Navaho Life* by the Leightons

is a pretty reliable presentation of some of the particulars of everyday Navajo life in the 1930s. Nevertheless, some of the information provided by certain informants is potentially questionable—such as one man's claim to be a diagnostician hand-trembler, who then describes his first hand-trembling "ceremony" more like a classic case of the shakes: "I wasn't feeling very good. You know some days you act like you are going to sleep, want to lie down. . . . After that my hands started shaking. . . . It all starts from the end of the toe and coming up through the knees and on up to the top of the head" (100–101); or the example of one of the Leightons' female informants, who demonstrated a clear disinclination to share personal information with the outside researchers: "One wonders why she was silent about her married life, which filled many years. Was it forbidden to speak of it? Was it too painful or too intimate an experience? One can only guess. She disposes of it in a single paragraph, with no mention of husband and children" (119). Regarding traditional hand-tremblers, perhaps the most interesting and complete treatment can be found in the Levy, Neutra, and Parker volume *Hand Trembling, Frenzy Witchcraft, and Moth Madness: A Study of Navajo Seizure Disorders*, as well as in other shorter discussions such as Gladys Reichard's *Navaho Religion*, Hill's "The Hand Trembling Ceremony of the Navaho," Morgan's "Navaho Treatment of Sickness: Diagnosticians," and Donald Sandner's *Navaho Symbols of Healing*. Each of these discussions deserves fuller critical analysis regarding the reliability of specific sources of information and the writers' interpretations of their data.

3.   There have been other ethnographers who have maintained ongoing relationships with tribal members and used their studies for the good of the tribes. For example, Julie Cruikshank's work in the Yukon has been important in tribal land-claims cases in Canada.

4.   The earliest discussion that I've found that touches on homosexuality among the Navajo is W. W. Hill's 1935 article "The Status of the Hermaphrodite and Transvestite in Navaho Culture." Hill explains it is based on information that "was gathered incidentally to research on Navaho material culture" (273). Hill asked one Navajo he had gotten to know to read his piece on the "traditional" hermaphrodite in Navajo culture. One of Hill's "informants," Albert Sandoval, told him that such behavior was "not respected nowadays" (274). Regarding what Hill had been told by other "informants" about the past acceptance of such behavior, Sandoval merely replied that the current attitude toward such behavior is that of "ridicule," noting that "Any child showing a tendency to a transformation is discouraged" (274).

This notwithstanding, Hill presents hermaphroditism and transvestism as accepted and valued conditions and behaviors among the Navajo, repeating some questionable stories told him as factual and reliable support for his views: "The genitals of hermaphrodite deer, antelope, mountain sheep, and sheep are rubbed on the ends of the tails of female sheep and goats and on the noses of male sheep and goats. This is believed to cause hermaphrodite sheep and goats to be born" (274). Presumably, herders would want physically sound animals to produce future generations of animals, not the production of potentially infertile animals. In this discussion, Hill's occasional informants also told him that Navajo families want hermaphrodite children (regardless of his regular "informant" Sandoval's correction to the contrary); that Navajos expect transvestites and hermaphrodites to be promiscuous and to behave unnaturally; and that they are respected because of this (one informant claimed sexual relations with over a hundred men and asserted that s/he was respected more than others because of this) (276). Such "scholarship" was published as factual information about the Navajo and subsequently cited by other scholars, even though Hill's other informants told him that none of this was true.

Here is it important to note the appalling degrees of hegemonic control and misrepresentation to which some of the past scholarship on the Navajo descended. A final example from Hill's paper will suffice, but readers are forewarned that this is an especially disturbing example that some readers might prefer to skip. Hill relates that a woman was brought to him and presented as a hermaphrodite. Hill then interrogated her for six days, during which she related nothing about herself personally. Finally he questioned her directly about being a hermaphrodite: "The result was that the informant gave instant evidence of acute emotional distress. She was visibly upset, very nervous, kept her eyes on the ground during the whole recital, kept rubbing her hands together, and squirming. She lost her voice completely for a few moments and when she began to talk, spoke in a whisper, and her accounts and answers were so incoherent that the interpreter had trouble in getting the sense and was forced to question her repeatedly" (277–78). A discussion of fieldwork that appears to be abusive is beyond the bounds of one endnote. Fortunately, such badgering of informants appears to be a relic of the past. Hill's published article unquestionably affirms the woman's condition as a transvestite. He concludes the article by asserting that this woman "has failed to make the personal adjustment which her culture makes possible [for such people]" (279). Oddly, Hill notes that this appears to be the case for all of the others so identified, but he does not consider other explanations about why this might be so—namely, that his "information" might, in fact, consist of tall tales that need to be interpreted as stories and not taken at the surface level of facticity, and that his conclusions might be entirely incorrect.

5.   At this point, let me reference a number of ethnographically produced
      Navajo autobiographies, many of which have been recently in print:
      Spiderwoman: A Story of Navajo Weavers and Chanters, Gladys A.
      Reichard (Glorieta, NM: Rio Grande Press, 1968); *Navajo Shepherd
      and Weaver*, Gladys A. Reichard (Glorieta, NM: Rio Grande Press,
      1984); *Lucky the Navajo Singer*, Alexander H. and Dorothea C.
      Leighton (Albuquerque: University of New Mexico Press, 1992);
      *Molded in the Image of Changing Woman: Navajo Views on the
      Human Body and Personhood*, Maureen Trudelle Schwarz (Tucson:
      University of Arizona Press, 1997); *Beyond the Four Corners of the
      World: A Navajo Woman's Journey*, Emily Benedek (New York:
      Alfred A. Knopf, 1996); and *The Fifth World of Forster Bennett:
      Portrait of a Navajo*, Vincent Crapanzano (New York: Viking, 1972;
      repr. Lincoln: University of Nebraska Press, 2003). Four ethnographi-
      cally produced Navajo autobiographies that I do recommend for their
      overall reliability include *Hosteen Klah: Navaho Medicine Man and
      Sand Painter*, Franc Johnson Newcomb (Norman: University of
      Oklahoma Press, 1964); *A Voice in Her Tribe: A Navajo Woman's
      Own Story*, Irene Stewart (Socorro, NM: Ballena Press, 1980); "A
      Navajo Life Story," Tom Ration, in *The South Corner of Time*, ed.
      Larry Evers (Tucson: University of Arizona Press, 1981), 62–71; and
      Bighorse the Warrior, Tiana Bighorse, ed. Noel Bennett, foreword by
      Barry Lopez (Tucson, University of Arizona Press, 1990).

Chapter Three

1.   "Stress Accent in Wishram Chinook" relies on some of the early lin-
      guistic work that Walter Dyk did as a doctoral student under Edward
      Sapir. He went to the Pacific Northwest to work on developing a
      Wishram grammar, which he presented as his Ph.D. thesis in 1933.
2.   For more information about Walter Dyk, the journal *American
      Anthropologist* provides a fairly extensive write-up on him in his
      obituary, written by Fred Eggan and Michael Silverstein (*American
      Anthropologist* 76 [1974]: 86–87).
3.   Interestingly, Dell Hymes notes that Wishram is virtually indistin-
      guishable from the language of the Wasco Chinook people, who lived
      across the river from the Wishram Chinook people. Dyk developed a
      grammar of the language he referred to as Wishram, and after going to
      Yale, Philip Kahclamet referred to the language as Wishram, even
      though that was not how he had previously referred to the language.
      It appears that in this case, scholars delineated linguistic and demo-
      graphic borders and named languages in ways that differed from the
      understandings of the Indian people themselves. The "Wishram" peo-
      ple lived across the river from the "Wasco" people, and according to
      Dell Hymes, who has worked extensively with the texts produced

from those peoples, "Linguistically, [the Wishram texts] are indistinguishable from Wasco texts" (19).

4.   While Dyk states here that prowling is a gendered activity limited to
Navajo men, elsewhere in his article he relates and notes that women
also "prowl," even though he asserts that the behavior is much rarer
among women.

5.   Kluckhohn laments the difficulties involved in obtaining rigorous and
accurate information on peoples' sexual behaviors: "Except to some
extent in the case of children, the anthropologist can seldom observe
overt sex acts" (90). I must admit that this statement leaves me quite
speechless. I include it to show the more egregious degrees to which
objective science descended in the era of psychoanalytic ethnography.

6.   While four of the family members offered their own interpretations
("associations") of their purported dreams, Kluckhohn and Morgan
note that the father of the family "could not or would not produce
any associations" (130). In noting the father's lack of associations in
relation to the dreams he recounted, Kluckhohn and Morgan explain
that this was due to the fact that he "had a very low anxiety level for
a Navaho" (130).

7.   For a more complete discussion of Wittgenstein's rejection of theory,
see my volume *Wittgenstein and Critical Theory* (Athens: Ohio
University Press, 1995), especially chapter 1, "Moving Beyond the
Modern/Postmodern Dialectic: Wittgensteinian Directives for
Literary Theory" (7–32).

Chapter Four

1.   There are a number of recent ethnographic publications that demonstrate a conversive approach in which the anthropologists/editors
worked collaboratively and intersubjectively with the Indian people
whose stories they transcribed. Three that I recommend as models for
future work include Julie Cruikshank's work with Angela Sidney,
Annie Ned, and Kitty Smith (Julie Cruikshank, *Life Lived Like a Story:
Life Stories of Three Yukon Native Elders* [Lincoln: University of
Nebraska Press, 1990]); James Kari and Alan Boras's work with Peter
Kalifornsky (James Kari and Alan Boras, *Peter Kalifornsky, A Dena'ina
Legacy, K'TL'EGH'I SUKDU: The Collected Writings of Peter Kalifornsky*
[The Alaska Native Language Center, 1991]); and Harold Courlander's
work with Albert Yava (Harold Courlander, ed., *Big Falling Snow: A
Tewa-Hopi Indian's Life and the History and Traditions of His People*
[Albuquerque, University of New Mexico Press, 1992]).

2.   As this chapter and the next indicate, it is significant that Left
Handed framed his stories about a young man's behavior among the
Navajo within the scope of three years, paralleling the time frame of
Dyk's fieldwork, which extended over the course of three years.

Chapter Five

1.   This information was related to me directly in a telephone conversation with Robert Young in the fall of 2005.

2.   This story is especially intriguing in light of Walter Dyk's psychoanalytic orientation. As a very capable storyteller, an ability that includes an astute awareness of one's listeners' reactions, cues, and interests, Left Handed might very well have developed stories that might fit interestingly into psychoanalytic theories (such as an Oedipal relationship between the son of Old Man Hat and his mother, or a castration complex). This does not mean that Left Handed was familiar with these theories, but rather that he was telling stories that responded to Dyk's inquiries and his responses to Left Handed's words, thereby telling stories that emphasized those elements of particular interest to the anthropologist.

3.   For a longer discussion of Berard Haile's ethnographic work among the Navajo, see chapter 2.

Chapter Six

1.   For a representative example of early drawings of Navajo sand paintings that were made without the authenticity and reliability of Newcomb's depictions, see Alfred Marston Tozzer's article "Notes on Religious Ceremonies of the Navaho," published in the 1909 *Putnam Anniversary Volume: Anthropological Essays*. In this essay, Tozzer reproduces a number of supposedly traditional and ceremonial Navaho sand paintings—this even though Tozzer explicitly notes that some of the sand paintings that his informants created for him were "entirely different" from those observed before by Washington Matthews. As Tozzer clarifies about one of the sand paintings he saw, "The sand picture made as the first of the three in the ceremony which I witnessed is, therefore, not the usual one painted at this time, and I have never seen it described. I cannot give any reason for its substitution in place of the usual picture" (323). In contrast to Newcomb's lived relationship as a member of the Navajo community in which she lived, Tozzer had no such developed connection to the tribe nor its people.

2.   I, too, met Kawano one day in the same manner. Driving up Mt. Taylor on the one-lane dirt road, I saw a man and a woman walking along the road. I stopped and asked if they wanted a ride to the top, an offer they accepted. The man with the backpack was Kawano—I imagine with a camera in his pack.

3.   It is important to note that the editorial work on the 1967 edition of *Miracle Hill: The Story of a Navaho Boy* is attributed to T. D. Allen. It is important to note that T. D. Allen was not the name of Mitchell's teacher at the Institute for American Indian Arts. Even

though, in his introduction to the 2004 edition, Paul Zolbrod refers to T. D. Allen as Mitchell's "English teacher and first-edition editorial guide" (xiii), it is important to clarify that T. D. Allen was actually "the corporate name of a husband-and-wife writing team" that consisted of Mitchell's teacher Terry Allen and her husband Don Allen (Allen, *Navahos Have Five Fingers* back cover). This fact makes the editorial mediation of Mitchell's 1967 book that much more complicated, since the extent of Don Allen's involvement in the editing has not been made evident.

4. For a recent and comprehensive overview of the literature about Navajo women, see Jennifer Nez Denetdale's "Representing Changing Woman: A Review Essay on Navajo Women" (*American Indian Culture and Research Journal* 25.3 [2002]: 1–26).

Epilogue

1. A more complete list of "Conversive Literary Structures" appears in appendix 1 of my volume *Contemporary American Indian Literatures and the Oral Tradition* (221–23).

Works Cited

Alcoff, Linda. "The Problem of Speaking for Others." *Cultural Critique* (Winter 1991–1992): 5–32.

Alfred, Taiaiake. *Peace, Power, Righteousness: An Indigenous Manifesto.* Don Mills, Ontario: Oxford University Press, 1999.

———. "Warrior Scholarship: Seeing the University as a Ground of Contention." *Indigenizing the Academy.* Eds. Mihesuah and Wilson. 88–99.

Allen, T. D. (Don and Terry). *Navahos Have Five Fingers.* Norman: University of Oklahoma Press, 1963.

Althusser, Louis. "Ideology and Ideological State Apparatuses (Notes toward an Investigation)." *Lenin and Philosophy and Other Essays.* Trans. Ben Brewster. London: New Left Books, 1971. 127–86.

Appiah, Kwame Anthony. *In My Father's House: Africa in the Philosophy of Culture.* New York: Oxford University Press, 1992.

Archibald, Jo-ann, and Ellen White. "*Kwulasulwut S yuth* [Ellen White's Teachings]: A Collaboration between Ellen White and Jo-ann Archibald." *Canadian Journal of Native Education* 19.2 (1992): 150–64.

Asad, Talal, ed. *Anthropology and the Colonial Encounter.* Atlantic Highlands, NJ: Humanities Press, 1973.

Ashcroft, Bill, Gareth Griffiths, and Helen Tiffin. *The Empire Writes Back: Theory and Practice in Post-Colonial Literatures.* London: Routledge, 1989.

Ballinger, Franchot. "Living Sideways: Social Themes and Social Relationships in Native American Trickster Tales." *American Indian Quarterly* 13.1 (1989): 15–30.

Barrett, John Mandel. "The Autobiographer's Art." *Journal of Aesthetics and Art Criticism* 27 (1968): 215–26.

Basso, Keith. *Western Apache Language and Culture: Essays in Linguistic Anthropology.* Tucson: University of Arizona Press, 1990.

Bauman, Richard. "Linguistics, Anthropology, and Verbal Art: Toward a
    Unified Perspective, with a Special Discussion of Children's
    Folklore." *Linguistics and Anthropology*. Ed. Muriel Saville-Troike.
    Washington: Georgetown University Press, 1977. 13–36.
———. "Verbal Art as Performance." *American Anthropologist* 77.2 (June
    1975): 290–311.
Beck, Peggy V., Anna Lee Walters, and Nia Francisco. *The Sacred: Ways of
    Knowledge, Sources of Life*. Tsaile, AZ: Navajo Community College
    Press, 1992.
Begay, Richard M. 1997. "The Role of Archaeology on Indian Lands: The
    Navajo Nation." *Native Americans and Archaeologists*. Ed. Swidler,
    Dongoske, Anyon, and Downer. 161–66.
Belenky, Mary Field, Blythe McVicker Clinchy, Nancy Rule Goldberger, and
    Jill Mattuck Tarule. *Women's Ways of Knowing: The Development of
    Self, Voice, and Mind*. New York: Basic Books, 1997.
Benedek, Emily. *Beyond the Four Corners of the World: A Navajo Woman's
    Journey*. New York: Alfred A. Knopf, 1996.
Bennett, Noël, and Tiana Bighorse. *Working with the Wool: How to Weave
    a Navajo Rug*. Flagstaff, AZ: Northland, 1971.
Berreman, Gerald D. "Is Anthropology Alive? Social Responsibility in Social
    Anthropology." *Current Anthropology* 9.5 (1968): 391–436.
Bhabha, Homi K. "Signs Taken for Wonders: Questions of Ambivalence and
    Authority under a Tree outside Delhi, May 1817." *Critical Inquiry*
    12.1 (Autumn 1985): 144–65.
Bighorse, Tiana. *Bighorse the Warrior*. Ed. Noël Bennett. Foreword by Barry
    Lopez. Tucson: University of Arizona Press, 1990.
Bird, Gloria. "Toward a Decolonization of the Mind and Text: Leslie
    Marmon Silko's *Ceremony*." *Wicazo Sa Review* 9.2 (1993): 1–8.
Bloom, Leslie Rebecca. "Locked in Uneasy Sisterhood: Reflections on
    Feminist Methodology and Research Relations." *Anthropology and
    Education Quarterly* 28.1 (1997): 111–22.
Bonaparte, Marie. "Some Psychoanalytic and Anthropological Insights
    Applied to Sociology." *Psychoanalysis and Culture*. Ed. Wilbur and
    Muensterberger. 145–49.
Bordo, Susan. "Feminism, Postmodernism, and Gender-Skepticism."
    Feminism/Postmodernism. Ed. Linda Nicholson. New York:
    Routledge, 1989. 133–56.
Bourdieu, Pierre. *Language and Symbolic Power*. Ed. John B. Thompson.
    Trans. Gino Raymond and Matthew Adamson. Cambridge, MA:
    Harvard University Press, 1991.
———. *The Logic of Practice*. Trans. Richard Nice. Stanford, CA: Stanford
    University Press, 1990.
Boyarin, Jonathan. "Voices around the Text: The Ethnography of Reading at
    Mesivta Tifereth Jerusalem." *Cultural Anthropology* 4 (1989): 399–421.

Bradburd, Daniel. *Being There: The Necessity of Fieldwork*. Washington, DC: Smithsonian Institution Press, 1998.

Bright, William. "Poetic Structure in Oral Narrative." *Spoken and Written Language: Exploring Orality and Literacy*. Ed. Deborah Tannen. Norwood, NJ: Ablex, 1982. 171–84.

Brill, Susan B. "Conversive Relationality in Bahá'í Scholarship: Centering the Sacred and Decentering the Self." *Journal of Bahá'í Studies* 7.2 (1995): 1–28.

———. "'Discovering the Order and Structure of Things': A Conversive Approach to Contemporary Navajo Poetry." *Studies in American Indian Literatures* 7.3 (1995): 51–70.

———. Review of *Native American Autobiography: An Anthology*, Arnold Krupat, ed. (Wisconsin Studies in American Autobiography. Madison: University of Wisconsin Press, 1994). *Biography* 19.3 (Summer 1996): 308–12.

———. *Wittgenstein and Critical Theory: Beyond Postmodern Criticism and toward Descriptive Investigations*. Athens: Ohio University Press, 1995.

Brill de Ramírez, Susan B. *Contemporary American Indian Literatures and the Oral Tradition*. Tucson: University of Arizona Press, 1999.

———. "The Resistance of American Indian Autobiographies to Ethnographic Colonization." *Mosaic* 32.2 (1999): 59–73.

———. Review of *Oratory in Native North America*, William M. Clements (Tucson: University of Arizona Press, 2002). *Studies in American Indian Literature* 16.4 (Summer 2004): 88–92.

Brooks, Peter. "The Storyteller." *Yale Journal of Criticism* 1.1 (Fall 1987): 21–38.

Brown, Alanna Kathleen. "Pulling Silko's Threads through Time: An Exploration of Storytelling." *American Indian Quarterly* 19.2 (Spring 1995): 171–79.

Brumble, H. David, III. *American Indian Autobiography*. Berkeley: University of California Press, 1988.

Burgos-Debray, Elisabeth. *I, Rigoberta Menchú: An Indian Woman in Guatemala*. New York: Verso, 1984.

Callaway, Helen. "Ethnography and Experience: Gender Implications in Fieldwork and Texts." *Anthropology and Autobiography*. Ed. Judith Okely and Helen Callaway. New York: Routledge, 1992. 29–49.

Carr, Helen. *Inventing the American Primitive: Politics, Gender and the Representation of Native American Literary Traditions, 1789–1936*. Cork, Ireland: Cork University Press, 1996.

Clark, David Anthony Tyeeme. "Not the End of the Stories, Not the End of the Songs: Visualizing, Signifying, Counter-colonizing." *Indigenizing the Academy*. Ed. Mihesuah and Wilson. 218–32.

Clements, William M. *Native American Verbal Art: Texts and Contexts*. Tucson: University of Arizona Press, 1996.

———. *Oratory in Native North America.* Tucson: University of Arizona Press, 2002.

Clifford, James. "Introduction." *Writing Culture.* Ed. James Clifford and George E. Marcus. 1–26.

———. "On Ethnographic Allegory." *Writing Culture.* Ed. James Clifford and George E. Marcus. 98–120.

———. "On Ethnographic Authority." *Representations* 1.2 (Spring 1983): 118–46.

———. *The Predicament of Culture: Twentieth-Century Ethnography, Literature, and Art.* Cambridge, MA: Harvard University Press, 1988.

Clifford, James, and George E. Marcus, eds. *Writing Culture: The Poetics and Politics of Ethnography.* Berkeley: University of California Press, 1986.

Cook-Lynn, Elizabeth. *Why I Can't Read Wallace Stegner and Other Essays.* Madison: University of Wisconsin Press, 1996.

Courlander, Harold, ed. *Big Falling Snow: A Tewa-Hopi Indian's Life and the History and Traditions of His People.* 1978. Albuquerque: University of New Mexico Press, 1992.

Crapanzano, Vincent. *The Fifth World of Forster Bennett: Portrait of a Navajo.* New York: Viking, 1972. Repr. with new Foreword. Lincoln: University of Nebraska Press, 2003.

———. "Life-Histories." *American Anthropologist* 86.4 (1984): 953–60.

———. "The Life History in Anthropological Field Work." *Anthropology and Humanism Quarterly* 2 (1977): 3–7.

Crick, Malcolm. "Ali and Me: An Essay in Street-Corner Anthropology." *Anthropology and Autobiography.* Ed. Okely and Callaway. 175–92.

———. "Shifting Identities in the Research Process: An Essay in Personal Anthropology." *Doing Fieldwork: Eight Personal Accounts of Social Research.* Ed. John Perry. Geelong, Australia: Deakin University Press, 1989. 24–40.

Cruikshank, Julie, in collaboration with Angela Sidney, Kitty Smith, and Annie Ned. *Life Lived Like a Story: Life Stories of Three Yukon Native Elders.* Lincoln: University of Nebraska Press, 1990.

Cruikshank, Julie. *The Social Life of Stories.* Lincoln: University of Nebraska Press, 1996.

Dasenbrock, Reed Way. "Intelligibility and Meaningfulness in Multicultural Literature in English." *PMLA (Publications of the Modern Language Association of America)* 102.1 (January 1987): 10–19.

De Lauretis, Theresa. *Alice Doesn't: Feminism, Semiotics, Cinema.* Bloomington: Indiana University Press, 1984.

Deloria, Vine, Jr. *Evolution, Creationism, and Other Modern Myths: A Critical Inquiry.* Golden, CO: Fulcrum, 2002.

———. *Red Earth, White Lies: Native America and the Myth of Scientific Fact.* New York: Scribner, 1995.

———. "Some Criticisms and a Number of Suggestions." *Anthropology and the American Indian: A Symposium.* Ed. Officer and McKinley. 93–99.

Denetdale, Jennifer Nez. "Representing Changing Woman: A Review Essay on Navajo Women." *American Indian Culture and Research Journal* 25.3 (2001): 1–26.

Devereux, George. "Institutionalized Homosexuality of the Mohave Indians." *Human Biology* 9 (1937): 498–527.

———. "Mohave Indian Autoerotic Behavior." *Psychoanalysis Review* 37 (1950): 201–20.

———. "Mohave Zoophilia." *Samiksa* 2 (1948): 227–45.

———. "The Primal Scene and Juvenile Heterosexuality in Mohave Society." *Psychoanalysis and Culture.* Ed. Wilbur and Muensterberger. 90–107.

Diamond, Stanley. *In Search of the Primitive: A Critique of Civilization.* New Brunswick, NJ: Transaction, 1974.

Dickinson, Emily. *The Poems of Emily Dickinson.* Ed. Thomas H. Johnson. Cambridge, MA: The Belknap Press of Harvard University Press, 1983.

The Diné of the Eastern Region of the Navajo Reservation. *Oral History Stories of The Long Walk: Hwéeldi Baa Hané.* Stories collected and recorded by the Title VII Bilingual Staff: Patty Chee, Milanda Yazzie, Judy Benally, Marie Etsitty, and Bessie C. Henderson. Crownpoint, NM: Lake Valley Navajo School, 1990.

Dinwoodie, David W. "Textuality and the 'Voices' of Informants: The Case of Edward Sapir's 1929 Navajo Field School." *Anthropological Linguistics* 41.2 (Summer 1999): 165–92.

Downer, Alan S. "Archaeologists' Native American Relations." *Native Americans and Archaeologists.* Ed. Swidler et al. 23–34.

Dumont, Jean-Paul. *The Headman and I: Ambiguity and Ambivalence in the Fieldworking Experience.* Austin: University of Texas Press, 1978.

Durham, Jimmie. "Cowboys and ... Notes on Art, Literature, and American Indians in the Modern American Mind." *The State of Native America: Genocide, Colonization, and Resistance.* Ed. M. Annette Jaimes. Boston: South End, 1992. 423–38.

Dwyer, Kevin. "Case Study: On the Dialogic of Field Work." *Dialectical Anthropology* 2.2 (1977): 143–51.

———. "The Dialogic of Ethnology." *Dialectical Anthropology* 4.3 (1979): 205–24.

Dyk, Walter. *A Navaho Autobiography.* Viking Fund Publications in Anthropology 8. New York: Viking Fund, 1947.

———. "Notes and Illustrations of Navaho Sex Behavior." *Psychoanalysis and Culture: Essays in Honor of Géza Róheim.* Ed. George B. Wilbur and Warner Muensterberger. New York: International Universities Press, 1951. 108–19.

————. *Son of Old Man Hat: A Navaho Autobiography.* Foreword Edward Sapir. 1938. Lincoln: University of Nebraska Press, 1967.

————, and Ruth Dyk. *Left Handed: A Navajo Autobiography.* New York: Columbia University Press, 1980.

Echo-Hawk, Roger. "Forging an Ancient History for Native America." *Native Americans and Archaeologists.* Ed. Swidler et al. 88–102.

Eggan, Fred. "Foreword." *Left Handed.* Walter and Ruth Dyk. ix–xiii.

————, and Michael Silverstein. "Walter Dyk: 1899–1972." *American Anthropologist* 76 (1974): 86–87.

Eisemon, Thomas Owen, Martin Hallett, and John Maundu. "Primary-School Literature and Folktales in Kenya: What Makes a Children's Story African?" *Comparative Education Review* 30.2 (1986): 232–46.

Ellis, Richard, and Ann McClintock. *If You Take My Meaning: Theory into Practice in Human Communication.* London: Edward Arnold, 1994.

Fabian, Johannes. "Culture, Time, and the Object of Anthropology." *Berkshire Review* 20 (1985): 7–23.

————. "Language, History and Anthropology." *Philosophy of the Social Sciences* 1 (1971): 19–47.

Fanon, Frantz. *The Wretched of the Earth: A Negro Psychoanalyst's Study of the Problems of Racism and Colonialism in the World Today.* New York: Grove Press, 1963.

Farella, John R. *The Main Stalk: A Synthesis of Navajo Philosophy.* Tucson: University of Arizona Press, 1984.

Faris, James C. *Navajo and Photography: A Critical History of the Representation of an American People.* Salt Lake City: University of Utah Press, 2003.

Finnegan, Ruth. "Literacy versus Non-literacy: The Great Divide? Some Comments on the Significance of 'Literature' in Non-literate Cultures." *Modes of Thought: Essays on Thinking in Western and Non-Western Societies.* Ed. Robin Horton and Ruth Finnegan. London: Faber and Faber, 1973. 112–44.

Fischer, Michael M. J. "Ethnicity and the Post-Modern Arts of Memory." *Writing Culture: The Poetics and Politics of Ethnography.* Ed. James Clifford and George E. Marcus. Berkeley: University of California Press, 1986. 194–233.

Foley, John Miles. "Explaining a Joke: Pelt Kid and Tale of Orasac." *Western Folklore* 53 (1994): 51–68.

————. "Word-Power, Performance, and Tradition." *Journal of American Folklore* 105.417 (1992): 275–301.

Follett, Wilson. "A Navaho Indian's Own Story." Review of *Son of Old Man Hat. New York Times Book Review*, 11 Dec. 1938: 33.

Forsman, Leonard A. "Straddling the Current: A View from the Bridge over Clear Salt Water." *Native Americans and Archaeologists.* Ed. Swidler et al. 105–11.

Frank, Gelya. "Finding the Common Denominator: A Phenomenological Critique of Life History Method." *Ethos* 7.1 (1979): 68–94.

Frey, Rodney. "Re-telling One's Own: Storytelling among the Apaalooke (Crow Indians)." *Plains Anthropologist* 28.100 (1983): 129–35.

Friedman, Susan Stanford. "Relational Epistemology and the Question of Anglo-American Feminist Criticism." *Tulsa Studies in Women's Literature* 12.2 (Fall 1993): 247–61.

Frisbie, Charlotte J. "Tales of an Endishodi: *Father Berard Haile and the Navajos, 1900–1961.*" Review of *Father Berard Haile and the Navajos, 1900–1961,* ed. and transcribed by Father Murray Bodo, O.F.M. *American Indian Culture and Research Journal* 23.2 (1999): 187–90.

———, ed. *Tall Woman: The Life of Rose Mitchell, a Navajo Woman, c. 1874–1978.* Albuquerque: University of New Mexico Press, 2001.

———, and David P. McAllester, eds. *Navajo Blessingway Singer: The Autobiography of Frank Mitchell, 1881–1967.* Tucson: University of Arizona Press, 1978.

Gardner, Ethel B. "Ka-im's Gift: A Sto:lo Legend." *Canadian Journal of Native Education* 15.3 (1988): 101–8.

Geertz, Armin W. "On Reciprocity and Mutual Reflection in the Study of Native American Religions." *Religion* 24 (1994): 1–7.

Geertz, Clifford. *The Interpretation of Cultures.* New York: Basic Books, 1973.

———. *Local Knowledge: Further Essays in Interpretive Anthropology.* New York: Basic Books, 1983.

Glaspell, Susan. "Trifles: A Play in One Act." Boston, 1927. Electronic Text Center, University of Virginia. 1 June 2006. http://etext.lib.virginia.edu/etcbin/browse-mixednew?id'GlaTrif& tag'public&images'images/modeng&data'/texts/english/modeng/parsed

Goldman, Anne E. *"Take My Word": Autobiographical Innovations by Ethnic American Working Women.* Berkeley: University of California Press, 1996.

Goodwin, Marjorie Harness. "'Instigating': Storytelling as Social Process." *American Ethnologist* 9.4 (November 1982): 799–819.

Goody, Jack, and Ian Watt. "The Consequences of Literacy." *Comparative Studies in Society and History* 5 (1963): 304–45.

Grant, Agnes. "Content in Native Literature Programs." Mokkakit Conference of the Indian Education Research Association. Winnipeg, 18 Oct. 1986. 1–16.

Gubrium, Jaber F., and James A. Holstein. "At the Border of Narrative and Ethnography." *Journal of Contemporary Ethnography* 28.5 (October 1999): 561–73.

Gumperz, John J. "Sociocultural Knowledge in Conversational Inference." *Linguistics and Anthropology.* Ed. Muriel Saville-Troike. Washington, DC: Georgetown University Press, 1977. 191–211.

Gupta, Akhil, and James Ferguson, eds. *Anthropological Locations: Boundaries and Grounds of a Field Science.* Berkeley: University of California Press, 1997.

Haile, Berard. *Navajo Coyote Tales: The Curly Tó Aheedlíinii Version.* Ed. Karl W. Luckert. Navajo orthography by Irvy W. Goossen. Lincoln: University of Nebraska Press, 1984.

———. *The Navaho Fire Dance or Corral Dance: A Brief Account of Its Practice and Meaning.* St. Michaels, AZ: St. Michaels Press, 1946.

———. *The Navaho War Dance: Squaw Dance.* St. Michaels, AZ: St. Michaels Press, 1946.

———. *Women versus Men: A Conflict of Navajo Emergence: The Curly Tó Aheedlíinii Version.* Ed. Karl W. Luckert. Navajo orthography by Irvy W. Goossen. Lincoln: University of Nebraska Press, 1981.

Hallowell, A. I. "Cultural Factors in the Structuralization of Perception." *Social Psychology at the Crossroads.* Ed. John H. Rohrer and Muzafer Sherif. New York: Harper, 1951. 164–95.

Handler, Richard. "On Dialogue and Destructive Analysis: Problems in Narrating Nationalism and Ethnicity." *Journal of Anthropological Research* 41.2 (Summer 1985): 171–82.

Hanks, William F. "Authenticity and Ambivalence in the Text: A Colonial Maya Case." *American Ethnologist* 13 (November 1986): 721–44.

Harding, Sandra. *Whose Science? Whose Knowledge? Thinking from Women's Lives.* Ithaca, NY: Cornell University Press, 1991.

Hastrup, Kirsten. "Writing Ethnography: State of the Art." *Anthropology and Autobiography.* Ed. Okely and Callaway. 116–33.

Hegeman, Susan. "Native American 'Texts' and the Problem of Authenticity." *American Quarterly* 41 (1989): 265–83.

Hill, Jane H., and Ofelia Zepeda. "Mrs. Patricio's Trouble: The Distribution of Responsibility in an Account of Personal Experience." *Responsibility and Evidence in Oral Discourse.* Ed. Hill and Irvine. Cambridge: Cambridge University Press, 1992. 197–225.

Hill, W. W. "The Hand Trembling Ceremony of the Navaho." *El Palacio* 38 (1935): 65–68.

———. "Navaho Trading and Trading Ritual: A Study of Cultural Dynamics." *Southwestern Journal of Anthropology* 4 (1948): 371–96.

———. "The Status of the Hermaphrodite and Transvestite in Navaho Culture." *American Anthropologist* 37 (1935): 273–80.

Hirsch, Bernard A. "'The telling which continues': Oral Tradition and the Written Word in Leslie Marmon Silko's *Storyteller.*" *American Indian Quarterly* 12 (1988): 1–26.

Hirsch, E. D., Jr. "Objective Interpretation." *PMLA* 75 (1960): 463–79.

Holmes, James R. "The Status of Persons or Who Was That Masked Metaphor?" *Advances in Descriptive Psychology* 6 (1991): 15–35.

Horowitz, Irving Louis. "Autobiography as the Presentation of Self for

Social Immortality." *New Literary History* 9.1 (1977): 173–79.

House, Deborah. *Language Shift among the Navajos: Identity Politics and Cultural Continuity*. Tucson: University of Arizona Press, 2002.

Hymes, Dell. *"In vain I tried to tell you": Essays in Native American Ethnopoetics*. Philadelphia: University of Pennsylvania Press, 1981.

———. "Reading Clackamas Texts." *Traditional American Indian Literatures: Texts and Interpretations*. Ed. Karl Kroeber. Lincoln: University of Nebraska Press, 1981. 117–59.

Irwin, Lee. "No Privileged Observers: A Reply to Geertz." *Religion* 24 (1994): 14–15.

Ivanitz, Michele. "Culture, Ethics and Participatory Methodology in Cross-cultural Research." *Australian Aboriginal Studies* 2 (1999): 46–58.

Jackson, Donald, ed. *Black Hawk: An Autobiography*. Urbana-Champaign: University of Illinois Press, 1990.

Johnson, Broderick H., Sydney M. Callaway, et al. *Denetsosie*. Ed. Broderick H. Johnson. Illus. Andy Tsinajinnie. Phoenix, AZ: Navajo Curriculum Center Press, 1974.

Justice, Daniel Heath. "Seeing (and Reading) Red: Indian Outlaws in the Ivory Tower." *Indigenizing the Academy*. Ed. Mihesuah and Wilson. 100–123.

Kari, James, and Alan Boras. *Peter Kalifornsky, A Dena'ina Legacy, K'TL'EGH'I SUKDU: The Collected Writings of Peter Kalifornsky*. Fairbanks: The Alaska Native Language Center, 1991.

Kawano, Kenji. *Warriors: Navajo Code Talkers*. Foreword by Carl Gorman. Intro. Benis M. Frank, USMC. Flagstaff, AZ: Northland, 1990.

Kelly, Jennifer. "Coming Out of the House: A Conversation with Lee Maracle." *Ariel: A Review of International English Literature* 25.1 (January 1994): 73–88.

Kluckhohn, Clyde. "As an Anthropologist Views It." *Sex Habits of American Men: A Symposium on the Kinsey Report*. Ed. Albert Deutsch. New York: Prentice Hall, 1948. 88–104, 233.

———. "Honest Insight to Navaho Life, With No Romantics." Review of *Son of Old Man Hat*. *Boston Evening Transcript* 19 Nov. 1938: 6.

———. "A Navaho Personal Document with a Brief Paretian Analysis." *Southwestern Journal of Anthropology* 1.2 (1945): 260–83.

———. *Navaho Witchcraft*. Cambridge, MA: Peabody Museum of Archaeology and Ethnology, Harvard University, 1944. Repub. Boston: Beacon, 1967.

———. "Notes on Navajo Eagle Way." *New Mexico Anthropologist* 5 (1941): 6–14.

———. Review of *Property Concepts of the Navaho Indians*, Berard Haile. *Ethnohistory* 2.4 (Autumn 1955): 386–87.

Kluckhohn, Clyde, and William Morgan. "Some Notes on Navaho Dreams." *Psychoanalysis and Culture*. Wilbur and Muensterberger. 120–31.

Kluckhohn, Clyde, and Katherine Spencer. *A Bibliography of the Navaho Indians.* New York: J. J. Augustin, 1940. Repr. New York: AMS, 1972.

Kroeber, Karl. *Retelling/Rereading: The Fate of Storytelling in Modern Times.* New Brunswick, NJ: Rutgers University Press, 1992.

———. *Traditional American Indian Literatures: Texts and Interpretations.* Lincoln: University of Nebraska Press, 1981.

Kroskrity, Paul V. "Growing With Stories: Line, Verse, and Genre in an Arizona Tewa Text." *Journal of Anthropological Research* 41.2 (1985): 183–99.

Krupat, Arnold. "The Dialogic of Silko's *Storyteller.*" *Narrative Chance: Postmodern Discourse on Native American Indian Literatures.* Ed. Gerald Vizenor. Albuquerque: University of New Mexico Press, 1989. 55–68.

———. *For Those Who Come After: A Study of Native American Autobiography.* Berkeley: University of California Press, 1985.

LaFarge, Oliver. "Left Handed's Story." Review of *Son of Old Man Hat. Saturday Review* 19 (24 Dec. 1938): 6.

Lakoff, Robin Tolmach. "Some of My Favorite Writers Are Literate: The Mingling of Oral and Written Strategies in Written Communication." *Spoken and Written Language: Exploring Orality and Literacy.* Ed. Deborah Tannen. Norwood, NJ: Ablex, 1982. 239–60.

Lamb, Susan Pierce. "Shifting Paradigms and Modes of Consciousness: An Integrated View of the Storytelling Process." *Folklore and Mythology Studies* 5 (Spring 1981): 5–19.

Larson, Sidner. "Native American Aesthetics: An Attitude of Relationship." *MELUS* 17.3 (1991–92): 53–67.

Lassiter, Luke Eric. "From 'Reading Over the Shoulders of Natives' to 'Reading Alongside Natives,' Literally: Toward a Collaborative and Reciprocal Ethnography." *Journal of Anthropological Research* 57.2 (Spring 2001): 137–49.

Lawless, Elaine J. "'I was afraid someone like you … an outsider … would misunderstand': Negotiating Interpretive Differences between Ethnographers and Subjects." *Journal of American Folklore* 105.417 (Summer 1992): 302–14.

———. "'Reciprocal' Ethnography: No One Said It Was Easy." *Journal of Folklore Research* 37.2/3 (2000): 197–205.

Left-Handed Mexican Clansman, with Howard Gorman and the Nephew of Former Big Man. *The Trouble at Round Rock.* Trans. and ed. Robert W. Young and William Morgan. Navajo Historical Series No. 2. N.p.: U. S. Dept. of Interior, Bureau of Indian Affairs, 1952.

Leighton, Alexander H., and Dorothea C. Leighton. *Lucky the Navajo Singer.* Ed. and annotated Joyce J. Griffen. Albuquerque: University of New Mexico Press, 1992.

———. *The Navaho Door: An Introduction to Navaho Life.* Foreword John Collier. New York: Russell & Russell, 1945.

Lévi-Strauss, Claude. "Anthropology: Its Achievements and Future."
   Current Anthropology 7.2 (1966): 124–27.

Lindfors, Bernth. "The Blind Men and the Elephant." *African Literature
   Today.* Vol. 7. New York: Africana, 1975. 53–64.

Mannheim, Bruce, and Dennis Tedlock, eds. *The Dialogic Emergence of
   Culture.* Urbana: University of Illinois Press, 1995.

Maranhão, Tullio. "Reflections of Fieldwork Conversations, or Authorial
   Difficulties in Anthropological Writing." *Responsibility and
   Evidence in Oral Discourse.* Ed. Jane H. Hill and Judith T. Irvine.
   Cambridge: Cambridge University, 1993. 260–88.

Marcus, George E. *Ethnography through Thick and Thin.* Princeton, NJ:
   Princeton University Press, 1998.

———, and Dick Cushman. "Ethnographies as Texts." *Annual Review of
   Anthropology* 11 (1982): 25–69.

Matthews, Washington. *The Night Chant: A Navajo Ceremony.* Salt Lake
   City: University of Utah Press, 1995.

Maud, Ralph. *Transmission Difficulties: Franz Boas and Tsimshian
   Mythology.* Burnaby, BC: Talonbooks, 2000.

M'Closkey, Kathy. *Swept Under the Rug: A Hidden History of Navajo
   Weaving.* Published in cooperation with the University of Arizona
   Southwest Center. Albuquerque: University of New Mexico Press, 2002.

McAllester, Mick. "Native Sources: American Indian Autobiography."
   Western American Literature 32.1 (1997): 3–23.

McClendon, Sally. "Meaning, Rhetorical Structure, and Discourse
   Organization in Myth." *Georgetown University Round Table on
   Languages and Linguistics 1977: Linguistics and Anthropology.* Ed.
   Muriel Saville-Troike. Washington, DC: Georgetown University
   Press, 1977. 155.

McGrane, Bernard. *Beyond Anthropology: Society and the Other.* New
   York: Columbia University Press, 1989.

McNeley, James Kale. *Holy Wind in Navajo Philosophy.* Tucson: University
   of Arizona Press, 1981.

Mead, Margaret. "The American Indian as a Significant Determinant of
   Anthropological Style." *Anthropology and the American Indian: A
   Symposium.* Ed. Officer and McKinley. 68–74.

———, ed. *Writings of Ruth Benedict: An Anthropologist at Work.* New
   York: Atherton Press, 1966.

Menninger, Karl A. "Totemic Aspects of Contemporary Attitudes toward
   Animals." *Psychoanalysis and Culture.* Ed. Wilbur and
   Muensterberger. 42–74.

Mihesuah, Devon Abbott. "Should American Indian History Remain a Field
   of Study?" *Indigenizing the Academy.* Ed. Mihesuah and Wilson.
   143–59.

———, and Angela Cavender Wilson, eds. *Indigenizing the Academy:*

Transforming Scholarship and Empowering Communities. Lincoln: University of Nebraska Press, 2004.

Mitchell, Blackhorse. *Miracle Hill: The Story of a Navajo Boy.* Foreword Paul Zolbrod. Tucson: University of Arizona Press, 2004. Orig. pub. *Miracle Hill: The Story of a Navaho Boy,* by Emerson Blackhorse Mitchell and T. D. Allen. Norman: University of Oklahoma Press, 1967.

Morgan, William. "Navaho Treatment of Sickness: Diagnosticians." *American Anthropologist* 33 (1931): 390–402.

Moore, David. "Myth, History, and Identity in Silko and Young Bear." *New Voices in Native American Literary Criticism.* Ed. Arnold Krupat. Washington, DC: Smithsonian Institution, 1993. 370–95.

Morris, Irvin. "The Blood Stone." *Neon Pow-Wow.* Ed. Anna Lee Walters. 20–27.

———. *From the Glittering World: A Navajo Story.* Norman: University of Oklahoma Press, 1997.

Morrison, Kenneth M. "They Act As Though They Have No Relatives: A Reply to Geertz." *Religion* 24 (1994): 11–12.

Motzafi-Haller, Pnina. "Writing Birthright: On Native Anthropologists and the Politics of Representation." *Auto/Ethnography.* Ed. Reed-Danahay. 195–222.

Mullen, Patrick B. "Collaborative Research Reconsidered." *Journal of Folklore Research* 37.2/3 (2000): 207–14.

Murray, David. *Forked Tongues: Speech, Writing, and Representation in North American Indian Texts.* Bloomington: Indiana University Press, 1991.

Nakhjavání, Bahíyyih. *Response.* Oxford: George Ronald, 1981.

Newcomb, Franc J. "Origin Legend of the Navajo Eagle Chant." *Journal of American Folklore* 53 (1940): 50–78.

Newcomb, Franc Johnson. *Hosteen Klah: Navaho Medicine Man and Sand Painter.* Norman: University of Oklahoma Press, 1964.

———. *Navaho Folk Tales.* Albuquerque: University of New Mexico Press, 1990.

Ngúgí wa Thiong'o. *Decolonising the Mind: The Politics of Language in African Literature.* London: James Currey Heinemann, 1986.

———. *Moving the Centre: The Struggle for Cultural Freedoms.* Oxford: James Currey Heinemann, 1993.

Noddings, Nel. *Caring: A Feminist Approach to Ethics and Moral Education.* Berkeley: University of California Press, 1985.

O'Connor, June. "On Studying and Being the Other: An Open Letter to Armin Geertz." *Religion* 24 (1994): 8–11.

Officer, James E., and Francis McKinley, eds. *Anthropology and the American Indian: A Symposium.* A Report of the Symposium on Anthropology and the American Indian at the Meetings of the American Anthropological Association, San Diego, California, November 20, 1970. San Francisco: The Indian Historian Press, 1973.

Okely, Judith. *Own or Other Culture*. New York: Routledge, 1996.

Okely, Judith, and Helen Callaway, eds. *Anthropology and Autobiography*. New York: Routledge, 1992.

Olson, David R. "From Utterance to Text: The Bias of Language in Speech and Writing." *Harvard Educational Review* 47.3 (1977): 257–81.

Ortiz, Alfonso. "An Indian Anthropologist's Perspective on Anthropology." *Anthropology and the American Indian: A Symposium*. Ed. Officer and McKinley. 85–92.

Ortiz, Simon J. *from Sand Creek: Rising in This Heart Which Is Our America*. Tucson: University of Arizona Press, 1981.

———. *Song, Poetry and Language: Expression and Perception*. Tsaile, AZ: Navajo Community College, n.d.

Ortner, Sherry. "Resistance and Ethnographic Refusal." *Comparative Studies in History and Society* 37.1 (1995): 173–93.

Ossorio, Peter. "An Overview of Descriptive Psychology." *The Social Construction of the Person*. Ed. Kenneth J. Gergen and Keith E. Davis. New York: Springer-Verlag, 1985. 19–40.

Parsons, Talcott, and Evon Z. Vogt. "Clyde Kay Maben Kluckhohn, 1905–1960." *American Anthropologist* 64.1 (1962): 140–61.

Pathak, Zakia, and Rajeswari Sunder Rajan. "Shahbano." *Signs: Journal of Women in Culture and Society* 14.3 (1989): 558–81.

Pepper, George H. "An Unusual Navajo Medicine Ceremony." *The Southern Workman* (Hampton, VA) (April 1905): 228–35.

Perry, Helen Swick. "Using Participant Observation to Construct a Life History." *Exploring Clinical Methods for Social Research*. Ed. David N. Berg and Kenwyn K. Smith. Beverly Hills, CA: Sage Books, 1985. 319–32.

Person, Raymond F., Jr. *Structure and Meaning in Conversation and Literature*. Lanham, MD: University Press of America, 1999.

Piquemal, Nathalie. "Free and Informed Consent in Research Involving Native American Communities." *American Indian Culture and Research Journal* 25.1 (2001): 65–79.

Polanyi, Livia. "Literary Complexity in Everyday Storytelling." *Spoken and Written Language: Exploring Orality and Literacy*. Ed. Deborah Tannen. Norwood, NJ: Ablex, 1982. 155–70.

———. "What Stories Can Tell Us About Their Teller's World." *Poetics Today* 2.2 (1981): 97–112.

Pratt, Mary Louise. "The Anticolonial Past." *Modern Language Quarterly* 65.3 (September 2004): 443–56.

Prus, Robert. *Symbolic Interaction and Ethnographic Research: Intersubjectivity and the Study of Human Lived Experience*. Albany: State University of New York Press, 1996.

Rabinow, Paul. "Representations Are Social Facts: Modernity and Post-Modernity in Anthropology." *Writing Culture*. Ed. James Clifford and George E. Marcus. 235–61.

Radner, Joan N., and Susan S. Lanser. "The Feminist Voice: Strategies of Coding in Folklore and Literature." *Journal of American Folklore* 100.398 (1987): 412–25.

Rapport, Nigel. "Edifying Anthropology: Culture as Conversation; Representation as Conversation." *After Writing Culture: Epistemology and Praxis in Contemporary Anthropology.* Ed. Allison James, Jenny Hockey, and Andrew Dawson. New York: Routledge, 1997. 177–93.

Ration, Tom. "A Navajo Life Story." *The South Corner of Time.* Ed. Larry Evers. Tucson: University of Arizona Press, 1981. 62–71. Initially printed in *Stories of Traditional Navajo Life and Culture* (Tsaile, AZ: Navajo Community Press, 1977).

Raugust, Mary C. "Feminist Ethics and Workplace Values." *Explorations in Feminist Ethics.* Cole and Coultrap-McQuin. Bloomington: Indiana University Press, 1992. 125–30.

Reed-Danahay, Deborah E., ed. *Auto/Ethnography: Rewriting the Self and the Social.* Oxford: Berg, 1997.

Reichard, Gladys A. *Navaho Religion: A Study of Symbolism.* New York: Bollingen Foundation, 1950. Princeton, NJ: Princeton University Press, 1977.

———. *Navajo Shepherd and Weaver.* Glorieta, NM: Rio Grande Press, 1984. First pub. New York: J. J. Augustin, 1936.

———. *Social Life of the Navajo Indians.* 1928. Repr. New York: AMS Press, 2001.

———. *Spiderwoman: A Story of Navajo Weavers and Chanters.* Glorieta, NM: Rio Grande Press, 1968. First pub. New York: Macmillan, 1934.

Retallack, Joan. "Poethics of Words and/as Music: Sam Beckett, John Cage." Presentation given at Modern Language Association Convention, San Francisco, 28 December 1991.

Review of *Son of Old Man Hat,* ed. Walter Dyk. *The New Republic* 9 Nov. 1938: 28.

Review of *Son of Old Man Hat,* ed. Walter Dyk. *New Yorker* 29 Oct. 1938: 67.

Riesman, Paul. "The Collaboration of Two Men and a Plant." *New York Times Book Review* 122 (22 Oct. 1972): 7, 10, 12, and 14.

Roberts, Mary Kathleen. "Worlds and World Reconstruction." *Advances in Descriptive Psychology* 4 (1985): 17–43.

Roessel, Ruth. *Women in Navajo Society.* Rough Rock, AZ: Navajo Resource Center/Rough Rock Demonstration School, 1981.

Rosaldo, Renato. "Doing Oral History." *Social Analysis* 4 (September 1980): 89–99.

Rosenblatt, Louise M. "The Poem as Event." *College English* 26.2 (1964): 123–28.

Ruppert, James. *Mediation in Contemporary Native American Fiction.* Norman: University of Oklahoma Press, 1995.

Said, Edward W. *Culture and Imperialism*. New York: Vintage, 1993.

———. *Orientalism*. New York: Vintage, 1979. Afterword. New York: Vintage, 1994.

Sandner, Donald. *Navaho Symbols of Healing*. New York: Harcourt Brace Jovanovich, 1979.

Sapir, Edward. *Navaho Texts*. Ed. Harry Hoijer. Iowa City: Linguistic Society of America, University of Iowa, 1942.

Sarris, Greg. *Keeping Slug Woman Alive: A Holistic Approach to American Indian Texts*. Berkeley: University of California Press, 1993.

———. "The Verbal Art of Mabel McKay: Talk as Culture Contact and Cultural Critique." *MELUS* 16.1 (Spring 1989–1990): 95–112.

Schipper, Mineke. "Culture, Identity, and Interdiscursivity." *Research in African Literatures* 24.4 (1993): 39–48.

Scholte, Bob. "Discontents in Anthropology." *Social Research* 38 (1972): 777–807.

———. "The Literary Turn in Contemporary Anthropology." Review of *Writing Culture: The Poetics and Politics of Ethnography*, ed. James Clifford and George E. Marcus. *Critique of Anthropology* 7.1 (1987): 33–47.

Schram, Peninnah. "One Generation Tells Another: The Transmission of Jewish Values through Storytelling." *Literature in Performance* 4.2 (1984): 33–45.

Schwarz, Maureen Trudelle. *Molded in the Image of Changing Woman: Navajo Views on the Human Body and Personhood*. Tucson: University of Arizona Press, 1997.

Scollon, Ron, and Suzanne B. K. Scollon. *Narrative, Literacy and Face in Interethnic Communication*. Vol. 7 in *Advances in Discourse Processes*, ed. Roy O. Freedle. Norwood, NJ: Ablex, 1981.

Scott, James C. *Domination and the Arts of Resistance: Hidden Transcripts*. New Haven: Yale University Press, 1990.

Sherzer, Joel. "The Ethnography of Speaking: A Critical Appraisal." *Georgetown University Round Table on Languages and Linguistics 1977: Linguistics and Anthropology*. Ed. Muriel Saville-Troike. Washington, DC: Georgetown University Press, 1977. 43–57.

Silko, Leslie Marmon. "Landscape, History, and the Pueblo Imagination." *On Nature: Nature, Landscape, and Natural History*. Ed. Daniel Halpern. San Francisco: North Point, 1987. 83–94.

———. "Language and Literature from a Pueblo Indian Perspective." *English Literature: Opening Up the Canon*. Ed. Leslie A. Fiedler and Houston A. Baker Jr. Baltimore, MD: Johns Hopkins University Press, 1981. 54–72.

———. *Storyteller*. New York: Arcade, 1981.

Silko, Leslie Marmon, and Dexter Fisher. "Stories and Their Tellers: A Conversation with Leslie Marmon Silko." *The Third Woman:*

Minority Women Writers of the United States. Ed. Derek Fisher.
Boston: Houghton, 1980. 18–23.

Simard, Rodney. "American Indian Literatures, Authenticity, and the
Canon." *World Literature Today: A Literary Quarterly of the
University of Oklahoma* 66.2 (Spring 1992): 243–48.

Smith, Linda Tuhiwai. *Decolonizing Methodologies: Research and
Indigenous Peoples.* London: Zed, 1999.

Smith, Sidonie, and Julia Watson. "Introduction: Situating Subjectivity in
Women's Autobiographical Practices." *Women, Autobiography,
Theory: A Reader.* Ed. Smith and Watson. Madison: University of
Wisconsin Press, 1998. 3–52.

Stacey, Judith. "Ethnography Confronts the Global Village: A New Home
for a New Century?" *Journal of Contemporary Ethnography* 28.6
(December 1999): 687–97.

Stanton, Domna C. "Autogynography: Is the Subject Different?" *The
Female Autograph: Theory and Practice of Autobiography from the
Tenth to the Twentieth Century.* Ed. Stanton. Chicago: University of
Chicago Press, 1987. 3–20.

Stein, Gertrude. *The Autobiography of Alice B. Toklas.* New York:
Vintage, 1961.

Stewart, Irene. *A Voice in Her Tribe: A Navajo Woman's Own Story.*
Foreword by Mary Shepardson. Ed. Doris Ostrander Dawdy. Socorro,
NM: Ballena Press, 1980.

Stoler, Ann Laura. "On Political and Psychological Essentialisms." *Ethos*
25.1 (March 1997): 101–06.

———. "Rethinking Colonial Categories: European Communities and the
Boundaries of Rule." *Comparative Studies in Society and History*
31.1 (January 1989): 134–61.

Surviving Columbus: The Story of the Pueblo People. Dir. Diane Reyna.
Narr. Conroy Chino. KNME-TV, Albuquerque, and the Institute
of American Indian Arts, Santa Fe, 1992. Videocassette. PBS
Video, 1992.

Swidler, Nina, Kurt E. Dongoske, Roger Anyon, and Alan S. Downer, eds.
*Native Americans and Archaeologists: Stepping Stones to Common
Ground.* Pub. in cooperation with Society for American Archaeology.
Walnut Creek, CA: AltaMira Press, 1997.

Tannen, Deborah. "Oral and Literate Strategies in Spoken and Written
Narratives." *Language* 58.1 (1982): 1–21.

Tapahonso, Luci. *Blue Horses Rush In: Poems and Stories.* Tucson:
University of Arizona Press, 1997.

———. *Sáanii Dahataał: The Women Are Singing.* Tucson: University of
Arizona Press, 1993.

———. Interview. WCBU-FM. Peoria, IL, 24 April 1996.

Tedlock, Dennis. "The Analogical Tradition and the Emergence of a

Dialogical Anthropology." *Journal of Anthropological Research* 42 (Fall 1986): 483–96.

———. *The Spoken Word and the Work of Interpretation*. Philadelphia: University of Pennsylvania Press, 1983.

Toelken, J. Barre. "The End of Folklore: The 1998 Archer Taylor Memorial Lecture." *Western Folklore* 57 (Spring/Summer 1998): 81–101.

———. "The 'Pretty Language' of Yellowman: Genre, Mode, and Texture in Navaho Coyote Narratives." *Genre* 2.3 (September 1969): 211–35.

———. "The Yellowman Tapes, 1966–1997." *Journal of American Folklore* 111.442 (1998): 381–91.

Toelken, J. Barre, and Tacheeni Scott. "Poetic Retranslation and the 'Pretty Languages' of Yellowman." *Traditional Literatures of the American Indians: Texts and Interpretations*. Ed. Karl Kroeber. Lincoln: University of Nebraska Press, 1981. 65–116.

Tomm, Winnie. "Ethics and Self-Knowing: The Satisfaction of Desire." *Explorations in Feminist Ethics*. Cole and Coultrap-McQuin. Bloomington: Indiana University Press, 1992. 101–10.

Tozzer, Alfred M. "Notes on Religious Ceremonials of the Navaho." *Putnam Anniversary Volume: Anthropological Essays*. Presented to Frederic Ward Putnam. New York: G. E. Stechert & Co., 1909. 299–343.

Trafzer, Clifford Earl. *Diné and Bilagáana: The Navajos and the First Anglos*. Tsaile: AZ: Navajo Community College Press, 1978.

Trinh T. Minh-ha. *Woman, Native, Other: Writing Postcoloniality and Feminism*. Bloomington: Indiana University Press, 1989.

Turner, Terence. "Anthropology and Multiculturalism: What is Anthropology That Multiculturalists Should Be Mindful of It?" *Cultural Anthropology* 8.4 (1993): 411–29.

Tyler, Stephen A. "On Being Out of Words." *Cultural Anthropology* 1 (1986): 131–38.

Underhill, Ruth M. *Papago Woman*. Prospect Heights, IL: Waveland Press, 1985. Repr. Holt, Rinehart & Winston, 1979; revised edition of *The Autobiography of a Papago Woman*, 1936 (*Memoir 46* of the American Anthropological Association).

Vizenor, Gerald. *Fugitive Poses: Native American Indian Scenes of Absence and Presence*. Lincoln: University of Nebraska Press, 1998.

———. *Manifest Manners: Postindian Warriors of Survivance*. Hanover: Wesleyan University Press, published by University Press of New England, 1994.

Wallace, Mark. "Black Hawk's *An Autobiography*: The Production and Use of an 'Indian' Voice." *American Indian Quarterly* 18.4 (1994): 481–94.

Walters, Anna Lee. *Ghost Singer*. Albuquerque: University of New Mexico Press, 1988.

———, ed. *Neon Pow-Wow: New Native American Voices of the Southwest*. Flagstaff, AZ: Northland, 1993.

————. *Talking Indian: Reflections on Survival and Writing.* Ithaca, NY: Firebrand, 1992.

Walton, Eda Lou. "An Indian's Memories." *The Nation* 148 (1939): 100.

Warrior, Robert Allen. *Tribal Secrets: Recovering American Indian Intellectual Traditions.* Minneapolis: University of Minnesota Press, 1995.

Wax, Rosalie. *Doing Fieldwork: Warnings and Advice.* Midway Reprint, 1985. Chicago: University of Chicago Press, 1971.

Weber, Max. *The Protestant Ethic and the Spirit of Capitalism.* Trans. Talcott Parsons. Foreword by R. H. Tawney. New York: Charles Scribner's Sons, 1958.

Welch, James. Interview with Kay Bonetti. American Audio Prose Library. Columbia, MO: n.d.

White, Hayden. "The Value of Narrativity in the Representation of Reality." *Critical Inquiry* 7 (1980): 5–27.

White Deer, Gary. "Return of the Sacred: Spirituality and the Scientific Imperative." *Native Americans and Archaeologists.* Ed. Swidler et al. 37–43.

Whiteley, Peter. "The End of Anthropology (at Hopi)?" *Journal of the Southwest* 35 (1993): 125–57.

Wilbur, George B., and Warner Muensterberger. *Psychoanalysis and Culture: Essays in Honor of Géza Róheim.* New York: International Universities Press, 1951.

Wilson, Angela Cavender. "Reclaiming Our Humanity: Decolonization and the Recovery of Indigenous Knowledge." *Indigenizing the Academy.* Ed. Mihesuah and Wilson. 69–87.

Witherspoon, Gary. *Language and Art in the Navajo Universe.* Ann Arbor: University of Michigan Press, 1977.

Wittgenstein, Ludwig. *Philosophical Investigations.* Ed. G. E. M. Anscombe and R. Rhees. Trans. G. E. M. Anscombe. 3rd ed. New York: Macmillan, 1968.

Womack, Craig S. *Red on Red: Native American Literary Separatism.* Minneapolis: University of Minnesota Press, 1999.

Wong, Hertha D. Sweet. "First-Person Plural: Subjectivity and Community in Native American Women's Autobiography." *Women, Autobiography, Theory: A Reader.* 168–78.

————. "Pre-literate Native American Autobiography: Forms of Personal Narrative." *MELUS* 14.1 (1987): 17–32.

————. *Sending My Heart Back Across the Years.* Oxford: Oxford University Press, 1992.

Wyman, Leland C., and Clyde Kluckhohn. "Navaho Classification of Their Song Ceremonials." *Memoirs of the American Anthropological Association* 50 (1938); Millwood, NY: Kraus Reprint, 1976. 1–38.

Young, Robert, and William Morgan. "Introduction." *The Trouble At Round*

Rock. Left-Handed, with Howard Gorman and the Nephew of Former Big Man. 1–22.

Zeiger, Carolyn Allen. "The Miss Marple Model of Psychological Assessment." *Advances in Descriptive Psychology* 6 (1991): 154–183.

Zepeda, Ofelia. Foreword: "Still Singing Down the Clouds." *Singing for Power*. Ruth Murray Underhill. vii–xiv.

———. *Ocean Power: Poems from the Desert*. Tucson: University of Arizona Press, 1995.

———. Personal correspondence. July 27, 1999.

Zolbrod, Paul G. Diné bahane': *The Navajo Creation Story*. Albuquerque: University of New Mexico Press, 1984.

Index

academy, viii, xxi–xxiv, 7, 25, 31,
  57–58, 88, 170, 204, 219; as
  colonialist, x, xvii,
  xxvi–xxvii, 77, 93, 120, 203,
  211; as empire-building,
  xxvi, 5, 110, 211
accessibility, xviii, 15, 31, 54–55,
  59–60, 115, 130, 173
accuracy, xviii, 36, 41, 57, 62, 79,
  174, 183, 197, 203, 205, 209
Alcoff, Linda, 75–76, 95, 96, 178
Alfred, Taiaiake, 91, 211
Allen, T. D., 164–65, 195–96,
  227n3
ambiguity, xiii, 56, 122, 129, 143,
  160, 215–16
animals, 23–24, 89, 97, 112, 116–28,
  185, 223n4. See also objectification; personification
anthropology, xxv, 7, 52–58, 59, 82,
  95–96; colonial, 15, 127, 164;
  history of, xii, 4–13, 35, 38,
  40; postcolonial, 171, 226n1;
  psychoanalytic, 39, 65–93,

226n5; revisionist, xxviii,
  4–13, 15, 27, 30; salvage,
  48, 103. See also fieldwork;
  ethnography; Navajo
  ethnography
appropriation, 1, 28, 61, 66
artifaction, 1, 48, 59, 175, 202
Asad, Talal, 55, 110, 126, 205
audience, 8, 18, 27–29, 51–60,
  76–87, 109, 168, 187–89,
  201. See also listener-readers
authenticity, xviii, xxix, 42, 52,
  144, 160, 174, 196, 204–5,
  227n1
autobiography, 1–2, 167, 175, 200;
  individualism of, 9, 141;
  monologic, 4, 102–3, 209;
  Native American, xi, 30, 57,
  208. See also ethnography;
  life histories; narrative
axiology, 10, 98, 207

Bauman, Richard, 20–21, 60
Beck, Peggy, 55, 130